~~DON'T~~ TOUCH THAT DIAL

The Impact of the Media on Children and the Family

by Barbara Hattemer and H. Robert Showers

HUNTINGTON HOUSE PUBLISHERS

Huntington House Publishers
P.O. Box 53788
Lafayette, Louisiana 70505

Library of Congress Card Catalog Number
Hardcover 92-73282
Quality Trade Paper 92-71225
Hardcover ISBN 1-56384-035-9
Quality Trade Paper ISBN 1-56384-032-4

Dedication

To my husband, Bob, and to our children, Elaine, Guy, Greg, and Beth.

—Barbara Hattemer

To my wife, Evie, and to our children, Robyn and Jessica.

—H. Robert Showers

Considering ourselves blessed and privileged to have lived our lives surrounded by family, we dedicate this book to our own families and to all the present and future families of our readers. May they value their families as we do ours, work to strengthen and protect them, and resist the many temptations in our culture to break them apart or abandon them.

We are deeply grateful to Dr. Dolf Zillmann and Dr. Jennings Bryant and to all the researchers who were so helpful in making the national conference and this book possible.

Contents

Preface

Cardinal Roger Mahony recently challenged the entertainment industry to reform the industry by urging its leaders to uphold high moral standards embodied in a set of criteria which he described as "human values." Many of these criteria were also a part of the Motion Picture Code of Hollywood's "Golden Age." The code was adopted by the Association of Motion Picture Producers, Inc., in February of 1930 and by the Motion Picture Producers and Distributors of America the following March. During the most successful years of Hollywood film-making, this code guided the contents of all feature films.

The statements at the beginning of each chapter of this book are actual quotes from that code as revised through the years up to 1948. They stand in stark contrast to the contents of today's media described in each chapter and as dramatic evidence of how far we have fallen as a society in reflecting the values put forth in that code.

In operation until 1966, the code was entirely voluntary; no producer was ever forced to comply. Hollywood executives recognized the influence of their films in the lives of their audiences and willingly accepted "high principles of public responsibility." They voluntarily concluded that the "development of higher moral and artistic standards in motion picture production has vastly improved the supply of popular entertainment and raised the artistic stature of the screen." It is a tragedy that this wisdom has been lost.

Recently, the National Family Foundation assembled twenty-five outstanding academic and clinical professionals to discuss scientific research and clinical data on the impact of the media. Reaching a remarkably clear consensus, they provided irrefutable scientific data to help concerned American citizens and lawmakers make sound decisions. They agreed that while we all cherish the First Amendment, we must distinguish between speech that promotes ideas, and acts of "entertainment," which harm individuals and society.

Whether or not the push for a new family film code is successful, the neglected principles of the old code—together with the accumulating evidence of harm to all members of society from today's media—is compelling evidence that demands a change.

Chapter 1

The American Family—
At Risk in the 1990s

The sanctity of the institution of marriage and the home shall be upheld. Pictures shall not infer that low forms of sex relationship are the accepted or common thing.

—The Motion Picture Code, 1930-1966

The American family today is clearly in trouble, but it is far from dead. It is still the best crucible for the nurture of children. Imperfect though it is, it remains at the heart of the dreams of millions of young people. Senior citizens look back to it as the source of their fondest memories. The single greatest tragedy of life is the loss of a spouse. It is the family that gives life meaning and provides a haven of emotional warmth from an often cold and uncaring world.

Every last shred of social science research supports the idea of strong families as the central component for effective outcomes for children and youth. (Dr. Onalee McGraw)[1]

Although divorce rose throughout the first half of the century, by 1950 it dropped from its peak. Dr. Margaret Andreasen reported that the 1950s were characterized by both a stabilized divorce rate and a rapidly rising birth rate. This was the era of the family and the child, and the dawn of television in the home.[2]

Surveys indicated that satisfaction with family life was strong during the 1950s; children and family life were high priorities.[3] Television families mimicked, or perhaps modeled, this idyllic life.[4]

The traditional family—Mom, Dad, Junior, and Sis with Mom and Dad sacrificing their wants for the good of the children— continued, but the 1970s saw the rise of a new breed of parents.[5] According to Dr. Andreasen, new-breed parents represented 43 percent of all parents in 1977. Differing from the traditionalists

9

who believed their main purpose was to nurture human growth, these parents were self-oriented and unwilling to sacrifice for their children. They believed children should not be pushed but should make their own decisions, that boys and girls should be raised alike. They regarded having children as an option, not a responsibility. College students ranked self-fulfillment and education above family and well above hard work and having children.[6]

This era can be characterized by a growth in enlightened self-interest, a "sexual revolution," and a decline in reported happiness with family life. In the fifties, people were confident that the family ideal characterized by "Leave It to Beaver" and "Father Knows Best" would endure forever. Today, the American way of life has shattered into a bewildering array of "lifestyles," which offer greater freedom but greater insecurity as well.[7]

The family system adapted to significant scientific, economic, and social phenomena in the 1960s and 1970s: the development of the birth control pill, greater sexual freedom for women as well as men, the adoption by many states of no-fault divorce laws, rapidly rising divorce rates, rising fertility rates for unmarried women, economic pressures on women to work outside the home, a desire for self-fulfillment in the work environment, and the glorification of material goods and their consumption.[8]

While the media can by no means be held responsible for all these dramatic changes, the increasing positive portrayal of divorce; sexual promiscuity; alternative anti-family lifestyles; sexual orientations of homosexuality, lesbianism, and bisexualism; and the emphasis on material goods and their consumption encouraged and promoted these trends. In time, these changes brought about a weakening of the family system, deficiencies in child rearing, and a host of sociological problems.

A study by the U. S. Census Bureau comparing the United States with other developed countries presents alarming statistical indicators of family fragmentation by the late 1980s. Our country has:

1. the highest divorce rate in the world, 64 percent higher than any other country studied;

2. the highest number of children involved in divorce;

3. the highest teen-age pregnancy rates;

4. the highest number of abortions in the world;

5. the highest percentage of youth abortions;

6. the highest percentage of children raised in single parent families;

7. the highest percentage of violent deaths among youth; and

8. a male youth homicide rate that is five times that of all other developed countries except Mexico.[9]

The latest count from the U.S. Centers for Disease Control on the nations AIDS epidemic is 218,301 cases, with 42,467 cases among young adults. The second 100,000 cases have come four times as quickly as the first, and experts guess there are ten times more cases than are known.[10]

A Rockford Institute study noted a significant decline in married couples remaining together throughout their lives, that one in four babies are now born out of wedlock, and half the marriages of the 1980s will fail.[11] These are staggering figures with staggering implications.

In 1960, 75 percent of all U.S. children lived with both their biological parents. By 1988, only 61 percent did. A number of studies found that children of divorce have more problems than single-parent children, but both suffer more depression, stress, anxiety, aggression, and other emotional and behavioral problems than children in two-parent families. Now a major children's health study has found that "children living with their biological parents perform better in school and have substantially fewer physical health and emotional/behavioral problems than other children."[12]

The 1988 National Health Interview Survey linked childhood psychological disorders with the growing number of children who experience parental divorce, were born outside of marriage, or are raised in conflict-filled families or single-parent households.[13] The study reported only on those problems recognized by parents or physicians in the overall child population. Because there are many young people whose problems are not recognized and are never treated, the figures are likely to be underestimated.

Essentially one in four adolescents and nearly three in ten male adolescents experience one of these disorders. The total number of U.S. children affected is approximately 10.7 million or 19.5 percent of American children.[14] While only 8.3 percent of children three to seventeen years of age living with both biological parents have significant emotional or behavioral problems, 23 percent of children in step-families have them.[15] By 1990, 15,867,000, or 24.7 percent, of the nation's children were living in single-parent families that also had high percentages of problems.[16] The number of children seeing a psychologist increased by 50 percent from 1981 to 1988. An estimated 2.5 million children suffer developmental delays, 3.4 million have a learning disability, and 7 million have had an emotional or behavioral problem that required psychological treatment.[17]

Department of Health and Human Services policy analyst Patrick Fagan noted that even in intact families emotional distancing between family members has increased. There is also a breakdown of cooperation between families, schools, churches, and communities. "This lack of intimate relating leads to acceptance of materialism, drugs, and sex—a one dimensional taking care of needs which makes people even less able to nurture the coming generation." The media, he believes, have a role in the isolation of the individual, because they absorb time that could be used to relate deeply to others.[18] The amount of time parents spend with their children has dropped 40 percent since 1965.[19]

This dismal picture, however, is not the whole story. While divorce is high, so is remarriage. The number of families is increasing. Rather than fewer families, there are actually more families in America than ever before, and more of them are "traditional" than are being reported.

According to a 29 January 1991 Census Bureau report, only 26 percent of American households are "traditional" families, defined as married couples living with one or more children under age eighteen. However, married couples who have successfully raised a traditional family are excluded from these figures and treated in the same manner as individuals living alone. Although the *percentage* of households that qualify as traditional families is still dropping, in actual numbers, families increased from 24.2 million to 24.5 million in the past decade.[20]

Translating these numbers into percentages, "70 percent of all Americans currently live in families headed by a married couple. Thus, reports of the traditional family's death have been wildly exaggerated—a fact made clear by another new report showing a dramatic four percent rise in marital births in 1990."[21] Population authorities claim to have no explanation for the increase. A Princeton professor, however, believes women in their twenties are not putting off having babies as long as their predecessors after witnessing the negative consequences of delaying childbearing.[22]

The growing homeschool movement is evidence that not all parents today are motivated by self-interest. Many young parents are willing to sacrifice income and time for the good of their children. Between 500,000 and 1,000,000 families are educating their children at home.[23] Numbers cannot be pinned down because some state laws do not permit homeschooling, and many parents do it very quietly. In addition, there are increasing numbers of young couples finding innovative ways of earning a living by working at home while caring for their children in their formative years.

Many homeschoolers do not have a television set. These young families understand the negative effect the media is having on families and are doing everything they can to help their children develop good character and a strong value system.

According to Dr. Dolf Zillmann, the family's most significant, enduring, and highly valued features include:

1. the male-female couple, living together potentially for life, remaining sexually exclusive, continually investing time and effort in the marriage, and resisting temptations that would place the family in disharmony; and

2. pursuing common economic objectives, providing loving care for their children, and supporting them to mental, emotional, moral, and economic independence.[24]

We are free to form a family, but once we have formed it, we are bound by a multitude of considerations and regulations.[25] We willingly sacrifice our freedom in the interest of the welfare of the family.

Dr. Zillmann, to those who embrace hedonism, the philosophy that pleasure is the chief good, "parenting in the traditional family context is not a winning formula."[26]

In the face of so many distressing statistics, polls surprisingly reveal that a majority of families are happy with their status and feel satisfied and fulfilled. A 1987 Phillip Morris/Lou Harris poll found 94 percent of family members "highly satisfied with their family relationships," with 85 percent of couples reporting "happy marriages." Similarly, a 1987 American Chicle/Roper poll found 84 percent of children reporting "positive attitudes about their home lives."[27]

According to Dr. Zillmann there is no better alternative.[28] Dr. Rinsley stated, "The family is the irreplaceable foundation for social progress, for society's preparation of its young, for the coming generation's acceptance of adult responsibilities, and for the transmission of the basic cultural values and traditions."[29] Research and common experience underscore the critical necessity of working to strengthen families rather than to weaken them.

Why then are so many individuals in our culture trying to redefine, weaken, or destroy the family? The most apparent reason is that those valuable, enduring qualities were missing in their families. Children of alcoholics and drug addicts, children who are abused or abandoned, children who are pawns in their parents' endless battles experience family not as a secure haven from which they can explore the world and return knowing they will be loved and encouraged, but as something from which to escape. They grow up in dysfunctional families.

According to Dr. Rinsley:

> There are still many highly functional healthy families who are doing an excellent job raising their children and preparing them for citizenship in the next generation. But I believe there is both a relative and an absolute increase in the

number of stressed, distressed and what we call "dysfunctional families"; that is, families that are not able, for a
variety of reasons, to fulfill their function as the nuclear
structure which permits their children to emerge as socialized citizens for the next generation.[30]

Dr. Rinsley defined dysfunctional families as those whose
members have never fully developed the inner controls necessary
for them to become fully socialized or to think before they act.[31]

> Parents who act impulsively . . . on a chronic basis, uncon-
> sciously teach their children to act this way. After all,
> children do what their parents want them to do. They try to
> conform to what their parents consciously or unconsciously
> communicate to them in order to get love.

While the term *dysfunctional* family has been overused and
often misused in our modern day vocabulary, the truth is that
such problem family structures exist in increasing numbers. Children of these families grow up without an adequate model of how
to properly nurture a child, passing on deficiencies rather than
strengths to the next generation.

While most of us experience a degree of dysfunction in some
area, truly dysfunctional families are those that produce *shame-
based* children. They have a poor self image, are confused and
anxious, and often experience intense psychological pressures that
create compulsive behavior patterns later on (see chap. 9). These
children are always trying to please others while keeping them
from discovering how inadequate they feel. Hungry for intimacy
and having few internal strengths, they reach outside themselves
for the nurturing they failed to receive as children.

Typically, they self-medicate by abusing drugs or using pornography to mask their pain. Too often they are seduced into
deviant lifestyles that eventually end in addiction. Unfortunately,
the fertile soil for substance abuse, sexual addictions, and other
psychological disorders is the dysfunctional family.[32]

Child psychologists have identified a progression of developmental stages—critical to the formation of character—that all
children must successfully navigate if they are to attain maturity.
Deficits in character development occur when conflict and anxiety
block the successful completion of one of these stages. Failure at
one stage makes it more difficult to successfully complete succes-
sive stages.

Further, the male child has an extra developmental task. His
first mirror of himself is his mother, but he must soon identify
with his father. When there is a very disturbed relationship in this
early process, the child tries to dominate his mother. Aggressive

tendencies that appear later in life might have their roots in this early disturbance. If the male child does not successfully separate from his mother and identify with his father, he might develop a fundamental sexual identity confusion, which predisposes him to unacceptable reactions.

Children who do not successfully navigate the stages of development grow up with personality flaws. Noting how widespread this has become, Charles Colson, during an address to the Harvard student body, said that, as a society, we face a crisis of character. We have lost the inner strengths and virtues that prevent us from giving in to our own darker instincts.[33]

Serial killer Ted Bundy is a classic example of a child who suffered from identity confusion and failed to develop integrity of character. His mother was single and tried to hide the fact. Posing as Ted's sister, she acted like his mother. He experienced emotional distress when separated from his grandfather who posed as his father. His name was changed when they moved away, only to be changed again when his mother married. After changing identity three times in his first five years, he was not sure who he was.[34]

His personality became compartmentalized and was never successfully integrated. He failed to successfully navigate the early stages of development and grew up with a major character flaw. Looking for comfort, he sought gratification in pornography. Without the inner strength to resist it, he was not only influenced by its dark messages, they took control of his life.

Such children are under supplied with parental love and nurture. They are more likely than other children to watch excessive amounts of television and less likely to receive parental monitoring of what they watch. They are overstimulated by what they see—overstimulated sexually before they are old enough to deal with feelings of sexual arousal, overstimulated commercially by the advertising of products that promise instant gratification, success, and popularity, and overstimulated by the constant action portrayed on television. The combination of being overstimulated by media images and undersupplied with loving nurturance makes these children more receptive to media messages and more likely to model them in actual behavior.

Because these children are angry inside, they are more susceptible to the world of violent television. Because they hunger for intimate relationships, they are susceptible to the enticements of sexual suggestion and pornography. By the time they reach adolescence, their inner worlds are chaotic, disorganized, and fragmented, and they are attracted to rock and heavy metal music, which reflects their inner turmoil. **Because they have no ap-**

**propriate real-life role models, they adopt the values glori-
fied in TV, movies, music, or the subculture.**

Children need boundaries. With parents spending less time
with children to establish those boundaries and the media sending
increasing signals that anything goes, we face a serious societal
problem. We must carefully examine the role of the media in
relation to the family and explore new concepts of media and
family interaction.

The solution will not be found in self-esteem programs. Early
parent-child interaction, societal recognition of family relationships, early intervention when problems are first revealed, and
reparenting of damaged children before they become parents will
provide the foundation for a reversal of trends. Healthy children
usually bond and attach successfully to their parents. By internal-
izing their parents' smiles and the perception that their presence
brings happiness to others, they build a reservoir of comforting
images within, which enable them to develop the capacity for
empathy and intimacy. They will draw from this reservoir to
comfort others throughout their lives.

For America's sake, the solution cannot be to destroy the
family and to encourage individuals in the unrestrained expression of their inner chaos. The solution must be to strengthen the
foundational unit of our culture, thus giving our children a more
secure and healthy start in life. We are challenged to lessen the
negative influences of the media, which undermine that goal,
and at the same time to encourage exciting entertainment
that promotes strong families.

Chapter 2

Right Media, Wrong Message

Motion picture producers recognize the high trust and confidence which have been placed in them by the people of the world. . . . They recognize their responsibility to the public because of this trust and because entertainment and art are important influences in the life of a nation.

—The Motion Picture Code, 1930-1966

The media's unprecedented potential for good has been virtually untapped. This was the overriding theme of the National Family Foundation Media Workshop: what our entertainment media *could* become and what the media *could* do to help families in this country.

The technological achievements of today's communications media can only be admired. Their ability to show us events that are taking place halfway around the world—a royal wedding in England, a students' revolution in China—is miraculous. Their ability to bring unsurpassing beauty into our homes—the skill of Olympic skaters, the grace of prima ballerinas, the fascination of nature's land and sea creatures—is a marvel. Their extraordinary ability to portray human emotion and create empathy in members of their audience is unparalleled. The power to tell a story of the impact of one human life upon another has never been greater. But the truly inspiring moments, the uplifting stories that offer hope and encouragement to a troubled world, are scarce. Yet, negative, socially destructive messages hit us with every turn of the dial.

While this book is about *all* of our entertainment media— magazines, movies, video, cable, satellite, radio, and television— much of it will focus on television, because it is so pervasive in our culture. It reaches millions of people at the same time, has the attention of most people for a part of every day, and has become a

17

focal point in the home. Cable comes via the same instrument, and most Hollywood movies end up on television as well.

Advertising research shows that "the power of television comes through loud and clear. . . . More time is spent with television than with all the other media combined."[1] Eighty-one percent of adults believe television has the most influence on people. Advertisers believe it brings their message home like no other medium because it delivers the message with the combined power of sight, sound, color, motion, and emotion.[2]

An article in the December *World Monitor* claimed that "TV is one of the most powerful cost-effective instruments of education the world has ever known."[3] It has been said that television has more influence on what a child learns than parents, church, and school combined. According to best-selling author Larry Woiwode,

> Television, in fact, has greater power over the lives of most Americans than any educational system or government or church. Children are particularly susceptible. They are mesmerized, hypnotized and tranquilized by TV. It is often the center of their world; even when the set is turned off, they continue to tell stories about what they've seen on it. No wonder, then, that as adults they are not prepared for the front line of life; they simply have no mental defenses to confront the reality of the world.[4]

Chapter 13 discusses television programs and films that have had positive effects in teaching the skills and behaviors that benefit individuals and society. Dr. J. Philippe Rushton, who did one of the first important reviews of this literature, concluded that

> television and film programs can modify viewers' social behavior in a prosocial direction. Generosity, helping, cooperation, friendliness, adhering to rules, delaying gratification, and a lack of fear can all be increased by television material. . . . Television does have the power to effect the social behavior of viewers in a positive, prosocial direction.[5]

Rushton noted that this conclusion provides the "evidence for a causal link between television and the viewer's social behavior."[6]

So many research studies have demonstrated this link that it is now clear that visual media have the power to influence behavior for good or for bad, depending upon the direction of their content.[7] Advertisers obviously believe television can influence how people think and act. Otherwise, they would not spend billions of dollars every year attempting to modify the behavior of viewers toward their products. The American Association of Advertising Agencies states clearly, "Television works in dollars returned."[8] Advertising executive Michael R. Smythe calls television "the world's most powerful advertising medium" and says it "has trained the baby boomers to a short attention span. It has dampened their patience with other media, making the marriage of pictures, words and music the most effective and powerful means of communications available to advertisers."[9]

Since the late 1950s advertisers have realized that television's blend of sight, sound, motion, and color produces such effective and convincing communication with the audience that they come to "accept what they see."[10] Not only are advertisers able to reach people physically with their message, television enables them to reach them psychologically, to "reach their minds and hearts," to become involved with the viewer so that they "hear what we say, feel what we feel, appreciate what we appreciate, accept what we say—and buy what we sell."[11] Research-based companies carefully check "to see what their advertising dollars buy in return."[12] They are convinced that television is doing a superior job of selling their message.

If television is so effective in communicating with its audience and therefore has the ability to bring about positive effects in the lives of its viewers, why does it so often portray what is the least desirable in society? The *bottom line* in network television, Hollywood films, cable, satellite, and radio is *profit!*

The mass media is largely owned and operated by individuals and corporations who stand to make money by attracting and holding the attention of audiences with whatever message it takes. According to Dr. Robert Kubey, their prime responsibility is to themselves and to stockholders. Only secondly do they operate in the public interest and to the varying and often minimal requirements of the FCC or Congress.[13]

Federal Communications Commissioner James Quello has appealed to the television industry:

> The sex trash, vileness and excessive violence flooding TV and radio today could . . . be considered a violation of the public trust. . . . The FCC has broad discretionary power to regulate broadcasting in the public interest. I believe we have an obligation to encourage constructive social values and to maintain reasonable decency on the airwaves. We also have an obligation to enforce the statutes against obscenity and indecency.[14]

American television, unique because it is run for profit rather than public interest, strives to remain free of either government regulation or accountability. According to one media researcher, it is "dominated by the powerful for the benefit of the powerful." It is a myth that television is "free entertainment dictated by public tastes and advertising support based on such tastes." The free market system does not exist in this realm because "only a few select American corporations" can afford network television advertising.[15]

The problem is worsened by the fact that much of the entertainment media is now owned by the news media. *Time* Magazine has merged with Warner Brothers. Time Warner owns Warner Brothers Pictures, which makes R-rated movies, and Warner Records, which produces Prince, Madonna, and Ice T recordings. Can *Time* now realistically gauge the negative impact of R-rated movies and dehumanizing lyrics on the nation's children? In the past, television news anchors presented themselves as protectors of the public's welfare. Will they now jeopardize their high-paying jobs to report on the irresponsible role of their employees in transmitting mind-polluting messages that negatively impact the lives of children?[16]

Commercial pressures create a particular kind of family image. In the 1970s it was commonly agreed among producers that a family program like Bill Cosby's could not succeed; it would be too boring. The main character had to be free to have sexual and romantic liaisons. This gave rise to a series of stories about single parents like "Bachelor Father," foreshadowing an increase in single families in the population at large. Dr. Kubey asked which came first. Did television reflect a change in society, or was it a model of a change to come?[17]

People don't really have the opportunity to decide what they want to watch. Many decisions are made well before the public decides whether or not to tune in. Like presidential candidates, the choice might be between two or three options, none of which the viewer would have chosen in the first place. The public never sees the stories Hollywood and network executives reject. According to producer James Brooks, only fifteen people in the entire country can decide to make a particular movie.[18] Some program decisions are based on how much disposable income the type of people have who watch certain types of programming. Groups with little disposable income have no voice in what is selected for commercial broadcast television.[19]

The audience, in fact, has little control over either the subject matter or the popularity of programming. Often the television networks control even the success of a program. If it has an unpopular actress or actor or high costs, they put it in a slot where it loses its audience and cancel it. Or they do the reverse. The "Lou Grant Show," after many weeks, was getting only a 14 percent share of the market. Because of their commitment to Ed Asner, instead of cancelling it as they normally would, the network re-tained the show until it began to build an audience.[20]

Rather than lifting the tastes of the country, the trend is toward the lowest common denominator. Whatever gives the most viewers a thrill and brings them back for more will be dished up again and again. When the thrill wears off, the line of what is acceptable is pushed back a little further. Myth or reality, the "let the market place decide" mentality works against programming that portrays positive values. This preoccupation with profit ac-counts for the fact that most television programming is stripped of politics and religion. Producers avoid alienating large numbers of people who hold particular political or religious views.[21]

David Larson, M.D., citing studies that showed that religion is highly protective against a host of social harms such as drug abuse, alcoholism, divorce, and physical disease, believes the me-dia are missing a unique opportunity to influence lives positively. Among other things, Dr. Larson reported that males who go to church on a regular basis live much longer than those who do not. When psychiatric journals looked at religion, they found it was associated with clinical benefit 70 percent of the time.[22] Yet there are almost no portrayals of religion as a positive influence in the lives of television or movie characters.

While it is accepted wisdom that the media's commercial orientation is in large part responsible for the loss of traditional values in most mainline shows, film critic Michael Medved has declared that in Hollywood, money is no longer the bottom line. In his provocative new book, *Hollywood vs. America, Popular Culture and the War on Traditional Values*, he points out that Hollywood never lost money on biblical pictures until *The Last Temptation of Christ*, a very unbiblical and blasphemous presentation of Jesus Christ as a "confused, lustful wimp." If Hollywood wanted solely to make money, they would produce mainstream American films that promote family, patriotism, religion, and a sense of purpose in life.[23] Films like *Chariots of Fire, Sound of Music*, and *Driving Miss Daisy* played to mass audiences. The country is so hungry for films with positive values, they flocked to see the cartoon *Beauty and the Beast*.

In discussing Hollywood's motivation and its ultimately de-structive and self destructive agenda, Medved finds Hollywood producers, directors, and actors profoundly out of touch with the American mainstream. He believes they choose their subjects from a desire to be taken seriously by their avant-garde colleagues rather than to appeal to the American public. The fact that movies have had the lowest attendance and their worst year at the box office in the last fifteen years is clear evidence that Hollywood is not listening to the public pulse.[24]

Medved has pointedly described Hollywood's vendetta against God and against religion. In addition to its total denial that religion plays a part in American life, it produces one antireligious film after another until, he says, it has offended just about everyone. After offending all Protestants with numerous caricatures of born-again believers, it has offended Catholics by portraying the pope as the gross and gluttonous father of a heavy metal rock star in *The Pope Must Die,* and Jews with *Naked Tango,* "the most anti-Jewish film since Hitler went out of business."[25]

The divergence in religious views between Hollywood movie makers and the American public is exceeded only by the clash of their political views. The great studio chiefs of the past—Louis B. Mayer, Sam Goldwyn, Darryl Zanuck, and Harry Cohn—were, according to film commentator and political columnist Richard Grenier, "American super patriots and vigorous anticommunists to a man." Now Hollywood is dominated by the politics of actors. Grenier says that the key element of change is that Hollywood actors, over these last few decades, have been annexed by America's "intellectual elite." The absorption of the film industry into the elite culture has resulted in the Academy honoring "what it considered to be the artistic, the idealistic, and the socially progressive no matter how mediocre the movie's record at the box office."[26]

Havana ardently espouses Castro's Cuba, and *The Russia House* condones treason. Both failed dismally at the box office because the American people still love their country. No cause has brought the nation closer together in recent years than the Gulf War, and yet, according to Michael Medved, by April 1992, there was not a single Hollywood film coming forth on that subject.

The gap in the views of Hollywood's elite and the American people has apparently grown even wider since a Lichter, Lichter, and Rothman study in 1982, which found them heavily weighted on the side of the liberal left.

	TV elite	Moviemakers
Political liberal	75 %	66 %
Religion "none"	44 %	55 %
Jewish *	59 %	62 %
Protestant *	25 %	—
Catholic *	12 %	—
Seldom or never attend worship	93 %	96 %
Pro-abortion	97 %	96 %
Homosexuality is wrong	5 %	7 %
Adultery is wrong	16 %	13 %

Government should redistribute income   69 %   59 %
TV should promote social reform   66 %   67 %
TV is too critical of traditional values   1 %   1 %

2 1/2 percent of the American population is Jewish, 67 percent is Protestant, and 22 percent is Catholic.

The authors of the study concluded, "This is perhaps the single most striking finding in our study. According to television's creators, they are not in it just for the money. They also seek to move their audience toward their own vision of the good society."[27]

This socializing institution is often seen as a "babysitter," or a "third parent," to which the child looks for guidelines. The cumulative effect of these media, left unchecked, threatens the stability of our culture. James Brooks, a successful writer, director, and Hollywood producer, in speaking of the values which proceed from Hollywood, said, "Hollywood is a place where the worst in all of us is nurtured and the best in all of us is ignored. . . . If you work in Hollywood, your values get battered." Amazed to learn that 42 percent of the population goes to church or synagogue every week, he concluded, "I guess there is nothing that Americans are doing more—and nothing that is represented less by Hollywood—than going to church."[28]

Radio reaches 98 percent of all Americans either at home, in the car, at work, in places of leisure, or in public places. In 1979 radios in the United States averaged less than one per household.[29] Today the average household contains 5.6 radios with an additional 167.8 million in cars, trucks, and vans.[30] Color television is now in 98 percent of all homes (92.1 million households), 65 percent have two or more sets, and customers spend over seven hours a day watching it. While the average daily viewing hours vary with age, average daily home use in November 1991 was 7 hours 26 minutes.[31]

More than 80 percent of children have a radio, and 44 percent have a television set in their bedrooms.[32] One half the adolescents in this country own a television set.[33] Cable is now available in 92 percent of television households, and 66.6 percent or 55.8 million homes currently subscribe.[34] Three quarters of households with children have a VCR.[35]

The FCC estimated that "children's unsupervised viewing ranges from 40 to 222 minutes each day. In certain age groups the amount of unsupervised viewing may average as much as six hours a day or more."[36] This makes parental supervision a source of frustration for all parents and a task beyond the capability of the 9.4 million single parents.

The Supreme Court recognized the pervasive presence of broadcast radio and television in the landmark *Pacifica* case in 1978. Because it could not reasonably be kept from children, broadcasting was held to higher standards of decency than other media. Cable and video were thought, at the time, to have a lesser presence in our lives because they had to be brought into the home by choice.

Today cable and video are almost as commonplace as network television and radio. In many areas, network reception is so poor that everyone has basic cable as a matter of course. In addition, many of the more educational and inspirational programs are available only on cable.

In 1986 a federal judge found that

> indecent programming is interspersed with programming generally thought suitable for minors. . . . It is unreasonable to shift an affirmative duty onto every parent to study all cable television program listings each week, even assuming that such listings provide adequate warning.

> As a developing medium, cable television provides a remarkable opportunity for viewing programming in other distant cities, recent movies, sports, and other features for a nominal fee. That opportunity should be available to all who are willing to subscribe, even those who object to patently offensive indecent material.[37]

The similarities between cable and broadcast television are growing rather than diminishing. To compete for the cable audience, which has gradually become desensitized to images of explicit sex and violence, the broadcast networks are lowering their standards and resorting to the same techniques to entice viewers.

A recent article in the *Arkansas Democrat Gazette* is clear evidence of what is happening. The reporter describes a visit to a publicist for an ABC-produced drama and a discussion regarding future programming:

> "I got a call just the other day from ABC," the publicist said. "They went on about how much they liked our show and how well-written our show is. They also mentioned that the reason our show had been doing so poorly (ratings-wise) was because ABC is such a young network (in regards to audience). They told me our show was geared more toward 50-year-olds."

> That's where the network contact gave the production company a little advice. "They said because ABC is such a young network that maybe we should start writing more scripts with prostitutes and serial murderers in them," the

publicist added. "I'm sitting here right now looking at a script about a serial murderer. Do you think I want to write something about that? Of course not. But what do you do when the network tells you your show needs more sex and violence to stay on the air?"[38]

Adults often do not realize how pervasive sexual, violent, and profane programming is in the lives of their children. Adults can avoid it if they choose to, but children come face to face with it, often unexpectedly, in the course of a normal social life. Before they have developed the self-confidence to say no and before they have the emotional maturity to understand what is harmful to them, they are often involuntarily exposed. When they spend the night at a friend's house and find themselves challenged by a "gross out" party, young boys may be made to feel their manhood will be questioned if they decline to watch horror movies. Young girls can be exposed to hard-R sexual videos long before they can handle them emotionally.

In speaking of the intrusiveness of materials in our lives today, Dr. Douglas Reed said, "It's like a freeway being built in your back yard—you don't have to get out on that freeway, but you have to watch your children so they don't climb over the fence and begin to play on it." Increasingly extreme forms of our mass media are being seen by our most vulnerable family members, young children and adolescents, during their formative years.[39]

According to psychiatrist Dr. Harold Voth, a great deal of social pathology is injected into American homes via television programs and movies. Pathology is a sickness or disease. Social pathology refers to social values that undermine the effectiveness of society and destroy rather than advance the culture. A lifetime of treating individuals and families has led Dr. Voth to conclude that psychologically healthy people create and embrace values that are constructive for both the individual and society. Psychologically sick people will do the opposite.[40]

A reciprocal relationship exists between the individual and society. Individual character, values, and beliefs create many of society's characteristics. Those qualities, in turn, reinforce individual characteristics. The media, particularly television, is a channel through which social influences continually and massively influence family life and the personality development of children.

Dr. Voth believes much of television is damaging to children and families.

The violence children see in such heavy doses unquestionably influences the child's view of how and when one should

give vent to hostility and aggression. . . . Sexuality is
displayed in a great variety of forms ranging from explicit
sex to behaviors which are highly suggestive or downright
lewd.[41]

According to Dr. Thomas Skill, the recent assault of TV mini-
series and evening soaps portray the worst of human relationships, and sensationalized specials show "the disease or pathology
of the week."

These specials focus on issues such as child abuse, teen
suicide, aging, the disabled, domestic violence and divorce.
The audience does not come to know what Dr. Skill calls
"the expendable families" that are beat up in the process of
exploring social issues. Their impact on the viewing audience has not yet been systematically studied.[42]

The new anti-family sitcoms thrive on feeding discord and
disharmony into the family living room. A *Time* article gives us a
glimpse of the sickness that pervades today's entertainment. "The
Bundys on 'Married with Children' take nastiness to new heights.
. . . Conversation in the Bundy Family is a torrent of verbal abuse."
Speaking of her children after a Thanksgiving get-together,
Roseanne of "Roseanne" says, "They're all mine. . . . Of course, I'd
trade any one of them for a dishwasher." In "The Simpsons," "a
grungy, bickering lot," Dad labels his family the worst in town and
drags them to a therapist where "they start giving one another
electric shocks." In these programs, Dad is "either a slob or an oaf,"
Mom is sarcastic and self-centered, and the children are "bratty
and disrespectful."[43]

There is a large part of the mass audience that is made up of
disturbed individuals who have grown up with major character
flaws. They want to see pathological personalities portrayed as if
they were normal, so they will feel better about themselves. Unfortunately for all viewers, monetary profit comes from playing to
their wishes.

The answer, then, is for responsible programmers to resist
feeding pathology back into society for the sake of making quick
profits and to produce programming that brings out and reinforces
the best in humankind. While the media may accurately reflect
the worst of our culture, they are potentially powerful causal
agents in the development of healthier culture-wide values and
beliefs.[44] If individuals and corporations within the industry would
catch this vision and accept responsibility for the power they have
been given, they could lead our society in healthier directions.

As this book goes to press, the American Psychological Association has just released a report summarizing television's effects on vulnerable groups in society. It affirms many of the themes and conclusions we are presenting:

> • Implied sexual activity on TV occurs most often between unmarried couples with little emotional attachment or commitment to one another.

> • Watching sexual violence or violence in a sexual context leads to increased acceptance of rape and other forms of social violence and can instigate anti-social values and behavior.

> • Children form stable patterns of viewing early in life largely on the basis of how parents and siblings use television.

> • Parents can enhance the positive effects of television by viewing, discussing and evaluating programs with their children.

> • However, the fact that parents can and should guide their children's viewing does not relieve the television industry and public policy makers from their responsibility to ensure that television offerings are diverse and free from clearly harmful content.[45]

It is yet another voice for a television policy that serves the public interest, meets the needs of viewers, and protects society from harmful effects. We would like to see these principles applied to all media entertainment.

Chapter 3

Media Effects on Personality, Perceptions, and Judgments

When right standards are consistently presented, the motion picture exercises the most powerful influences. It builds character, develops right ideals, inculcates correct principles . . .

—The Motion Picture Code, 1930-1966

How early does television impact a child's world? Dr. Andrew Meltzoff exposed infants fourteen and twenty-four-months-old to behavior modeled on television (the taking apart and reassembling of an unfamiliar toy). Both age groups repeated the manipulation of the toy, even after a twenty-four hour time delay, whereas infants who had not seen the action on television did not. This research established that early in their second year, infants can use information they acquire from looking at television as a guide to real-world action. It suggests that television exposure in the home might influence young children even earlier than we realize.[1]

While children under two on average watch television only two hours a day, their viewing is scattered throughout their daily routines. Typical two-to five-year-olds increase viewing to twenty-eight hours per week. By age three, three-quarters of them can name their favorite TV program.[2]

According to Dr. Harold Voth, mature parents and solid family life can, to some extent, ward off damaging external influences on children, but weak, dysfunctional, or part-time families cannot. Children are highly vulnerable, and proper psychological development can easily be damaged when they fail to receive the emotional nurturing and shielding mature parents and healthy family life provide.[3]

28

Parents who take refuge from parental responsibilities by losing themselves in television deny children important nurturing experiences that ultimately lead to healthy personality development. Parents further avoid responsibilities by sending children off to the TV set. Television watching promotes passivity in children at a time when they should be developing patterns of active mastery and learning social skills.[4] With this in mind, it is alarming to note that one study found that *a third of all parents find one of the major advantages of television to be babysitting.*[5] Thus, excessive TV watching by either parents or children or both deprives children of the parental nurturing they so desperately need.

Dr. Charles Ashbach sees the family as the *buffer, benchmark, and lens* for the child across his entire span of development.[6] Parents act as a *buffer* to protect the young child from the messages of society, from overwhelming stimulation, seductions, and confusion. They help to neutralize, interpret, and exclude messages from the media.

As the *benchmark*, the healthy family provides a guide by which the child can judge the difference between health and sickness, love and hate, truth and lies. The family is the originator of conscience, the source from which internal controls are created. These controls enable the child to become a self-regulating member of a complex and changing social world.

Whether healthy or dysfunctional, the family is also the *lens* through which all media influences are brought. The family helps the child focus and prioritize the multitude of influences that compete for his attention. Since many of these have commercial agendas, which ignore the best and highest interests of the child to achieve economic ends, parents must help children understand the motivation behind the presentations.

Healthy personality development is dependent on the quality of the parent-child relationship, the quantity of time spent together, and the integrity and health of the family system. These are fundamental to building a healthy inner image world and a strong sense of identity. The tasks needed to accomplish healthy personality development include:

1. taming the child's impulses and cravings through the creation of boundaries that will regulate appetites and passions;

2. developing an adequate sense of reality—the ability to distinguish between real and imaginary, safe and dangerous; and

3. accepting sexual identity and an internal moral order by identifying with parents and their values and standards.[7]

The transition from a totally dependent infant to a relatively independent, self-regulating, happy, and masterful child is brought about by the construction of an *inner world of images and emotions.*

The first images of the child's inner domain are fantastic and distorted. Through gradual growth, development, and interaction with parents and others, the inner world is transformed into increasingly realistic images. When a child is violently or sexually abused at any time during childhood, his inner image world is distorted. It can become bizarre, destructive, sexual, and sadistic. Such an individual often seeks external images that confirm this distorted inner life.

Highly respected forensic psychiatrist Ismond Rosen, M.D., has said, "Pornography and violent imagery can be understood as one means that such traumatized individuals use to both regulate and stimulate their chaotic, impoverished, and fragmented inner worlds. The formation of perverse character structure and the use of bizarre, external activities, and media would seem to be clearly linked."[8]

Media images and scenes have the greatest influence on a person when they deal with themes and emotions similar to those that fill his inner image world. These emotions are primarily of two kinds: *pleasure*, on the positive side, and *pain, anxiety, guilt, and shame,* on the negative side.

Even in the best of homes, parents do and say things that make children anxious. In addition, parental anxiety or dissension produces great anxiety within, which children tend to deal with in isolation.[9] When a media story resonates with such pressing inner concerns, it captures the rapt attention of young viewers.

The healthy child from eighteen months to four years experiences the assimilation of his basic personality structures to form an integrated personality. During this period of vast changes, a child needs his parents to validate, explain, support, mirror, and limit his experiences.

The amount of time he spends viewing videos and television can be as important as the content of specific messages. *Excessive consumption of media during early childhood points to a "gap" in the child's relationship to parents.* Media, in many cases, is used by the child as a "fix" to compensate for a lack of emotional closeness with his parents. It can become a compulsive or defensive habit to ward off dissatisfaction, anger, or loneliness.[10]

> The child who merely sits in front of the television set for hours without any verbal exchange with another person is not challenged to think or create. He merely absorbs. The child, on the other hand, who plays with his blocks and creates a castle on a hill or a runway for a plane, picturing the adventure of a perfect landing is stimulating his capacity for imagination and creativity.

It is the task of parents to filter out, explain, or exclude the most damaging and overstimulating imagery that is encountered in the media world. Even the most violent and brutal media images can be neutralized if adequate emotional communicating occurs.

If, however, violent and sexual images reverberate with themes that are powerfully at work within the child's own family rather than explained away by loving parents, they will reinforce the child's feelings that the world is an unsafe place that cannot be trusted. Because they act out the trauma the child is experiencing, he will be drawn to watch them, perhaps looking for an answer or a way out. Unfortunately, such images, once committed to memory, might serve as models for later behavior (see chap. 9 and 10).

According to Dr. Jean Piaget, the thinking of preschool children (two to six) is "concrete, irreversible, egocentric, self-centered, and present-oriented."[11] They are unable to abstractly evaluate the messages they receive. They have a difficult time foreseeing consequences of their actions or understanding another's perspective. At this stage, children merely take in what they see and hear and accept it as normal.[12]

Children of preschool age use symbolism to deal with much of reality. Consequently, they find television highly persuasive. Middle children, age six to twelve, according to Dr. Piaget, begin to develop theories about the world, always tying them to concrete objects and social relationships they can see, test, and categorize. Though they do not have full abstract understanding, their memory is excellent. They will remember every socially "prohibited" word they hear and use it. They will imitate the actions of others without an adequate understanding of the consequences of that behavior.

Unable to distinguish reality from fantasy until they are in the fifth or sixth grade, children at this stage do not understand that scenes on television are only "play acting."[13] They believe what they see is really happening.

A recent study of seventh and ninth graders in Rhode Island illustrates how easily children are influenced by constant media messages that present premarital sex as the accepted standard. The idea that forced sex is acceptable and enjoyed by the victim is a standard theme in pornography, which is increasingly finding its way into mainstream entertainment. Of seventeen hundred children, 65 percent of the boys and 47 percent of the girls agreed that "it was acceptable for a man to force sex with a woman if he had been dating her for more than six months." One quarter of the boys and one-sixth of the girls said "it was acceptable for a man to force a woman to have sex if he has spent money on her."[14]

Middle or latency-aged children turn to peer relations and begin to experience the world beyond family. For boys, conflicts emerge in the form of fantasies, games, war games, robberies, attacks, car crashes, karate, knives, and other forms of defense. Their consumption of media images will naturally reflect these themes.[15]

The mastery of skills and the acquiring of new capacities are all important. Latency-aged children watch how older children and adults handle life. They look for cues that define their nature as male or female.[16] Since both parents and teachers discuss sexuality in an intellectual manner, children look to the experiential messages of the media to help discover their own sexuality.[17] They are especially vulnerable to media messages that portray them as "little adults." If, because of media exposure, ten-year-olds begin to see themselves as fifteen or twenty-five before they have adequately identified themselves as ten, they will become confused about the kind of behavior that is appropriate for their age.[18]

At this stage, a love of repetitiveness makes children prone to slogans and ideal targets for advertising. Children want "instant gratification," so they expect action and excitement. Their perceptual apparatus is accustomed to short, choppy imagery and information. MTV's rapid fire scenes are particularly appealing and powerful at this age (see chap. 11). Constant identification with sexually explicit images results in the "disappearance of childhood" at increasingly earlier ages.[19]

Dr. Melvin Anchell warned that overstimulating children with sexual images during the latency period may both diminish their desire to learn and cause serious problems with the development of compassionate feelings for others. At first directed toward parents or those who care for them, stirrings of compassion eventually extend to others. Later in life, it becomes the capacity to love. The results of over-feeding our youths sexually stimulating entertainment can be seen in their increasingly anti-social behavior.[20]

From ages thirteen to eighteen, the adolescent is engaged in a battle between giving up childhood and developing the personal and social skills necessary for adult living. With the decrease in the child-parent bond comes a greater dependence on the peer group and greater vulnerability to group influences. What the group wears, watches, smokes, drinks, and thinks strongly affects the child who is still unsure of himself. Advertising images are accordingly more persuasive, compelling, and seductively reassuring.[21] Developing an independent adult identity in relationships is often accompanied by considerable anxiety.[22]

Adolescence is also the developmental period when disorders

of regulation—alcoholism, drug abuse, eating disorders, gambling, compulsive work, and sexuality patterns—are all given final form. The poorly nurtured adolescent is especially vulnerable to media messages promising freedom from restraint or suggesting an entitlement to pleasure and reward.[23]

Dr. Lawrence Kohlberg's theory of moral development provides another framework for understanding the potential harm that sexually explicit programming does to children.[24] He describes three distinct stages of moral development: 1) the pre-conventional child obeys rules either to avoid punishment or to obtain rewards; 2) the conventional child conforms to avoid disapproval by others or conforms to avoid censure by authorities; or 3) the post-conventional person conforms in order to maintain social order or to avoid self-condemnation because of his belief in universal principles.

Sexually explicit programming will affect people differently, according to their level of moral development. People in Kohlberg's first two stages are highly susceptible to imitating the sexual behavior of others. They have not developed the internal controls or values that help them evaluate that behavior and be guided by their own beliefs. Upon hearing or seeing sexual messages, the pre-conventional child would conform unless he fears punishment or perceives other behaviors as more rewarding. If a parent did not know that a child was listening or watching such programming, the child might feel free to imitate the sexually explicit behavior.

Responding to sexually explicit media, the person in the conventional stage (middle child to adult) tends to look to his peers or to an authority figure for acceptable standards. Some children would use profanity or imitate sexually explicit behaviors if they thought they were endorsed by peers. Other children would look to an authority figure to tell them if the behavior or language was appropriate.

Only some late adolescents (seventeen- or eighteen-year-olds) reach Kohlberg's last stage, where they begin to evaluate and integrate the values of others into their own belief systems. Thus, it appears morally responsible and scientifically justifiable to limit the sexually explicit messages of the media to those who are this age or older, who have the skills to adequately judge them for themselves.

The messages of fantasy-based print ads and television commercials offer the consumer an opportunity to momentarily slip off the chains of cause and effect, for a short time rise above his normal limitations, and believe that anything is possible and attainable. This type of advertising sells its products by tapping into deep-seated aspects of personality, fantasy, and desire. It sends a message that not only will you be gratified in a way you never thought possible, you will be relieved of the pain, uncertainty, and effort of life. Fantasy-based commercials resort to any combination of stimuli—magic, awe, love, happiness, sex—to surround the product with a cluster of associations that "compel" the customer to purchase it.[25]

Eventually, this hallucinatory-based experience must be frustrated. The high that accompanies the purchase of the product diminishes and reveals that you are still the same person. When the euphoria ends, the momentary feelings of being safe, happy, proud, or serene give way to frustration, boredom, resentment, anger, an increase in appetite, and a renewed search for gratification.

Such advertisements create confusion about roles, resources, and expectations; conflict between generations; and unreal attitudes of entitlement (guaranteed gratifications). Beliefs, values, and enduring symbols are trivialized as the sacred and profane are mixed to sell the commercial product.

The constant weaving of images creates confusion between what is important and what is inconsequential. The increasing reports of violence—even murder—surrounding specific fashion products: shoes, coats, eyeglasses, necklaces, and the like, show how important these items are becoming for some groups in our society—enough to kill for. This is simply the logical extension of creating motivated consumers: "I've got to have that; I'll do anything to get it!" So they do.

Fantasy-based advertising seems to have as one of its hidden agendas the creation of massive numbers of "spoiled children" unable to regulate desire and unable to differentiate between luxuries and necessities. Because they function at a low stage of moral development, their internalized values are not strong enough to resist these external messages, establish limits, and tolerate frustration.

Dr. Charles Ashbach believes untold millions of addicted and compulsive individuals in our society are related to the torrent of hyperstimulation and appetite manipulation lying at the core of fantasy-based advertising. "The millions of alcoholics, drug addicts, eating disordered, gamblers, sex addicts, and chronic overworkers bare brute testimony to the effectiveness and impact of over thirty years of relentless manipulation of the fundamental structures of need, hunger, and desire."[26]

Fantasy-based advertising produces individuals who enjoy prolonged emotional arousal in a context of reduced critical and moral judgment. This capacity makes the person hungry for new stimulation and increasingly indiscriminate about the content of the next stimulation. In this moral climate, pornography, sexual exploitation, and all forms of seduction and abuse are likely to flourish.

Advertisements are designed to create an appetite. Program content is not, but it might touch the emotions even more deeply than ads, because viewers develop relationships with people they see in the stories week after week. That viewers identify with characters in situation comedies and primetime serial dramas was clearly demonstrated when a line of "Dynasty" perfume and clothing was promoted in Bloomingdales. Police were called to control the crowds because customers who came to buy the products were so highly charged.[27]

Mounting evidence indicates that some of the most durable effects of watching television come in the form of subtle, incremental, and cumulative changes in the way we view the world. Unnoticed in their early stages, subtle shifts in our perception of social reality change the way we think about things.[28]

Dr. Jennings Bryant conducted important research studies to try to understand potential shifts in moral judgment in teen-agers who watch sexually oriented programs. Because television is a readily available consultant for teen-agers who watch it approximately twenty-two hours per week—far more than the average parent is available—Dr. Bryant asked two questions: "What do teen-agers learn in terms of moral judgment from primetime television programming?" and "Can the sexually oriented messages of primetime entertainment . . . change adolescents' moral judgment?" His first investigation established that media exposure influences moral judgment.

For three hours on five consecutive evenings, thirteen- and fourteen-year-old boys and girls were shown fifteen hours of episodes from evening serial dramas from the mid-to late-1980s. Later they answered questions which disguised the study's true purpose. Divided into three groups, they saw 1) scenes that dwelt on sexual relations outside of marriage, 2) sexual relations between married partners, or 3) nonsexual relationships between adults.

From three to seven days after the viewing, they were shown seven brief segments featuring nonsexual transgressions or crimes and seven scenes featuring unwise or improper sex-related behaviors. They were asked to rate how bad they were, morally speaking, and how much the victim had been wronged. Both boys and girls, who were exposed to episodes of sexual relations between unmarried partners, rated sexual misconduct as significantly less bad than their peers who had seen either sexual relations between married partners or nonsexual scenes. They also found the victims of sexual transgression to be less severely wronged than their peers in the control groups.

A second study attempted to determine which factors could lessen those media effects on moral judgment. It was guided by two suppositions: 1) an active rather than passive viewing style will lead to more critical media consumption and, therefore, more resistance to attitude change; 2) families who establish open lines of communication between all family members create environments that help children resist messages designed to manipulate and to persuade them.

This study used teen-agers who differed widely in active vs. passive viewing and open vs. closed family communication styles.

The findings were similar to the first study but the special factors studied made a difference. *Both active viewing and open family communication style lessened the effects of exposure.* Active viewing teen-agers, who were from homes in which family members communicated openly, appeared to be relatively unaffected by being immersed for fifteen hours in an alternative value culture. Their moral judgment did not change. Active viewing plus an open family communication environment apparently provided resistance to being influenced by the programs viewed.

A third study incorporated two "politically sensitive" factors: (a) whether or not the teen-agers came from families with a clear, well-defined value system, and (b) whether the orientation of that value system was liberal or conservative.

Teen-agers from families with unclear or ill-defined value systems were strongly affected by exposure to programming featuring sexual relations between unmarried partners. They saw the sexual improprieties featured in the video scenes as less bad and the victims as less seriously wronged than their peers did. On the other hand, the moral judgment of subjects from homes with well-defined value systems were only minimally affected by viewing the same programs. The type of value system they believed in was not as critical as the fact that they knew some value system well.

Overall, Dr. Bryant concluded that "for young teenagers, heavy exposure to primetime television programming featuring sexual intimacy between unmarried people can clearly result in altered moral judgment."[29] Teen-agers, then, are vulnerable to media messages. Pairing these findings with the high number of sexual messages that the average teen-ager is exposed to every year, as reported in the next chapter, there is cause for deep concern. It is encouraging, however, to learn that several individual and family factors can lessen potential shifts in values from watching television.

Dr. Bryant concluded that a warning label could be put on sexually oriented primetime television fare: *"Teenagers beware. Watching too much television programming featuring pre-marital, extra-marital, or non-marital sex can be hazardous to your moral health."* While neither Dr. Bryant nor the authors are seeking such a literal label, this is the message that producers and parents must hear.

Chapter 4

Sexual Trends in the Media

Pictures shall not infer that low forms of sex relationship are the accepted or common thing.

—The Motion Picture Code, 1930-1966

Dr. Robert Kubey pinpointed the primary messages of the commercial media:[1]

1. *Materialism*: In order to be happy, one must own things and avail oneself of services. Unfortunately, a society obsessed with material goods might have difficulty recognizing that non-materialistic family life can also be rewarding.

2. *For everything there is a quick fix*: Ads promise a quick solution for everything that ails us. The need to resolve problems within the time slot of a scheduled program contributes to the expectation that we should obtain gratification immediately and solutions should come easily and quickly.

This orientation conflicts with the basic commitments and gradual processes necessary to sustain the family. People who have been conditioned thus may not learn to be patient, to persist, to endure difficult times, or to handle complexities—all of which are basic qualities required for marriage and parenthood.

3. *Young is better*: Television teaches that the next developmental stage children should aspire to is adolescence, not adulthood. Older people, therefore, are obsolete, not "with it." Mass media detract from a recognition of the value of older family members.

4. *Open and unfilled time is not desirable; in fact, it cannot be tolerated*: Children must compete with people on TV for the attention of other family members. Women must compete with TV beauties for their husband's attention. Sometimes both men and women begin to think they are missing something and look outside of marriage for fulfillment.[2]

38

5. *Violence is acceptable*: Throughout the media, violence has become a tolerated norm and an acceptable way of resolving problems. More often than not, it is the preferred method of attacking a problem.

6. *Religion is unacceptable*: Most television shows and movies simply ignore the element of religious faith, as if it does not exist in modern America. If a religious character is portrayed, he is more often the villain, a rapist, a deceiver, or at best, a fool.

7. *Sex is only good outside of marriage*: The media devalue the idea of marriage. On television, sex outside of marriage is portrayed five times as often as sex within marriage. References to prostitution, rape, and sex crimes are standard fare on adventure and drama programs. "Women characters use eroticism to entrap men and achieve their goals. Erotic relationships between people are seldom seen or discussed in the context of warm, loving, stable relationships."[3]

Deviant sex as normal and acceptable has long been the subject of soft and hard-core pornography. It came to television via cable and now is spilling over to broadcast television. In the United States, until forty years ago, sexual material was confined to a few explicit novels, European films shown in out-of-the-way art cinemas, and an underground market of "dirty" postcards and stag films. American children could grow up totally ignorant of their existence.

Today's youth cannot avoid such materials and parents who try to protect their children from them take on an impossible task. *Playboy Magazine* in the 1950s birthed hundreds of sexually explicit magazines that are sold in grocery stores, family convenience stores, gas stations, bookstores, and on street corners. The movie *Deep Throat* generated the pornographic film industry, which has gained greater and greater acceptability through the video market and influenced the breakdown of standards restricting sexual explicitness throughout the media. Verbal and visual depictions of explicit sex bombard American children from the radio, television, cable, satellite, movies, videos, telephone, and computer.

During the last thirty years, the media has become more and more graphic in sexual content. This change has occurred in daytime soaps and primetime television as well as in X-rated videos, "porn rock," and pornographic outlets.

Not long ago, pornography—sexually oriented material intended to arouse the viewer—was available only on the "black market" and was confined to the decaying areas of large cities. With the advent of new technology and the sexual revolution, it has spread to most suburban regions, small towns, and nearly every neighborhood of the United States via local video outlets, convenience stores, cable, satellite television, telephones, and home computers. It has been accompanied by an ever-escalating severity in content, including increasingly degrading, violent, and exploitative depictions with predominantly anti-family, anti-marriage, and deviant themes.

It has also seeped into mainline media. After extensive research on sexual trends in the media, Dr. Bradley Greenberg concluded that today's teen-agers are exposed to at least three thousand to four thousand sexual references per year in mainstream media alone.[4]

Dr. Greenberg's analysis of daytime soap operas popular among junior and senior high-school students revealed an average of four sex acts per hour. Intercourse occurred two to three times per hour and accounted for 62 percent of all sexual activity. "Unmarried intercourse was twice as frequent as married intercourse."[5]

Only one fourth of the characters were married to each other, leaving 75 percent of the sex acts divided evenly between extramarital and premarital intercourse. Finding that marriage is not a strong value on soap operas, Dr. Greenberg concluded, "sex between married people appears to be of interest to no one."[6]

Dr. Greenberg also studied the nineteen network primetime series viewed most often by ninth and tenth graders. They contained an average of just under three sexual activities per hour. Married intercourse was infrequent, accounting for only one sixth of the activity. Homosexuality and prostitution acts were identified once every two hours.[7] Of nine visual acts involving intercourse, seven were in action-adventure series, and none were in situation comedies.[8]

An exhaustive study done at American University and funded by the Office of Juvenile Justice and Delinquency Prevention revealed that from 1954 until 1984, images linking children with sex significantly increased in men's magazines. In all, the research team counted over six thousand images linking children with sex or an average of 8.2 times in each issue of *Playboy*, 6.4 times in each issue of *Penthouse*, and 14.1 times in each issue of *Hustler*. *"Child imagery" in men's magazines increased nearly 2,600 percent from 1954 to 1984, with nearly two-thirds of the child scenarios sexual and/or violent.* The dominant age bracket was three to eleven-year-olds, with girls more prevalent than boys and most likely associated with sex with adults. Although 80 percent of the children were actively involved in sex scenes, each magazine portrayed children as unharmed and/or benefited by adult-child sex.[9]

The authors of an earlier, similar study concluded that there exists the possibility that such materials contribute to a "cultural climate" that sanctions acts of violence against women.[10] These studies are especially alarming given the new conclusions confirming that pornography motivates, promotes, and is often used and imitated in the sexual seduction of children and the rape of women.

The increase sexual content and the number of sexually explicit magazines has influenced trends in general magazines as well. The sheer number of sex references in magazines like *Reader's Digest, McCall's, Life, Time, Newsweek,* and the *Saturday Evening Post* increased 84 percent from 1950 to 1960, 16 percent from 1960 to 1970, and another 68 percent from 1970 to 1980. The ratio of sex references per editorial page increased from seventeen references in one hundred pages in 1950 to eighty-eight references in one hundred pages in 1980, almost one per page.[11]

Dr. Greenberg noted that the shift in emphasis in these magazines suggests where sex is on the agenda of the American reader. At least, it is on the agenda of writers, editors, and publishers of magazines who desire to market their product more aggressively.

In 1986 Dr. Greenberg selected sixteen strong box office films rated R for sexual content, which had special appeal to young viewers. Nine of the sixteen films had been seen by 53 to 77 percent of the ninth and tenth graders surveyed; six of the remainder had been seen by 35 to 46 percent of the sample.[12]

They found 17.5 sex acts per film and 10.8 acts per film hour. Eight acts per film, or 46 percent of sexual activity, involved sexual intercourse between unmarried partners. Sexual intercourse between marriage partners occurred only four times altogether, making the ratio of unmarried to married intercourse thirty-two to one.[13] There was an average of 45 uses of profanity per film and the frequencies ranged from 11 to 101 uses of profanity in just one film.[14]

Dr. Greenberg noted that teen-agers see these films in the theaters away from the family context where an open communication system might well lessen the impact. Many people believe young teens are prohibited from seeing these films. However, during debriefing sessions, when Dr. Greenberg typically asked if thirteen- and fourteen-year-olds had any trouble getting into R-rated movies, they laughed.

> If they are tall enough, if their head is above the ticket counter, they can buy a ticket. Restriction is totally a local management decision. Don't expect the NC17 rating to

have any effect on their ability to get into even X-rated movies.[15]

Studies that document the high percentage of readership and viewership of hard-core pornography by junior and senior high-school students confirm this finding.

Since the attitudes of the participants in the films, in contrast to the soaps and primetime shows, are very positive toward having sex, they send a much stronger and clearer message, which undoubtedly has a stronger impact on moral values. These movies are also available for video rental and are often watched in the dating situation.[16]

A study of offerings from MTV and other television music programs found suggestive sexual content in 60 percent of their sample of sixty-two videos.[17] Another study focused on the presence of visual sex and violence (not lyrics) in 166 "concept" videos. Sexual intimacy was presented in over 75 percent, 71 percent of it heterosexual, 26 percent homosexual. There were five sexual activities per video—twice the rate that occurred on conventional TV.[18] Four of every five videos containing violence also contained sexual imagery.

MTV, available on basic cable in 80 percent of homes that have children, presented over six scenes per video.[19] At six sexual references per video, an "hour per day of viewing MTV would add 1,500 more video sex experiences on an annual basis to the teenager's imagination"[20] (see chap. 11).

The 1970 Commission on Obscenity and Pornography concluded that "adults only" paperbacks represented "one of the largest areas of pornography production in the U.S."[21] A 1976 study of 428 "adults only" paperback books published from 1967 through 1974 took every fifth book from the shelf of one store in eight communities in five states. In 1967 sex episodes consumed twenty-nine of every one hundred pages. By 1970 it had risen to sixty-four of every one hundred pages. Only 9 percent of the sex acts expressed some form of love. Sixty percent described gratuitous sex with no involvement or commitment. Physical or mental coercion was described in one third of the paperbacks.[22] Men often coerced women into lesbian acts, masturbation, fellatio, anal intercourse, and bestiality.[23]

Retaining this imagery, consider contemporary X-rated video fare. An analysis of 443 explicit sex scenes in 45 X-rated videos found over half dealt primarily with domination or exploitation, mostly by men toward women.[24] Sex scenes lasted four to five minutes, compared to seventeen seconds on broadcast television. The videos averaged ten sex scenes per video, which took up thirty-six minutes per hour, or 60 percent of each film. Of the sex scenes, 78 percent were heterosexual, 11 percent lesbian, 2 percent bisexual, and 9 percent autosexual. The authors concluded,

> The fusion of sex and aggression present in these videotapes, including the portrayal of rape, bondage, female submission and verbal abuse, supports the ideology that sexuality includes domination and abusive treatment of women. . . . A significant level of hatred of women is now available for viewing in our living rooms and bedrooms.[25]

Another study compared "adult" movies with triple-X titles. "Adult" and XXX titles averaged eleven sex scenes each, with XXX video scenes twice as long and more than twice as explicit. Nudity was shown in two thirds of both, but other kinds of sex were more frequent in XXX titles: 4.2 times more oral-genital contact, 1.5 more fondling of breasts or genitals, 1.9 more genital-genital intercourse, 2.7 more masturbation, and 10 times more anal intercourse.[26]

The "adult" videos contained more aggression (hitting, kicking, using weapons, attempted and actual murders, kidnaping, severe beatings, and torture) and more sexual aggression (verbal humiliation and bondage). Triple-X videos, while more sexually explicit, are less violent and less sexually violent than "adult" movies.[27]

The content of hard-core pornography has dramatically changed over the past twenty years.* The 1986 Commission on Pornography and a Harvard University scientific content survey both discovered that "mainstream" pornography freely available in the 1980s was virtually unavailable in 1970.[28] In 1970 the vast majority of "hard-core" pornography magazines featured a nude woman posing alone.[29] Today hard-core pornography features sexually deviant or violent behavior including child sexual abuse, bondage, torture, rape, incest, group sex, sex with animals, excretory functions, lesbian, homosexual, and transsexual activity, and a wide variety of violent and degrading sexual practice, which can only be described as extremely "unsafe."

One commissioner (Dr. James Dobson) described the debasing, violent content of today's mainstream pornography this way:

---

* At this point we would like to apologize for the few graphic descriptions we have included in this book. We have tried to tone them down. One of the great difficulties with this issue is that citizens, legislators, and policy makers are largely unaware of just how graphic the material has become. Unless you understand that, you will not fully understand this issue.

X-rated movies and magazines today feature oral, anal and
genital sex between women and donkeys, pigs, horses, dogs
and dozens of other animals. In a single sex shop in New
York City, there are forty-six films and videos available
which featured bestiality of every type. Other offerings
focused on so-called "bathroom sports" including urination,
defecation . . . mutilation of every type (involving "voluntary" amputation, fish hooks through genitals, fists in rec-
tums, mouse traps on breast), oral and anal sex between
groups of men and women. . . .

Simulated child pornography depicts females who are actually eighteen or older but appear to be [young teen-agers].
They are shown with shaved genitalia, with ribbons in their
hair and surrounded by teddy bears. Their "fathers" are
often pictured with them in consummate, incestuous settings. . . . The magazines in sex shops are organized on
shelves according to topics, such as Gay Violence, Vomiting,
Rape, Enemas, [Bondage and Domination (B&D) Torture]
and topics that I cannot describe even in a frank discussion
of this nature.[30]

After studying 430 magazines in Time Square bookstores, Dr.
C. A. Winick concluded, "practically all the magazines were clearly
intended for men." One fourth catered to individuals interested in
specific sexual deviant behavior like bondage, torture, sadomasochism, lesbianism and homosexuality, fetishes, and foreign object
insertion.[31] Another study surveyed thirteen randomly selected
pornography outlets in four major cities. Studying 5,132 different
magazine, film, and book titles, they concluded:
    1. The average commercial pornography outlet carried ap-
proximately 1,000 nonduplicative titles, on average 324 magazines, 292 books, and 267 films. Had pamphlets, photo packets,
tabloid newspapers, and other merchandise (such as dildos, penis
rings, whips, artificial vaginas, etc.) sold in the shops been included, the average would have been much higher.
    2. The magazines contained the following content:
        3 percent—use of force (rape, whipping, spanking, and
    women fighting),
        5 percent—implements of violence (whips, guns, knives,
    hoists, or racks),
        10 percent—sexual bondage (gags, blindfolds, hoods, or
    masks, neck restraints, handcuffs, leg irons),
        12 percent—sadomasochistic imagery (torture, forcible
    rape, the sexual use of piercing, whipping, or weapons, or
    sexual depictions of bruising or blood),
        13 percent—violence (bondage, sadism evidenced other

than by bondage, spanking, women fighting, or fisting),

10-15 percent—sexually deviant imagery (excluding sadomasochistic imagery): corpses; enemas; feces or defecation; diapers or diapering; bestiality; anatomically normal men wearing female clothing; leather, rubber, latex, or exaggerated shoes and boots; and childlike clothing, props, or settings and shaved pubic hair,

Approximately 15 percent—male homosexual imagery,

Approximately 11 percent—group sexual activity,

Approximately 10 percent—focus on particular body states.

Less than 5 percent of all merchandise depicted vaginal intercourse between only one man and one woman.

3. Twelve of thirteen outlets sold books on child sexual abuse and incest with detailed sexually explicit written descriptions of sexual activity between children and adults.

4. In general, film packages depicted less deviant imagery than magazine or book covers, perhaps because film packaging is designed to increase acceptability in the "family" video sale and rental market.

Concerning paraphilic imagery (for sexual deviants), a 1985 study of 2,173 pornographic magazines determined that 562 titles involved paraphilia (sexual deviations). Sadomasochism was the most common deviation (47.8 percent), and incest and pedophilia were next, each claiming 13 percent.[32] Over one-fourth of the market is designed for sexual deviants. Of that part, three-fourths depicts bondage and torture of women or sex with children.

Dr. Greenberg concluded that teen-agers see or hear a minimum of fourteen hundred references to sexual activity every year on primetime, one thousand more on soaps, fifteen hundred more from just one hour daily of MTV, a minimum of one hundred more from six R-rated movies a year, for a total of four thousand references to sexual activity even if they avoid pornography altogether.[33]

While subtle in presentation, sexual content in network programming is increasingly explicit. Though more time is spent in front of television, movies contain stronger sexual messages and more concrete models than television. What television suggests, movies and videos do. Exposure to sexual programming on television establishes an acceptable mood or tolerance for increased sexual activity, which is intensified and instructed by explicit movies.

R-rated films, like the popular *Pretty Woman*, introduce thirteen- or fourteen-year-olds to content they do not have the capacity to process. At the same time, they send a very misleading message. For younger children to be introduced to sexuality by an

X-rated video would be even more traumatic (see chap. 3 and 6).

Dr. Greenberg offered the following hypotheses for further research. Regular viewers of television programs, music videos, and movies with high sexual content are more likely:

1. to be preoccupied with sex, to spend more time thinking and talking with peers about sex, and to believe that others are more preoccupied with it;

2. to have stronger beliefs that sex is a regular and popular activity among young people, especially sexual intercourse;

3. to develop beliefs that premarital, extramarital, and postmarital sex, prostitution, and rape are more frequent and that sex within marriage is rare;

4. to erroneously think they know more about sex and are better able to counsel others about romance, love, etc;

5. to be uncaring about the sanctity of marriage;

6. to think that extramarital and deviant encounters accompanied by romanticized music are more attractive, appealing, and acceptable; and

7. to be less satisfied with their own sex life or progress.

Themes of divorce, illegitimacy, deception, and general hanky-panky are pervasive across all media, making marriage seem unimportant. However, these themes plus regular exposure to successful sex encounters outside of marriage undoubtedly encourage young people to more actively seek out illicit opportunities for sexual satisfaction. Dr. Dolf Zillmann's research has already found that college students and nonstudents who viewed X-rated videos became "less satisfied with their partners—with their affection, physical appearance, sexual performance, and sexual curiosity (see chap. 8).

While Dr. Greenberg confined his observations largely to the impact of mainstream, nonpornographic sexual content on teenagers, Dr. Judith Reisman described the effect of pornographic magazines on adult coders in her research on *Images of Children, Crime and Violence in Playboy, Penthouse and Hustler*. Mature men and women in the university, who identified themselves as having no problem with handling this material, were exposed to pornographic magazines eight hours a day over an extended period of time.[34]

A psychologist met with the coders once a week to make sure they were not developing problems. Nonetheless, almost all coders had problems before the study was completed, the worst developing for those who coded scenes in *Hustler*. Some women experienced flashbacks of homosexual material; others had dreams or experienced problems after work, which they realized were connected with viewing the magazines. They became confused about what they were feeling in terms of sexual arousal and disturbed and anxious about how they were handling themselves after they left the coding situation. Those who coded *Playboy* and *Penthouse* developed more subtle problems related to body comparisons. Even attractive, slender women became more self-conscious about their own images.

Trying to help the coders, researchers played soft music, hung pleasing pictures on the walls, and continuously counseled them. In spite of constant debriefing, none could work on *Hustler* for very long. Even though they were disturbed by the material, it began losing its shocking quality. Becoming habituated to it, they began passing by pictures that were obviously violent and had to be constantly reminded of their original guidelines.[35]

Dr. Bryant similarly experienced the habituation of graduate student participants in a study of X-rated films at the University of Houston:

> The first few hours we were in the room the temperature got invariably hot from people being very, very strongly affected by the material. Over time we clearly saw habituation revealed in body temperatures. After they became desensitized to the sexual content, these same people could code, in the same room for twenty hours and the temperature would stay the same.[36]

The change in the content of lyrics in rock and roll and rap music evidences a rapid breakdown in standards. The Beatles sang about holding hands. Now people are singing about rocking in the cradle of love and driving in a Mercedes Benz (a popular word for vagina).[37] The rap lyrics of 2 Live Crew, which drew so much public comment, were so profane and brutal, newspapers could not print them. Columnist George Will was one of the few writers who let the public know what they actually were. Asking how the young men who gang raped the Central Park jogger could call it fun, he quoted the following lines:

> "To have her walkin' funny we try to abuse it
> A big stinking p——y can't do it all
> So we try real hard just to bust the walls."
> 2 Live Crew's lyrics exult in busting women—almost always called bitches—in various ways, busting vaginas, forcing anal sex, forcing women to lick . . . That's entertainment.[38]

A December 1991 *New York Times* article detailed how far advertising has gone toward breaking down long-honored standards of good taste and marketing strategy. More conservative companies have been spurred on by the success of Calvin Klein whose ads for Obsession perfume have been breaking barriers for years. Not content with showing naked bodies that hint at hetero-sexual, homosexual, and group sex, he recently put out an ad supplement for his jeans that was so "hot," some thought it should be covered by a brown wrapper like pornographic magazines. The article calls it "nearly as steamy as R-rated movies," and says it "now defines the outer limits:" nude "images of men and women touching themselves and each other."[39]

Advertisers are apparently looking for the right "shock level" to catch viewer attention to sell their products. "The search for the boundary lines of propriety has evolved into a process that is part test, part tease and part double dare . . . the fringe keeps getting further out as ads that have shock value today lose their sting by tomorrow."[40]

Like the display of naked body parts that can be lathered with Lever soap and Klein's seemingly nude young men photographed on top of the Ocean Drive's Breakwater Hotel in Miami, a wide range of companies are trying various stages of undress to sell soap operas, beer, perfume, underwear, paper, shower heads, and detergent.

Partially blaming "the growing preponderance of homoerotic imagery in the mainstream, sexually graphic material in movies and on television . . . [and] the slickly sensual quality of music videos shown on MTV," advertisers are claiming they are merely reflecting society. The article concluded:

> Perverse, erotic, or simply a little bit naughty, sexy ads are clearly here to stay. . . . What is not clear is just how perverse, erotic or naughty ads will have to be to sell products next year, the year after that and the year after that. . . .[41]

The most recent development is the sensational televised trial where public figures are subjected to the most explicit questioning of their private sex lives while the whole country listens. Even the newspapers, which are normally to be applauded for their re-straint in reporting sexual crimes, left nothing to the imagination in describing Jeffrey Dahmer's grizzly deeds as his trial domi-nated the news in February 1992. Every day there was a rehash of the details of the murders, sex with dead bodies, dismemberment, and cannibalism. The unnecessary repeating of these details long after they were "news" is indicative of the media's focus on sensa-tionalism and their desire to feed appetites that are out of control.

On 7 June 1991, CNN had a special day to discuss problems of morality. One of the topics discussed was nude dancing in bars. Presented as a serious news story at midday, this segment was interspersed with scenes of nude or nearly nude dancers performing with all their suggestive and erotic movements.

In the 5 to 6 P.M. segment when everyone is home watching, CNN introduced the latest in cable entertainment: interactive voyeurism. This outrage is confined to New York's leased access channel Manhattan Cablevision, at 11:00 at night, but CNN brought it to the living rooms of the nation in the late afternoon. It consists of an erotic female lying on a couch dressed in a sexy one piece garter belt. Sharing sexual fantasies with her telephone audience, she does what they ask her to do. Her conversation is crude, sexy, and arousing as is her every movement.

A voyeur is sexually excited by seeing the sex organs or intimate acts of others—a sexual perversion usually combined with exhibitionism. While it is normal conduct for a five-year-old, in adults, it is evidence of arrested sexual development.[42] If present sexual trends in the media continue, we may become an entire nation of voyeurs.

Chapter 5

Pornography— A Research Case for Harm

Obscenity in word, gesture, reference, song, joke, or by sug-
gestion (even when likely to be understood only by part of the
audience) is forbidden.

—The Motion Picture Code, 1930-1966

According to the industry, pornography is affordable, readily available, highly profitable, and highly appealing entertainment.[1] Scientific research on the effects of pornography, however, tell a different and disturbing story. Social science is demonstrating its harmful effects, clinicians are having to deal with the shattered lives of its addicts and victims, and society is reeling from a loss of its moral and sexual bearings.

After studying scientific research literature, the 1986 Commission on Pornography divided pornography into four primary categories and assessed its effects as follows:[2]

1. Child pornography is universally harmful.

2. Sexually violent material increases the likelihood of aggression towards women. It fosters and perpetuates the rape myth— the notion that women actually enjoy being raped; degrades the class and status of women; encourages a modeling effect (once a viewer sees specific activities portrayed, he tends to act them out); and causes aggression towards women.

3. Sexual activity without violence but with degradation, submission, domination, or humiliation has a similar impact.

4. Materials without sexual violence or images of degradation, subordination, submission, and humiliation have varying effects. While some commissioners concluded erotica, which depicts mutually consensual vaginal intercourse between a man and a woman, was not harmful, others found harm associated with any material in this category. The commission found the quantity of materials

50

identified as both non-violent and non-degrading to be relatively small.

The commission divided pornography's harms to victims into three categories:

1. Major *physical harms* are rape and child molestation. Noting that some hard-core obscenity (when a "performer" is misled about what is expected during the photographic session) is itself the photographic documentation of a rape, the commission found the pornography industry's abuse of performers to be systematic and extreme. With no apparent concern for health and safety, women were subjected to multiple acts of prostitution with multiple partners in very short periods of time. No precautions were taken to protect the health of women in any meaningful way.

The fastest growing physical harm from pornography is *"date rape."* To consumers of pornography, the consent to date means consent to have sexual intercourse and to engage in deviant sexual behavior, a fantasy not shared by most women.[3] When persons married to the victim act out behavior depicted in pornography, they commit *spousal rape*. Other physical harms that flow from the consumption of pornography include forced sexual performance and sadism (as reported by scores of women), battery, torture, murder, imprisonment, transmission of sexually-related diseases, masochism, and prostitution.

2. *Psychological harms* suffered by the victims of pornography include suicidal thoughts and behavior; fear and anxiety caused by seeing pornography; feelings of guilt and shame; fear of exposure through publication or display of pornographic materials; amnesia; denial and repression of abuse; nightmares; compulsive reenactment of sexual abuse; inability to feel sexual pleasure outside of a context of dominance and submission; inability to experience sexual pleasure in any context; feelings of sexual inadequacy; feelings of inferiority and degradation; and feelings of frustration with the legal system.

3. *Social problems* suffered by these victims include loss of jobs or promotions, financial losses, defamation, loss of status in the community, promotion of hatred against women and minorities, loss of trust within a family, divorce, promiscuity, compulsive masturbation, prostitution, and sexual harassment.

The commission removed the veil of silence from the women of America. It is now clear that many thousands of women have been battered and abused as a direct consequence of pornography (see chap. 7). It is also abundantly clear that thousands of children have been sexually exploited and victimized by pornography. Many have been left with permanent scars and ruined lives (see chap. 6).

Following the 1986 Commission, the Surgeon General published a Workshop Report that focused on the public health dimensions of pornography. A group of nineteen nationally and internationally respected experts on all aspects of pornography were charged to summarize what, if anything, the social and behavioral sciences can say with certainty about the effects of pornography. "Surprisingly, the Surgeon General's report [and its five conclusions] has attracted little notice in the media, although each of its conclusions is the unanimous opinion of the experts."[4]

1. *Children and adolescents who participate in the production of pornography experience adverse, enduring effects.*

According to Dr. James Mason, Assistant Secretary of Health, Department of Health and Human Services, "These effects include what is called 'traumatic sexualization' which is the result of a child being coerced into viewing and participating in a broad range of sexual experiences. This experience can produce an obsession with, or aversion to, sex and intimacy."[5]

Clinical studies of children suffering from traumatic sexualization show a range of pathological responses: sexual dysfunction, preoccupation with sexual activity, sleep disorders, withdrawal from other children and adults, and an inclination to act out what they have seen or experienced. Convincing long and short term clinical studies demonstrate that these disorders may last a lifetime.[6]

2. *Prolonged use of pornography increases beliefs that less common sexual practices are more common.*

Repeated exposure causes people to believe that other people frequently engage in the behaviors depicted in pornography. This results in acceptance of deviant behavior as normal and exciting, and increases the chances of experimentation with abnormal sexual activity. Many people, including children and teen-agers, learn about sex from pornography; it shapes their beliefs, attitudes, expectations, and behavior. The current violent, abusive, and degrading content of hard-core pornography could instill beliefs that torture, bondage, anal intercourse, and paraphilia are not only common, but acceptable. The implications for future generations of children are frightening.

3. *Pornography that portrays sexual aggression as pleasurable for the victim increases acceptance of the use of force in sexual relations.*

Graphic depictions of rape—including the victim's initial resistance and later willing and excited participation—are commonplace. They promote the "rape myth" that all women are potential sex partners even when they refuse.[7]

Sexual violence in pornography is related to the development of anti-social attitudes and behavior in males. Specifically, men who use pornography develop attitudes of callousness towards women and accept force as a means to achieve sexual gratification. When gratification is the sole consideration, the sexual partner is reduced to the status of a sexual object who deserves and likes to be abused.

A summary of over 145 scientific papers published during the last ten years on the development of sexual callousness from consuming violent and non-violent pornography follows:

• Rape is seen as a less serious criminal offense. Shorter sentences are recommended for a convicted rapist by both men and women.

• Most sexual practices seem more prevalent than they are.

• Callousness toward women and the sexual abuse of women increases.

• There is heightened dissatisfaction with existing sexual relationships and diminished caring for and trust in one's partner.

• Evaluations of the victim's "worthlessness" are significantly increased.

• There is an increase in callousness toward the suffering experienced by child victims.

• There is a self-reported increase in the likelihood of forcing sexual acts on a woman.

Even very brief exposure to standard pornography featuring attractive women changed the way men perceived their female sexual partners:

• They significantly under appraised their mate's sexual appeal.

• They showed less affection for their mates.

• Dissatisfaction with their intimate partner increased.[8]

Similar concerns exist when children are involved. Many pedophiles and child molesters use three rationalizations for their behavior, which stem directly from pornography use—these may be referred to as the "molester myth."

First, they contend that sexual activity/abuse is "fun" for the child; second, that it is educational, and finally, that the child really "seduced" the molester or was responsible for initiating the conduct. These three themes are commonly promoted in pornographic magazines and paperbacks and demonstrated in child pornography or simulated child pornography.

4. *Acceptance of forced sex in pornography appears to be related to sexual aggression in real life.*

Pornography promotes the idea that all women are potential sex partners and will eventually enjoy sex even though they initially refuse to participate. To a "hyper-eroticized" mind, a casual smile from a woman is a signal that she finds him sexually attractive. If she accepts a date or invites him into her apartment, he is convinced that she is inviting him to have sex. When she refuses, he knows this "no" really means "yes" and thus proceeds to rape her. As Dr. Mason concluded: "When the fantasy world of pornography meets the world of real life, there is conflict and all too frequently, victimization."[9]

5. *In laboratory studies measuring short-term effects, exposure to violent pornography increases punitive behavior toward women.*

There are strict, ethical limitations to exposing individuals to hard-core pornography and recording their sexually violent acts against others outside the laboratory. However, despite these limitations, many rigorous, well-designed experiments have clearly demonstrated that men exposed to violent pornography subsequently behave in an aggressive, punitive, and retaliatory manner towards women.

The two national commissions of 1986 reached similar conclusions that pornography is harmful. Some social scientists, however, disagreed with the interpretations of existing data and accused the commission of going beyond the social science research in formulating its conclusions.

In order to bring greater clarity to this important issue, Dr. John Lyons and David Larson, M.D., who have no research bias or background in pornography effects, undertook a systematic review of the empirical studies (studies founded upon experiment in the laboratory) in the social science literature. A systematic analysis, in any research field, is effective because it can take a diverse body of research and present the findings in terms of a simple whole that is easily understood. Their purpose was to determine whether or not there is experimental evidence that exposure to pornography has a harmful effect on the attitudes and behaviors of its viewers.

Like the 1986 Commission and *Webster's Dictionary*, they defined pornography as "material that is predominantly sexually explicit and intended primarily for the purpose of sexual arousal." Aggressive pornography was defined as materials that contain "images of sexual coercion in which physical force is used or implied, usually against a woman in order to obtain certain sexual acts."

Through computerized literature searches and personal conversations with recognized authorities, Drs. Lyons and Larson identified 152 empirical studies on the effects of pornography from 1971 to the present. As a form of quality control, they used only peer-reviewed studies, but these included most of the important studies in the field.[10] Thus, the final analysis was based on eighty-one research studies of audio or visual pornographic materials, all of which had previously been published in peer-reviewed scientific journals.

The studies were classified into three categories of results based on evidence of effects on arousal, attitudes, or behavior: "a) positive—pornographic stimuli produced a statistically significant effect, b) negative—pornographic stimuli produced no statistically significant effects, c) mixed—evidence of both positive and negative."[11]

The majority of the studies used college students as the sample. Other samples included convicted rapists and married couples. The average exposure time was 51.8 minutes, the range being from 2 to 420 minutes. The type of pornographic material varied: 58 percent was visual—films, pictures, or slides; 17 percent written passages; 17 percent audio-taped passages; and 7 percent mixed media.[12]

The authors of the review concluded, "Systematic research results suggest that exposure to pornography does have important causal impact." The majority of studies found a causal association between exposure to pornography and both aggression towards women and the development of rape myth attitudes and beliefs. This means that pornographic material not only arouses sexually, as it was designed to do, it arouses to the point that it changes attitudes and beliefs and causes more aggressive behavior.

The causal impact was particularly pronounced for exposure to violent pornography. While less consistent, studies of non-violent pornography also show harmful effects. Non-violent pornography contributes to aggressive and callous attitudes and behavior towards women.[13]

A significant relationship was found between type of material and evidence of causal effects. Evidence of causal effects was found in 100 percent of the studies that used written passages, in 76.9 percent of studies using audio-tapes, and in 66 percent of the studies using pictures. These findings suggest that written and audio material give the individual more room to personalize the sexual fantasies. This may account for the fascination both children and adults have for dial-a-porn and pornographic rock music.

However, other research has shown that visual material has the greatest impact, particularly on children and teen-agers.[14] Further research is needed to understand what appears to be conflicting results. There are a complex of factors, including the general impact of music and the essential difference in men and women in receiving visual and written messages. Men respond more to visual material and raw sex, and women respond more to written romance material. What we can conclude with certainty is that all of these forms of pornography have substantial impact.

The conclusions of this systematic review were decisive. A total of 82 percent of the studies showed harmful effects from exposure to pornography.[15] The greatest causal effects were evidenced when aggressive, rape-myth sexual material was studied for its effects on aggressive behaviors and attitudes towards women. Fifteen of seventeen studies or 88 percent reported causal effects in sexual arousal,[16] in negative attitudes,[17] and in aggressive behaviors toward women.[18] Higher levels of arousal were produced by rape scenes in which the rape victim became aroused.[19]

In studying rapist populations, Dr. Lyons found that rapists "were equally aroused to [depictions of] rape and [portrayals of] consenting sex." While nonrapists were less aroused by images of rape, "rapists did not show a preference for rape [depictions]." Other studies have shown that "rapists and nonrapists are similar in their arousal patterns to [portrayals of] rape and consent scenes" and that "rapists show similar or less arousal to rape depictions compared to nonrapists."[20]

According to Drs. Lyons and Larson, the most surprising finding was that there were *any* adverse effects of pornography given the serious restrictions on pornography research. Experimental laboratory studies

1. cannot ethically study subjects most likely at risk from harmful effects of pornography such as children, teen-agers, sexual deviants, and psychologically unstable individuals;

2. most often used soft-core or erotica rather than hard-core and violent pornography, which may have produced more adverse effects;

3. did not study the cumulative effect of heavy exposure to visual pornography over long periods of time (Dr. Lyons stated that it "would be reasonable to propose that if there are effects of a little exposure there should be bigger effects with more exposure."); and

4. did not study the effect of hard-core pornography consumption paired with masturbation, which is often the real-life practice.[21]

Given these obvious limitations, Drs. Lyons and Larson stated that they would have expected to find no harm in the majority of the studies. Instead, "the empirical research on the effects of aggressive and non-aggressive pornography show, with fairly impressive consistency, that exposure to these materials has a negative effect on attitudes toward women and perceived likelihood to rape."[22] In fact, when rape and aggression toward women were measured, almost all the studies showed harm (88 percent), and regardless of the variable measured, the vast majority (82 percent) demonstrated consistent short-term effects. Thus, methodological restrictions suggest that real-life effects would be even greater than demonstrated in the lab.

Systematic analysis of the most reliable studies on the effects of pornography is significant because it puts an end to the debate about whether or not harm results from the consumption of pornography. We can no longer say that half the studies do and half the studies do not show harm; therefore, we don't really know. The disagreement is resolved by the much larger quantity of peer-accepted studies that do show harmful effects. It also presents the scientific studies in a way they have not been presented before. We see 80 to 90 percent of the research projects on pornography demonstrating adverse affects of one fashion or another. If a pharmaceutical firm found such evidence, it would move immediately to action.

A study by Dr. James Check, undertaken in 1984 for the Canadian Frazer Committee on Pornography and Prostitution, is the single most important study that compares the impact of violent and nonviolent pornography. It is the only study that makes a direct comparison after prolonged consumption. Three classes of pornography were shown to samples of male students and nonstudents for three 30-minute sessions within one or two weeks. Four or five days later, the subjects were tested.[23]

Figure 1 shows that commonly available, non-violent, mainstream hard-core pornography and violent pornography had exactly the same effect on men's inclination to commit rape. They both significantly elevated a man's likelihood of committing rape. When it came to the inclination to force women into unwanted sex acts, commonly available, non-violent pornography had a substantially greater impact than violent pornography. While the effect of the ideal pornography (material used in sex education without offensive elements) was not as great, it was clearly in the same direction.[24]

This study also revealed that men who score high in terms of psychoticism—those who tend to be solitary, hostile, lack empathy, and disregard danger—were those most influenced by both common and violent pornography. In addition, Dr. Check found that those who were already regular pornography consumers were more strongly affected than those who were not. Dr. Zillmann concluded from his results that "those who take a keen interest in erotica seem to constitute the population at risk of becoming coercive and violent in their sexuality."[25]

Dr. Check found that "subjects who viewed sexually explicit videos or films at least once per month (relative to those who rarely viewed such materials) were more accepting of rape myths and violence against women, more likely to endorse adversarial

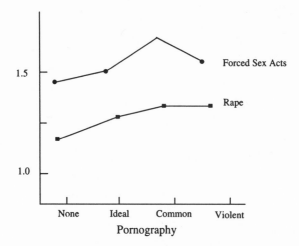

1.5

1.0

None   Ideal   Common   Violent

Pornography

Forced Sex Acts

Rape

*Figure 1. Reported inclination to force sexual acts on
uncooperative partners (circles) and to rape (squares.)

sex beliefs, more likely to report that they would rape and force
women into unwanted sex acts, and were more sexually callous."[26]
Those who regularly watched pornography and were exposed to
non-violent common pornography "were particularly likely to report that they might rape, were more sexually callous and reported engaging in more acts of sexual aggression." The effects of
exposure to sexually violent pornography were the same for consumers and nonconsumers. The greatest effect, and perhaps the
greatest cause for alarm, was in response to commonly available,
non-violent pornography, the type "most prevalent in mainstream
commercial entertainment videos."[27]

The American public is concerned about the big business sex
industry. A Gallop Poll (*Newsweek*, March 1985) reported 73 percent of respondents said they think sexually explicit materials
lead some people to commit sex crimes, while 93 percent called for
strict control of magazines that depict sexual violence.

Woman's Day polled its readers (August 1986) and found that
90 percent of six thousand respondents felt pornography encourages violence against women. Roughly 25 percent of women respondents had experienced sexual abuse as a direct result of
someone's access to pornographic entertainment, and about 50

---

* Graph taken from: Dolf Zillman, *Pornography: Research Advances
and Policy Considerations* (Hillsdale, N.J.: Lawrence Erlbaum Associates, Inc.), 149.

percent had children harmed by pornography. A Harris Poll (1987) found roughly 75 percent of the U.S. population felt theaters, video cassettes, and magazines that showed "sexual violence" should be "banned."

Americans—especially American women—are saying that whatever triggers sexual violence discriminates against women and children and should be eliminated. They seem to be arguing that pornography, the $8-10 billion big business product, shares responsibility for today's toxic sexual environment. Society is just beginning to understand how environmental pollution (e.g. air, water, second-hand smoke) impacts all citizens. Similarly, media sex and violence pollution may yet emerge as the impetus for pandemic adult and teen-age sexual activity. It could encourage skyrocketing levels of out-of-wedlock pregnancy, divorce, suicide, AIDS, sexually transmitted diseases, rape, abortion, and sex crimes by and against children and adults.

Some critics of pornography claim that were the public fully aware of the nature of the images in these materials, the public pulse would reflect an even more intense concern and outrage than already identified.[28]

Chapter 6

Children and Pornography: A Deadly Combination

*Many scenes cannot be presented without arousing danger-
ous emotions on the part of the immature, the young or the
criminal classes. Even within the limits of pure love, certain
facts have been universally regarded by lawmakers as outside the limits of safe presentation.... Children's sex organs
are never to be exposed.*

—The Motion Picture Code, 1930-1966

My father was my pimp in pornography. There were occa-
sions, from ages nine to sixteen when he forced me to be a
pornography model. . . .[1]

He'd pin a picture on the easel and like a teacher he would
tell me this is what you're going to learn today. He would
then act them out on me. . . .[2]

Viewing the [pornographic] pictures seemed to click something for him. . . . He whipped out his Polaroid camera, and
proceeded to take pictures of me in these various [sexual]
positions. . . .[3]

The changing world of children now includes casual, promiscuous sex at earlier and earlier ages, alcohol and drug abuse,
sexual exploitation and abuse, pornography consumption, and
violent crime. For many, these are normal occurrences within
their own families and among their peers. A simple comparison
between growing up in the 1950s and 1990s highlights the "cultural gap that is a million miles wide." A well-known child psychologist recounted his adolescent experience:

60

I attended high school during the "Happy Days" of the1950s, and I never saw or even heard of anyone taking an illegal drug. It happened, I suppose, but it was certainly no threat to me. Some of the other students liked to get drunk, but alcohol was not a big deal in my social environment. Others played around with sex, but the girls who did were considered "loose" and were not respected. Virginity was still in style for males and females. Occasionally a girl came up pregnant, but she was packed off in a hurry and I never knew where she went. . . . Most of my friends respected their parents, went to church on Sunday, studied hard enough to get by and lived a fairly clean life. There were exceptions, of course, but this was the norm.[4]

The decade of the 1990s, however, paints a different and much darker picture for children now growing up. Over half of all girls have experienced sexual intercourse by age fifteen, up 50 percent in less than a decade.[5] Births out of wedlock rose 618 percent from 1950 to 1986 to a total of 878,477.[6] The birth rate for teens doubled between 1960 and 1985.[7] The proportion of births by teen-agers versus total births out of wedlock have tripled in recent years. Now almost one third of all illegitimate births are by teen-agers.[8]

Child sexual abuse is at epidemic levels. Reported cases tripled between 1980 and 1986. The 138,000 confirmed cases in 1986 were just a fraction of the actual number since the majority of cases are unreported.[9] Researchers, law enforcement, and public officials estimate that between 1/1.5 million children are sexually abused each year. Between one hundred thousand and three hundred thousand children in the United States are used in juvenile prostitution annually, and an estimated three hundred thousand children are photographed in sexually explicit poses for child pornography.[10] Today, it is predicted that one out of three girls and one out of seven boys will be sexually abused during his or her lifetime.[11]

The changing world of children includes teen-agers who have become accustomed to pornography. According to recent surveys, virtually all high-school students and most junior high students have seen hard-core or X-rated material. How do children obtain pornography? They find it in the homes of their parents, friends, and relatives or discarded on a garbage pile. They view it in bookstores, family convenience stores, greeting card shops, movies, video stores—on the covers of videos whether they rent them or not—in newscasts on television, blatantly on cable, and only somewhat less blatantly on television. In many cases, they buy or rent it. In Austin, Texas, a local group reportedly sent forty fifteen-year-olds into convenience stores and video stores to obtain hard-core pornography and thirty-eight of the under-aged teen-agers were successful.[12]

Both the 1970 President's Commission on Pornography and recent research found that of all age groups twelve-to seventeen-year-olds are the *largest* consumers of pornography.[13] With such massive early exposure to graphic sexual material, the impact on children's sexual development and mores is enormous. Not surprisingly, surveys have found 62 percent of junior high boys and 54 percent of girls approve of pre-marital sex. Almost half of eighth graders admitted to already experiencing sexual intercourse. The average age of first intercourse was twelve and one half.[14] A study by Dr. Judith Reisman of the content of men's magazines from 1954 to 1984 revealed that the messages of pornographic magazines are both directed toward and are about children.[15] Surprisingly, during that period, popular adult pornographic magazines *Playboy*, *Penthouse*, and *Hustler*, contained an average of nine child images per issue for a total of over six thousand child images since their inception in the 1950s. These were strategically placed side by side with fifteen thousand violent scenes and forty five thousand sexual scenes. The message was clear: adult sex with small girls and boys is fun, harmless, and beneficial to children. Even more alarming, one-sixth of the child images showed children and adults in a sexual encounter.[16] These magazines not only mainstreamed child pornography through cartoons and fairy tales, they portrayed toddlers and children aggressively seeking out sex with adults.

Illustrated by the "progressive" handling of the Wizard of Oz theme, the change in magazine content over the years broke every major taboo. In 1968 *Playboy* published an implied sexual innuendo in black and white. By 1978 *Playboy* insinuated that the little girl Dorothy had been gang raped by her three companions—the lion, the tin man, and the scarecrow. By 1984 a full color *Penthouse* cartoon showed her enjoying sex with the scarecrow while their companions watched and admired his sexual prowess.[17]

Surprisingly, "adult cartoons" draw children to what Dr. Reisman calls "*child magnets*"—Santa Claus, child heroes, fairy tales, coloring book inserts, and pop ups—images that have special appeal to the average boy or girl. "When viewed from this 'child's perspective,' at least 30 percent of *Playboy*, 40 percent of *Penthouse*, and 50 percent of *Hustler's* imagery overall were *child magnets*."[18]

Unfortunately, our culture fails to realize that the seeds of callousness, child sexual abuse, sexual violence, sexual deviance,

and physical violence can all be planted in our children by magazines. For increasing numbers of children, they are watered by
hard-core pornography. Eventually, society reaps a full harvest of
sexual violence and deviant behavior.

Evidence of the true motivation for child images and child
magnets in adult pornography surfaced during the child molestation trial of Dwaine Tinsley, author of the infamous *Hustler* cartoon, "Chester the Molester." He was found guilty of molesting a
thirteen-year-old girl in Ventura, California, on 8 January 1990.
Although he claimed his child pornography cartoons were merely
social commentary, he admitted, "You can't write about this stuff
all the time if you don't experience it."[19] Tinsley's young victim was
his daughter, who testified that Tinsley's "Chester the Molester"
cartoons were an ongoing record of five years of her incestuous
victimization.[20]

After the uproar from the Reisman study and the 1986 Commission on Pornography, the magazines virtually eliminated child
images (see Illustration I). A 1990 study, however, found they still
contain pictures of women who deceptively resemble children
posed beside text that "recalls" the woman as a "child" or as
reliving teen-age bobby-sox sexual adventures.[21] Such images will
henceforth be referred to as "pseudo-child."

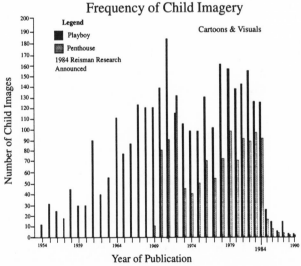

After the content review of this "harmless entertainment," the
correlation between increasing rape and child molestation and
readership rates of men's magazines became more understandable

and increasingly alarming. Researchers have found, for instance, an unusually high correlation between the sex magazine readership index and the Uniform Crime Report rape rates per state. They concluded that such "pornography endorses attitudes and behaviors that increase the likelihood of rape and sexual violence."[22]

In order to make child pornography, at least one child victim must be sexually abused. According to the recent National Commission on Pornography,

> Child pornography is not so much a form of pornography as it is a form of sexual exploitation of children. The distinguishing characteristic of child pornography, as generally understood, is that actual children are photographed while engaged in some form of sexual activity, either with adults or with other children.[23]

In simple terms, child pornography is child sexual abuse in progress and in pictures—a crime scene photograph permanently recorded. Under state and federal law, it is defined as a "visual depiction of a minor [under age eighteen] engaged in sexually explicit conduct." Explicit sexual conduct is defined as "1) sexual intercourse; 2) bestiality; 3) masturbation; 4) sadistic or masochistic abuse; or 5) lascivious exhibition of the genitals or pubic area."[24]

These visual depictions come in many forms: photographs, videotapes, developed or underdeveloped film, magazines, computer images, etc. Children range in age from a few months to eighteen years. Child molesters or pedophiles, those who have a sexual preference for children,* are often selective about the age, sex, race, or looks of their victims (e.g., a ten- to thirteen-year-old white girl with blue eyes and blond hair). However, sexual exploitation of children transcends all economic, social, ethnic, and religious lines.[25]

The distribution and sale of child pornography harms children in ways which some researchers believe are more severe and long lasting than harm from production. The United States Supreme Court in the landmark case on child pornography, *Ferber v. New York*, noted:

> Because the child's actions are reduced to a recording, the pornography may haunt him [or her] in future years, only after the original misdeed took place. A child who has posed

---

*Child molesters and pedophiles are not synonymous terms. Pedophilia is a psychiatric disorder of a sexual perversion in which children are preferred sexual objects. Child molestation is a criminal offense.

for a camera must go through life knowing that the recording is circulating within the mass distribution system for
child pornography. . . . [I]t is the fear of exposure and the
tension of keeping the act secret that seems to have the
most profound emotional repercussions and increases the
emotional and psychic harm suffered by the child.[26]

From a child's perspective, the whole process of being used for
child pornography is devastating. Being molested is bad enough.
The child suffers both immediate and long term harm, sometimes
physical, always emotional. The production of a picture of the
sexual act captures the abuse permanently, and the distribution of
the picture or pictures throughout the underground network of
child molesters and pedophiles is still worse. Often it haunts the
child throughout his or her life.

The most common characteristic of pedophiles and child molesters is the use and consumption of pornography. As one FBI
behavioral scientist concluded:

. . . child pornography exists primarily for the consumption
of pedophiles [and child molesters]. If there were no
pedophiles [or child molesters], there would be little or no
child pornography . . .[27]

A 1982 case confirms this conclusion:

A postal inspector asked a young North Carolina prosecutor
to stop an investigation of explicit photos discovered in a
national photo developing business. Busy with high priority
drug trafficking and public corruption cases, he did not
close the case as the investigator wanted but referred it to
the state to be handled locally. In the process, he discovered
that the state pornography law had serious shortcomings,
making prosecution virtually impossible.

Trying to be diligent, he asked the investigator to further
research the case before he closed it. That investigation
uncovered the largest child pornography case in the South-
east. The suspect, twice decorated as state employee of the
year, was running an "uncensored" photo developing business in which he received pornographic negatives from all
over the United States, Canada, and Mexico. He had molested, photographed and recorded the abuse of, at least,
eighteen girls including his own recently adopted six-year-
old daughter. He was a deacon and church youth worker
who always befriended the church and neighborhood children. After his conviction, at his sentencing, he testified at
length about his pornography addiction and how he pro-

gressed to harder and harder pornography until he finally
acted out his fantasy of seducing and molesting a little girl.
He used the pornography to arouse himself, seduce the girls
to have sex, and teach them different forms of sex.

I was that prosecutor (H. Robert Showers). When I asked him
how we could stop him from doing this to children, he said, "Take
away my pornography!"

Prosecutors and investigators across the nation have confirmed that pornography is the key link and catalyst in the chain
of child sexual abuse.[28] Former Judge Gene Malpas in Florida's
Dade and Broward Counties prosecuted close to one thousand
child sexual abuse cases; only four did not involve some type of
pornography. Judge Malpas said pornography fueled and assisted
the seduction process that led to molestation. Many molesters
confirmed, "without pornography, the molestation would not have
occurred or been possible to accomplish."[29]

Research confirms the experiences of prosecutors and investigators as well. A 1983 study by Dr. William Marshall revealed
that 87 percent of child molesters of girls and 77 percent of child
molesters of boys admitted regular use of pornography. Pornography was reportedly used for three main purposes: (1) to stimulate
the child molester, (2) to lower the natural inhibitions to sexual
activity in their intended child victim, and (3) to teach the child
victim to imitate the conduct in real life sexual encounters with
adults or other children.[30]

According to the Congressional Subcommittee on Child Pornography and Pedophilia, "no single characteristic of pedophiles is
more pervasive than the obsession with child pornography."[31]
Another common trait of pedophiles and child molesters is collect-
ing child pornography and child erotica.* These sexually explicit
collections are always kept in secret. Often catalogued and well
organized, they are generally used for stimulation, seduction,
validation of the deviant behavior, blackmail of the child victim to
keep his/her secret, and trade/sale in the underground pedophile
network.[32]

Pedophiles and child molesters have two additional traits in
common: 1) *they desire access to children,* and 2) *they seduce rather*

---

* Child erotica, which is a broader and more encompassing term than child
pornography, is any material, relating to children, that serves a sexual purpose. Child erotica can be published material on child development, man-boy
love, nudism, personal advertisements, men's magazines, adult pornography
advertisements, access to children, etc., and unpublished material such as
diaries, letters, newsletters, telephone and address books.

than force. The child abuser meets the children on their own "turf" and begins the process of "seduction" that leads to sexual exploitation and picture-taking.

The seduction process lowers the natural inhibitions to sex and instructs the child in sexual poses and conduct. Pornography, both child and adult, is critical to successfully complete the seduction process and to accomplish the goal of "consensual sexual participation by the child" usually in front of the camera. This seduction process generally has eight steps as shown in Illustration II.

Illustration II

SEDUCTION PROCESS FOR CHILD MOLESTATION

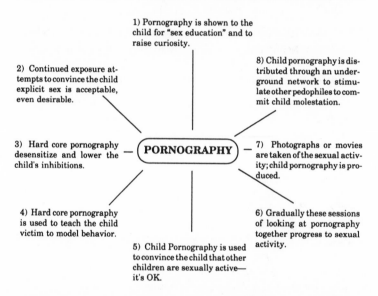

1) Pornography is shown to the child for "sex education" and to raise curiosity.

2) Continued exposure attempts to convince the child explicit sex is acceptable, even desirable.

3) Hard core pornography desensitize and lower the child's inhibitions.

4) Hard core pornography is used to teach the child victim to model behavior.

5) Child Pornography is used to convince the child that other children are sexually active—it's OK.

6) Gradually these sessions of looking at pornography together progress to sexual activity.

7) Photographs or movies are taken of the sexual activity; child pornography is produced.

8) Child pornography is distributed through an underground network to stimulate other pedophiles to commit child molestation.

PORNOGRAPHY

Children are often surprised and bewildered when shown "child imagery" in adult men's magazines, but it serves to convince them that sexual behavior is normal and acceptable.[33] Progressively introduced to harder material, the child's inhibitions are lowered to a point where he allows the molester to kiss and touch him sexually. Eventually, if successful, the seduction process progresses to more explicit activity between the child victim and adult or other children.[34] Finally, pictures of these activities are made for the enjoyment of the molester and for distribution to other seducers. In short, pornography is at the center of the sexual exploitation of children.

Pornography's use for enticement, seduction, instruction, blackmail, and trade/sale has been confirmed by numerous law enforcement surveys.[35] A 1984 survey of fourteen hundred child molestation cases in Louisville, Kentucky, revealed that in all forty major selected cases of sexual exploitation outside the family, adult pornography was involved. In most cases, child pornography or child erotica were found in the molester's home.[36]

In a comprehensive Los Angeles child sexual exploitation survey from 1980 to 1989, pornography was indicated in 62 percent of preliminary investigations and child pornography in 23 percent. Especially significant was the discovery that pornography was recovered in almost 55 percent of the cases regardless of whether initially indicated. When indicated in the preliminary investigation, pornography was recovered 88 percent of the time.

The Los Angeles Police Department study concluded:

> Clearly pornography is an insidious tool in the hands of the pedophile population. The study merely confirms what detectives have long known: that pornography is a strong factor in the sexual victimization of children.[37]

In summary, a form of pornography almost always plays a catalytic, key role in child molestation. It serves to justify the deviant conduct, to assist molesters in seducing their victims, and to provide a means of blackmailing the victim to prevent disclosure.

Even more alarming than rising rates of child sexual abuse, and the connection of pornography to child abuse, is the *cycle or chain of child victimization*.[38] As previously discussed, most sexually exploited children are seduced into participating in sexual activity with adults. Some are missing children (runaways, throwaways, non-family abductions) who are exploited through prostitution and pornography, and some are relatives or children in the neighborhood of the molester.[39] While no conclusive studies or statistics are available, it is clear that a significant number of sexually abused children become molesters if not treated early and adequately.

The Los Angeles Police Department reports that most child molesters (80 percent) were themselves molested as children and that they generally seek out victims of the same age and sex as when they were first molested.[40] Scientific research has verified this law enforcement study by finding that 57 percent of the child molesters studied reported they were themselves molested as children.[41]

Before being caught for the first time, homosexual and heterosexual child molesters average between thirty and sixty child victims respectively. Preferential child molesters sexually abuse an average of 380 children in their lifetimes.[42] If even a small number of the 380 children become molesters, who in turn sexually abuse 380 children, the exponential increase of sexual exploitation in the second and third generations would be staggering. This clearly indicates that our children are seriously at risk, and if the chain of sexual abuse is not broken, each year the risk will be greater.

Illustration III

CHAIN OF SEXUAL ABUSE

Molesters/Rapists

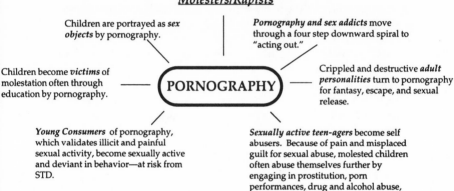

Children are portrayed as *sex objects* by pornography.

Pornography and sex addicts move through a four step downward spiral to "acting out."

Children become *victims* of molestation often through education by pornography.

PORNOGRAPHY

Crippled and destructive *adult personalities* turn to pornography for fantasy, escape, and sexual release.

Young Consumers of pornography, which validates illicit and painful sexual activity, become sexually active and deviant in behavior—at risk from STD.

Sexually active teen-agers become self abusers. Because of pain and misplaced guilt for sexual abuse, molested children often abuse themselves further by engaging in prostitution, porn performances, drug and alcohol abuse, eating disorders, etc...

Not only is pornography the engine that drives the cycle of sexual victimization, it is the lock that holds the chain of abuse together. The keys to unlock the chain are education, victim assistance, legislation, and enforcement. To stop the avalanche of abuse and reverse the trend, pornography's removal from society is essential.

Evidence is mounting that both psychological and physical injuries are inflicted on children who participate in child pornography. The *Ferber* court concluded:

It has been found that sexually exploited children are unable to develop healthy affectionate relationships in later life, have sexual dysfunctions, and have a tendency to become sexual abusers as adults . . . . Sexually exploited children are predisposed to self-destructive behavior such as drug and alcohol abuse or prostitution . . . [43]

Frequently, the emotional distress caused by child sexual abuse results in identifiable behavior changes,[44] but fewer than 6 percent of these cases are reported.[45] Children fail to speak out about sexual molestation either because they believe they did something wrong to bring about the abuse, or they are threatened into silence by their molesters.[46]

Most disturbing is the discovery that sexually abused children are more likely when they reach adulthood to victimize young children, particularly their own.[47] In fact, of all sexual crimes, the recidivism rate (falling back into prior criminal habits) for pedophile offenders is second only to exhibitionists.[48]

The end-result of pedophiles acting out pornographic sexual/ sadistic depictions of children can be death. One series of child pornography photographs shown to the Attorney General's Commission on Pornography "focused on a cute, nine-year-old boy who had fallen into the hands of a molester. In the first picture, the blond lad was fully clothed and smiling at the camera. But in the second, he was nude, dead, and had a butcher knife protruding from his chest."[49] Unfortunately cases have been reported in which a sex-related murder followed a pattern detailed in pornographic magazines or films.

Harm to children occurs simply from the existence of the material. Having a life of its own, child pornography is timeless and may be distributed and circulated for years after initially created. Each time it is exchanged, the children involved are victimized again.

Pornography is also luring runaway and throwaway children into juvenile prostitution. In twentieth century America, a child does not have to grow up to become a prostitute. Instead, many children "grow up" while forced to survive as prostitutes.[50] While the exact number of children involved in prostitution is hopelessly elusive, the best estimate from all sources is between one hundred thousand to three hundred thousand.[51] Although no clear profile of a juvenile prostitute exists, most juvenile prostitutes are in their mid-to-late teens. They run away from home because of an abusive atmosphere and remain far from home in metropolitan areas such as Los Angeles, Miami, New York, Chicago, and Washington, DC.[52] For example, there are thirty thousand children walking the streets of Los Angeles every night.[53]

The families of these teen-agers are generally in disarray. The majority come from broken homes,[54] but are not necessarily poor economically. Most juvenile prostitutes said in interviews that they came from "middle-class," "comfortable," and occasionally even "wealthy" homes.[55]

A large Canadian study revealed that 60 percent of both male and female juvenile prostitutes had been asked to participate in the making of pornography and 12 percent of the girls and 20 percent of the boys had actually been so used.[56] Two smaller American studies emphatically confirmed that there is a significant link between juvenile prostitution and child pornography. For example, an American study found that 75 percent of male teen-age prostitutes had participated in pornography.[57] The Canadian Badgley Report concluded that "juvenile prostitutes are at high risk of being exploited by pornographers."

Numerous studies of junior and senior high teen-agers dramatically demonstrate their wide exposure to pornography. Dr. Bryant's study in Evansville, Indiana, found that every high-school male and 97 percent of the females had seen some form of pornography. The average per boy was sixteen issues. Ninety percent of the boys and 80 percent of the girls had been exposed to "hard-core" pornography, with thirteen the average age of first exposure.[58]

Among junior high students, 92 percent of the boys and 84 percent of the girls had seen soft-core magazines. The average age for exposure to *Playboy* for boys was eleven and for girls twelve. Junior high students had seen an average of six R-rated films, 70 percent of them having seen their first film before the age of thirteen.[59]

An important finding was that the desire for imitation increased as age decreased. An even larger percentage of junior high boys (72 percent) and girls (44 percent) reported wanting to try something they had seen than did high-school boys and girls. Alarmingly, 31 percent of the high-school boys and 18 percent of the girls reported that they had, in fact, acted out something they had seen depicted within a few days of exposure.

Pornography is a primary source of sex education for children. A 1979 study by Aaron Hass interviewed teen-agers across the country and found that 91 percent of the girls and 95 percent of the boys had received their sex education from pornography.[60]

Today, explicit sex is even more pervasive in our culture, and children are continually exposed to it. It is acted out in living color on cable and video in their own homes. Children learn the details of the physical act long before they are prepared to deal with them emotionally.

What kind of sex education do our children receive from pornography? According to Dr. Park Elliott Dietz, a member of the Attorney General's Commission on Pornography who has degrees in medicine, public health, and sociology,

> a person who learned about sex in today's pornography outlets would never conceive of a man and woman marrying or even falling in love before having intercourse. He could not imagine tender foreplay or having children as a purpose of sexual union. He would learn that sex at home means sex with children, parents, siblings, pets, members of the extended family, servicemen, or burglars. He would learn that one in five sexual encounters involved spanking, whipping, fighting, tying, chaining, gagging, or torture; that one in ten sexual acts involve more than two people; and that urine and excrement are erotic materials. He would learn that the instruments of sex are chemicals, hand cuffs, restraints, harnesses, knives, guns, whips and that photographers and cameras should always be present to capture the action unless children are involved. Then secrecy is required.[61]

In January 1989, national news carried the story of serial rapist-murderer Ted Bundy. Prior to his execution, he claimed that pornography helped change a vulnerable boy into a pornography addict, then into a man who acted out sexual fantasies that had become violent, and finally into a brutal mass murderer of over thirty women and girls. While the media downplayed and cynically joked about this bizarre assertion, law enforcement knew that Bundy was only one of a long list of serial rapists and murderers for whom pornography was the catalyst. In fact, an FBI study of serial sex murderers revealed that pornography use was one of the most common profile characteristics, occurring in 81 percent of the criminals studied.[62] Almost all of the men had started pornography consumption before eighteen, and many of them were exposed as early as six, seven, and eight-years-old.

Younger and younger children are becoming sexual offenders and victimizing children even younger than themselves. According to the 1989 Uniform Crime Report, from 1986 to 1988 forcible rape arrests of children twelve and under increased by over 25 percent, while murder arrests for those under 18 jumped 22 percent between 1983 and 1987. Now, according to the 1991 FBI Uniform Crime Report, almost half of all sex offenders are under 18.

A 1988 report on Sex Offenses by Youth in Michigan reports a dramatic increase of juvenile sex offenses in the last ten-year period. The report stated that 681 juveniles who averaged fourteen years of age were convicted of sexually assaulting children who averaged seven years of age. Ninety-three percent of the offenders were acquaintances, babysitters, friends, or relatives of the victims.[63]

Modern technology has promoted pornography from the back alleys of urban inner cities to the living rooms, kitchens, and bedrooms of suburbs and small towns through local video outlets, cable television,[64] satellite TV, telephones, and even home computers.

The $2.4 billion per year telephone sex industry, called dial-a-porn, has activated over five hundred thousand calls per day. In 1985 one company reported six to seven million calls per month at 50 cents per call. Most of the callers are believed to be children. In fact, during a trial on the West Coast, two dial-a-porn services admitted that 75 to 85 percent of their customers were children.

Not surprisingly, the incidence of sexual violence perpetrated by children is increasing at an alarming rate. In New York City, for example, rape arrests of thirteen-year-old boys have increased by 200 percent between 1986 and 1988.[65] According to the FBI, the number of arrests for rape committed by boys eighteen and under rose by almost 15 percent between 1982 and 1987.[66] A Utah juvenile court analysis revealed a 55 percent increase in the number of juvenile sex offenses from 1984 to 1989. The analysis noted:

> the fastest growing adolescent offense is sexual abuse. . . . We hardly ever get a first time referral; they just haven't been caught before. When we check, we sometimes find hundreds of [sex] offenses.[67]

From 1950 to 1979, serious crimes by children increased by 11,000 percent.[68]

When the pornographic media is blamed for the rapid rise in child sex offenders, critics point their finger at parents. However, parental control has become increasingly difficult since passage of the days of one television and telephone in the house of a two parent family. Over 44 percent of all children now have a TV in their own bedroom, and over half the teen-agers have their own television. More than three-fourths of all households with children have a VCR, which provides a great challenge for the almost 9.4 million single parents who try to supervise their children's viewing (and work for a living).[69] The FCC estimated that for all ages, children's unsupervised viewing averaged about two hundred minutes per day with the average rising to six hours a day for older age groups.[70]

A recent story from Ohio illustrates the problem:

For two years, starting at the age of four, a child watched cableporn in his own living room before he was caught. He got up late at night and turned on the cable without sound so he wouldn't be heard. Wanting to imitate what he saw, he started undressing his sister who was two years younger than he and still in diapers. He would pull her diapers off, take his clothes off and lie on top of her. Later he started playing with body parts. As she grew older, she watched the movies and played with him.

The children were six and four when they coaxed a neighborhood boy into their bedroom and asked him to expose himself and participate in a touch and feel game. The boy was scared and fled but returned later in the day to hit his former friend with a baseball bat. When confronted, the child who had watched the cable movies said, "Big people do it, I just wanted to be big."[71]

In chapter 9 we will see that pornography addiction is often the result of being raised within a dysfunctional family structure. However, for the young child, pornography can have a developmental or causal influence on the path to addiction. According to research, if pornography is seen by a child or used by a child before the age of twelve, it actually becomes the predisposing factor.[72] This means that exposure to pornography can have a devastating effect on any normal child, even the very well-nurtured child.

A clear example is the entrapment of many children by telephone sex or dial-a-porn. Dr. Victor Cline, in a 1985 field study for the U.S. Department of Justice, found an "addiction effect" in every child who had become involved with dial-a-porn. Nearly all the children had clear memories of the content of calls even one or two years later, and many of them acted out what they had learned. For example,

One 12-year-old boy in Hayward, California listened to dial-a-porn for nearly two hours on his church phone between Sunday meetings. Later he sexually assaulted a 4-year-old girl in his mother's Day Care Center. He had never been exposed to pornography before. He had never acted-out sexually before, and he was not a behavior problem at home. From a family with conservative values, he had never heard of oral sex before, but this he performed on the girl, in direct imitation of what he had heard on the phone.[73]

The very first sexual learning experiences are incredibly powerful. If the first experience is of deviant sex, it will be highly related to later sex offenses. Early sexual abuse of a boy by a male can result in a homosexuality disorder. If the experience is perceived as good, it will have an even greater impact. For example, often people who become addicted to gambling are those who happen to hit the jackpot the first time they gamble.[74]

Children's exposure to pornographic materials in the media today may be creating a whole generation of dysfunctional individuals. Young voyeurs, molesters, and rapists are an increasing reality. Statistics, research, and real life stories leave no one in doubt that a constant diet of explicit sex and graphic violence in the media affect the attitudes and behavior of children and teenagers. Can we reverse this trend? Absolutely! But we must take decisive action now.

Already, child pornography has become a separate *per se* law—it is illegal without regard to community standards—and its enforcement across the nation has driven its production, distribution, and use underground. However, more must be done.

The following are ways we can protect our children:

1. Pass harmful matter *per se* laws that make explicit sex and graphic violence in any media illegal for children under age eighteen. These laws would eliminate the "subjective variable obscenity test of today's harmful to minor laws and replace it with objective, easy to apply standards as to what material cannot be shown, rented, or sold to minors. These laws and regulations should apply to cable, satellite, and broadcast media as well as to video stores, convenience stores, and movie theaters. Simply put, all sexually explicit depictions such as intercourse, masturbation, sexual violence, and lewd exhibition of private areas will be illegal to be sold, rented, or shown to children. While X-rated and "hard R" material may be made available to adults, there is nothing to be gained and much to be lost by exposing children to such harmful materials.

2. All states should define children as under age eighteen and pass felony laws against production, distribution, receipt, and possession of child pornography. With the new *per se* child pornography laws and aggressive enforcement, child pornography can be eliminated from our society.

3. Every state should require convicted sex offenders to register their location when released from prison, and a national registry should be created to prevent molesters and rapists from having access to additional children to repeat their crimes.

4. Long-term treatment programs should be extended to better understand and help sexually abused children. Further, vertical prosecution systems and child victim/witness laws that require everyone involved in the system (social service workers, investigators, prosecutors, and psychologists) to question the child at one

time should be instituted in every state so that child victims are not further traumatized by constant retelling of their abuse stories.

5. Parents must monitor what their children watch and listen to and guide them to healthy content and value filled themes.

6. Churches, schools, parents, and civic groups should make children and parents aware of molester's ploys without scaring them.

7. They should cooperate to help teach children acceptable attitudes and behavior while making clear statements about unhealthy and dangerous attitudes or conduct.

8. Finally, parents and teachers must become aware of indications of sexual abuse in children's behavior in order to be able to stop it and get effective treatment. Knowing the signs and what to do could literally save that child's life.

While no one advocates programming children or repressing opportunities for them to learn about the world around them, we must reestablish and communicate to our children the basic principles and values that are necessary for a democratic society to survive and prosper. Parents need help from all our institutions to protect their children. Both our pervasive media, and those who feed on its worst elements, have the potential to destroy their innocence forever. We have the power "through the purse," law, public pressure, and education to stop and reverse this devastating trend, but we must act aggressively; and we must act now.

Chapter 7

Women and Pornography

*Seduction or rape . . . should never be more than suggested.
And only when essential for the plot, and even then never
shown by explicit method.*

—The Motion Picture Code, 1930-1966

My name is Andrea Dworkin. I am a citizen of the United
States, and in this country where I live, every year millions
of pictures are being made of women with our legs
spread. . . . Millions and millions of pictures are made of us
in postures of submission and sexual access so that our
vaginas are exposed for penetration, our anuses are exposed for penetration, our throats are used as if they are
genitals for penetration. . . . Real rapes are on film and are
being sold in the marketplace. And the major motif of
pornography as a form of entertainment is that women are
raped and violated and humiliated until we discover that
we like it and at that point we ask for more . . .

There is a pornography of the humiliation of women . . . a
form of sexual pleasure for the viewer and for the victim . . .
where women are tortured for the sexual pleasure of those
who watch and those who do the torture, where women are
murdered for the sexual pleasure of murdering women, and
this material exists because it is fun, because it is entertainment, because it is a form of pleasure, and there are
those who say it is a form of freedom.

Pornography is used in rape—to plan it, to execute it, to
choreograph it, to engender the excitement to commit the
act. Pornography is used in gang rape against women. . . .

We see pornography in the harassment of women on jobs, in
the harassment of women in education, to create terror and

77

> compliance in the home . . . where more violence is commit-
> ted against women than anywhere else.
>
> We see pornography having introduced a profit motive into
> rape. We see that filmed rapes are protected speech. We see
> the centrality of pornography in serial murders . . . boys
> imitating pornography. . . .
>
> We see the average age of rapists going down . . . sexual
> assault after death . . . because the man believes that he
> will get a particular kind of sexual pleasure having sex with
> a woman after she is dead.
>
> When your rape is entertainment, your worthlessness is
> absolute. . . . One lives inside a nightmare of sexual abuse
> that is both actual and potential, and you have the great joy
> of knowing that your nightmare is someone else's freedom
> and someone else's fun. . . . I live in a country where women
> are tortured as a form of public entertainment and for
> profit, and that torture is upheld as a state-protected right.
> Now that is unbearable.[1]

Andrea Dworkin offered this eloquent statement before the
Attorney General's Commission on Pornography in 1986. But in
spite of increased efforts by the Justice Department to prosecute
hard-core pornography since then, the humiliation and torture of
women are still considered entertainment and defended as protected speech in the United States.

Just across our northern border, however, a ground breaking
case has been upheld by the Supreme Court of Canada. It offers
hope to millions of women who are daily living in fear of rapists
and in bondage to husbands and lovers who are hooked on pornography and are forcing their women to try out everything they view
and read in pornographic materials—women like the speaker
below:

> After ten years of a relatively happy marriage, George
> began to request sexual favors Susan was unwilling to
> deliver. . . . As his requests became more deviant, Susan
> became more resistant. During marital counseling no ex-
> planation was ever offered as to why George was demand-
> ing such deviant activities. When his demands continued to
> go unmet he began violently raping Susan. As the divorce
> became final, it was disclosed that the children had also
> been sexually abused by their father. George finally admit-
> ted he had been using pornography since he was nine and
> hard-core pornography since he was sixteen.

Susan explained, "Even though he knew intellectually that he risked the loss of everything he stood for, he could not control his addiction. My entire family has now joined the ranks of those who are numbered as victims of pornography."

On 27 February 1992, by unanimous vote, Canada's Supreme Court decided it is legitimate to suppress materials that harm women, even though freedom of expression is involved. According to University of Michigan law professor Catherine MacKinnon, this means "what is obscene is what harms women, not what offends our values." Materials that subordinate, degrade, or dehumanize women and children are now obscene in Canada.[2]

Lawyer Kathleen Mahoney, who argued the case, explained:

The court said that while the obscenity law does limit the charter's freedom of expression guarantee, it's justifiable because this type of expression harms women personally, harms their right to be equal, affects their security and changes attitudes toward them so they become more subject to violence. . . . [The court said the harm caused by] the proliferation of materials which seriously offend the values fundamental to our society is a substantial concern which justifies restricting the otherwise full exercise of the freedom of expression.[3]

Community standards will still decide which materials are obscene, that is, which show "undue sexual exploitation" and are therefore harmful. "Harm in this context means that it predisposes persons to act in an antisocial manner as, for example, the physical or mental mistreatment of women by men."[4]

Similar ordinances in Indianapolis, Minneapolis, and Bellingham, Washington, in the early 1980s failed to be upheld in the United States, but the judge who wrote the Indianapolis opinion "apparently accepted the argument that pornography could harm women." He wrote:

Depictions of subordination tend to perpetuate subordination. . . . The subordinate status of women, in turn, leads to affront and lower pay at work, insult and injury at home, battery and rape on the streets.[5]

A newly proposed bill for the state of Massachusetts would allow women to recover damages from publishers and purveyors of pornography if they can prove it influenced the assault.[6] Several pieces of legislation based on this harm approach will be before the state legislatures and the United States Congress in the 1990s.

The Pornography Victim's Compensation Act was introduced by Senator Mitch McConnell of Kentucky after hearing Ted Bundy's story of how pornography fueled his appetite for violence against women.

> The most damaging pornography is that which depicts sexual violence . . . it molded and shaped my thought process . . . it crystallized it inside and I got to the point of acting it out.[7]

The bill would make producers and distributors of pornographic material financially accountable for the harm they cause. It would enable victims of sexual abuse and rape to sue pornographers if it can be proven that the material helped to cause the crime.[8] A logical conclusion that the explicit material influenced the commission of the offense may be reached if:

1. there are unusual similarities between the actual crime and certain acts described or depicted in the material;

2. the sexual offender testifies that the material did in fact influence or incite him to commit the offense;

3. the victim testifies that the pornography was used in the commission of the offense; or

4. an expert who has examined the offender testifies that the material influenced or incited the commission of the offense.[9]

An important societal question is: How is it that viewing materials of torture and abuse of women ever came to be accepted as a legitimate activity in a civilized nation? Feminists claim that most pornography is "pro-rape propaganda."[10] Men quickly become bored with repeated viewings of semi-nudity, nudity, and mild, sexually explicit conduct.[11] They increasingly desire and seek novel materials.[12] To hold viewer attention, the industry has provided increasingly explicit materials. In search of novelty, it has turned to bizarre presentations containing elements of violence. For example, *Penthouse* portrayed Asian women bound and gagged and hung upside down in trees. That this is not mere artistic presentation is strongly suggested in a *New York Times* article two months later:

> The December 1984 issue of *Penthouse* carried this eroticized torture into the "men's entertainment" forum with a series of photographs of Asian women bound with heavy rope, hung from trees, and sectioned in parts. It is not known whether this pictorial incited a crime that occurred two months later wherein an eight-year-old Chinese girl living in Chapel Hill, North Carolina, was kidnaped, raped, murdered and left hanging from a tree limb.[13]

Research has verified that men who are exposed to beautiful women in pornography become less satisfied with their wives and girlfriends.[14] Not only are women diminished by pornography, men are demeaned as well. A man cannot love a woman and think pornographically about her. He becomes more concerned about the sex act than the woman with whom he has it. Nowhere is this more evident than in the testimonies of women who thought they were marrying the man of their dreams only to find out on the honeymoon that pornography was more important to their new husband than they were:

> He chose Las Vegas for our honeymoon. We made love one time during that week. The rest of the time he dragged me to burlesque shows, to topless shows, and to peep show machines that ate quarters. He ran from show to show until he was too exhausted to have sex.
>
> Back home, he locked himself in the bathroom with *Playboy*. He received magazines in brown wrappers in the mail. I found stacks of X-rated magazines and videos. Eventually he spent his evenings peering into the neighbor's bedroom with a high powered telescope. There was almost no love-making . . . .
>
> From the honeymoon on, I felt inadequate. I thought, "Oh, my god, I'm not woman enough for this man." I had breast surgery, anything I could do to become woman enough. When I came home, he said, "I wish you'd have gone bigger." I thought, "There is no way to please this man!" I eventually put a gun to my head. . . .
>
> The counselor said he was not admitting he had a problem, he was only saying, "My wife is jealous when I look at other women." It hurt even worse that he wouldn't admit that the women in pornography were replacing me.
>
> After 13 years of marriage and three separations that failed to produce a change, the counselor said I had three choices. "You can have an emotional breakdown, you can commit suicide, or you can be like a great race horse and run." I ran and I've never been sorry.[15]

While pornography is the province of men, women become active in it; most are introduced to it by men. They look at it and try to act it out in order to please their men. Some are so repulsed, they have nothing to do with it. Often, however, in a desperate attempt to save their marriages and retain the "love" of their husbands, they rent X-rated videos to learn how they are expected to perform.

Helen Singer Kaplan, the sexologist who taught Dr. Ruth, advised wives in the December 1985 *Redbook* to enjoy their husband's girlie magazines, see the kinds of things he likes, and use his fantasies to make their sex lives more satisfying. She frightened thousands of women by telling them that resistance to his sexual needs could drive him to women who would be more willing to accept his fantasies. Because of propaganda like this and because they are trying to be good wives, many women go along with bizarre and violent behavior.

Two-thirds of the women a Florida psychologist counseled complained about their husbands' viewing habits and unrealistic sex demands.[16] Women experience rejection, anger, hurt, and pain when their men prefer impersonal pictures to the care, warmth, and love they would like to give them. They feel devalued and dehumanized, related to only as sex objects. They suffer silicone implants and become anorexic or bulimic, not out of vanity, but to compete with airbrushed pictures, which are more beautiful than reality. They never feel loved and accepted for themselves, and they learn to distrust all men.[17] According to clinical psychologist Dr. Gail Stevenson, "Increasing numbers of women are entering psychotherapy with problems specifically related to the shame that results from their forced exposure to, but inability to counteract, pervasive pornographic denigration."[18]

Pornography gives a vivid portrayal of what is perceived as the willingness of women to give men access anytime, anywhere, and in every circumstance. In so doing, it offers scientifically inaccurate, false, and misleading information about female sexual nature and response. It promotes sex devoid of all the things women value in sexual relationships: foreplay, tenderness, caring, love, and romance.[19] It encourages men to think they are entitled to fulfill their desires, and even when activities that are commonly thought to inflict discomfort and pain are shown, it is almost always their ultimate conversion into extreme euphoria that is featured."[20] Many male consumers eventually come to feel justified in imitating those behaviors.

The purpose of sexual fantasies is to generate sexual excitedness. According to Dr. Dolf Zillmann, some sexual fantasies have a haunting quality that drives men "to force upon nonconsenting, resisting partners actions that promised much gratification when imagined."[21]

Research findings show that pornography influences a man's imagination long after exposure.[22] It plants "the idea that women are sexually provocative and nondiscriminating in their partner

choice [which] leads many men to believe that women tend to
bring rape upon themselves and that women's allegations of having been violated are not to be trusted."[23]

Thus, to male consumers, women appear permissive and promiscuous, and such wrong perceptions lead to callous attitudes in
males toward the sexual victimization of women and makes them
believe that coercive sexual actions against women are not serious
offenses.[24]

Some writers have long contended that pornography makes
men lose respect for women: "If one sees these women (in pornography) as symbolic representatives of all women, then all women
fall from grace."[25] "Once fallen from grace, once branded as promiscuous, women become 'public property.'"[26] This perception of
women encourages sexual harassment on the job, sexual callousness on dates and at home, the inclination to rape, and the act of
rape, itself.

The term "sexual harassment on the job" covers a wide range
of male-female behaviors and accusations. Feminists believe pornography on the job serves as "an instruction manual for violent
men that shatters women's civil rights."[27] In 1985, the Attorney
General's Commission on Pornography received numerous complaints of social injuries from women who were humiliated and
degraded by the presence of pornographic materials in the working environment. These materials obviously motivated inappropriate remarks and aggressive behavior. The following example
illustrates what women must endure because of the existence of
pornography in the workplace:

> I was working as a telephone repairwoman for Southern
> Bell in Florida. Porn was everywhere. They use it to intimi-
> date you, to keep women out of their territory. They had
> pin-ups in the workrooms. Male workers would draw porno-
> graphic pictures of women workers in the cross-boxes and
> write comments about what we would do in bed. One day . . .
> [a man] shoved a photograph at me of a woman's rear end
> with her anus exposed and asked, "Isn't this you?" I was
> humiliated and furious.[28]

Largely because of the feminists' emphasis on women's rights
to safety and dignity, sexual harassment on the job is now recognized legally as a prosecutable offense. In January 1991, in Jack-
sonville, Florida, a federal judge ruled that:

> a welder named Lois Robinson was harassed by male co-
> workers who put up graphically sexual posters and calen-
> dars, some showing women being abused. Among the offen-

84

sive materials was a poster with a frontal view of a nude
woman and the imprinted words "USDA choice."[29]

This is one more in a long line of pornographic images of
women as pieces of meat; for example, the album cover called
"Choice Cuts" or the beach towel of a woman's body segmented and
labelled like a butcher's cow. Perhaps the most famous was the
June 1978 *Hustler* cover of a woman being ground in a meat
grinder. The centerfold of that issue featured a woman covered in
blood red ketchup on a hamburger bun.

Feminists claim, "Supreme Court rulings on obscenity, meaning prurient material that offends community standards, provide
no impediment to the increasing violence directed against women."[30]
They have made a valuable contribution to the national debate by
spotlighting the fact that the pornography problem is one of real
harm to women, not merely a matter of freedom of expression.

Sexual callousness is "the disregard of, if not disrespect and
contempt for, women's right to deny access for whatever reason, at
whatever time, and under whatever circumstances."[31] As we saw
in chapter 5, pornographic themes—standard non-violent, violent,
even idealized sex—can produce undesirable changes in men's
attitudes toward women.

The myth that women enjoy being raped—that a woman's
initial reactions of distress are transformed into sexual arousal,
then into enjoyment—is one of the dominant themes in violent
pornography. It molds the attitudes of men toward women,[32] encouraging the young men in our culture to force themselves on
their dates, because the young women will eventually relax, enjoy
it, and be grateful.

Other violent themes like biting, hitting, spanking, and verbal
abuse as part of "normal" sexual behaviors transmit the message
that pain enhances pleasure.[33] A testimony given before the Attorney General's Commission on Pornography dramatically illustrates this point:

> Pain, in most pornographic paperbacks, is depicted by capi-
> talized letters when women are screaming because of some
> form of torture. When I would make a trip to the newsstand
> for these books, I would pay no attention to the cover—only
> the amount of time I could find agony portrayed in its
> pages ... Bondage entered into my bedroom as extra
> activity ... But I still could not find what I was searching
> for out of those books. You see, every woman that screamed
> in pain in those books eventually gave in to pleasure beyond
> all reality. So it was easy to imagine raping my wife ... the
> end results had to be pleasure.

Looking at specific research, Dr. Weaver's 1990 study planted female-degradation cues in questions asked of half the subjects. The other half responded to neutral questions. For example, after viewing the same erotic violent scene from contemporary movies, half were asked "how degrading to women was this scene?" and half "how well produced was this scene?" Subjects who were given cues suggesting the scene was degrading reported significantly less compassion for a female assault victim. They also more strongly endorsed the idea that a victim of rape is a "lesser woman."[34]

This study illustrates how easily cues can influence men's perceptions of women. Reading into the dating situation cues that are prevalent in pornography may strongly influence male expectations.

A 1990 study by Drs. McKenzie-Mohr and Zanna found that exposure to pornography effects men's behavior toward women in nonsexual contexts as well. Male college students were exposed to a standard-fare pornographic video or a nonsexual one and then interviewed by a female research assistant. The interview concerned students' transition from high school to college and did not involve questions pertaining to sexual matters. Yet, from their behavior, the female interviewer could readily distinguish between men who had seen the sexually explicit video and men who had seen neutral fare. The former moved their chairs closer to her and afterward could recall her physical features much more clearly.[35]

Studies have established that exposure to pornography displaying sexual openness of the female[36] and exposure to rape-myth portrayals[37] intensify aggressive reactions against women. A study in 1987 found that 84 percent of college students who had been raped were acquainted with the rapist and two thirds of the rapes had occurred on a date.[38] Dr. Diana Russell found that "even more frequent (than rape or attempted rape) is the use of physical force by men for the attainment of particular sexual services from their intimate female partners—services that these women consider objectionable and repugnant."[39] Speaking of crimes on college campuses, Michael Clay Smith recognized a prevalent attitude in college males, which he believed sometimes breeds rape: "I continue to be shocked that male students very often feel that it's the norm that they expect sexual activity from a casual date or even just a casual female companion."[40]

Dr. Russell in 1984 found that less than 10 percent of rapes reported in the San Francisco survey had been reported to the police. In 1987 Dr. Mary Koss found that only 5 percent of women college students who reported forced sex during the previous year had reported the incident to the police.[41] Several studies up to

1982 found that "about one-fourth of male college students admitted to having made forcible attempts at intercourse."[42] In 1984 "more than half of all college men acknowledged the use of force in getting their dates to perform with them sexual acts to which the women objected vigorously."[43] Dr. Koss, who studied date rape at the University of Arizona, confirmed research conclusions: "They get the idea from pornographic magazines that a woman likes to be roughed up and if she resists, she's just putting on an act."[44]

The research suggests several practical implications. Contemporary pornography is a potent catalyst for sexually abusive behaviors such as rape, resulting in both loss of respect and aggressiveness toward women. These are prominent factors in the profiles of sexually abusive and aggressive individuals.[45] It is probable that pornography-induced, women-hating perceptions negatively influence the welfare of women in everyday, nonsexual circumstances. Pornography—with its seemingly factual, documentary style presentation of sexual behaviors—has usurped most other socialization agents to become a primary institution of sexual indoctrination in many societies.[46]

Field data indicates that as pornography becomes more available in society, sex crimes against women increase.

Critics of any restrictions on the flow of pornography quickly point to Dr. Kutchinsky's 1973 study, which erroneously concluded that, as sexual materials in Denmark increased, sexual offenses, rape, and child molestation dropped. "In fact, some serious sex crimes such as rape actually increased in number and rate following the legalization of pornography in Denmark."[47]

Moreover, when pornography was legalized, a number of sex crimes against children were decriminalized. For example, it is now unlawful to molest children under age twelve, not sixteen or eighteen as before. This appeared to drop the sex crime rate although such sex offenses continued to occur. Unofficial changes in police handling of sex crimes also reduced the number of cases reported, increasing the illusion of decreased sex offenses.[48] Thus, the increase in serious sex crimes after the decriminalization of pornography in Denmark could have been even greater than reported.

"When your rape is entertainment, your worthlessness is absolute," said Andrea Dworkin.

"When rape is promptly and severely punished, as in China, Japan, and many Islamic nations, its incidence rate is extremely low. Where punishment is unlikely, or thought to be so, rape is a common occurrence."[49] The United States leads the world in rape statistics, with a rape rate four times that of Germany, thirteen times that of England, and twenty times that of Japan.[50] There is now substantial evidence of a link between the availability of sexually explicit materials and the occurrence of criminal sexual offenses.

Dr. John Court in 1984 collected data from many countries that provides evidence that the availability of pornographic materials corresponds positively with the reported occurrences of rape.[51] Drs. Scott and Schwalm found a significant positive relationship between the incidence of rape in this country and the number of sexually explicit magazines sold.[52] Drs. Baron and Straus found a direct relationship between circulation rate of sex magazines and rape rates in states across the nation. Alaska, for example, has the highest male readership of pornographic magazines *and* the highest rape per capita in the nation.[53] It also spends more money on shelters from domestic violence than any other state.

Time magazine summarized the growing problem of rape and violence against women in the fall of 1990:

> According to the Senate Judiciary Committee this past June, the rape rate is increasing four times as fast as the overall crime rate. One in five adult women has been raped, one in six by someone she knows. Between three million and four million women are beaten each year, one million so severely that they seek medical help. More than half of all homeless women are fleeing domestic violence.[54]

Since 1960 the rape rate has risen 526 percent, from 8.7 in 1960 to 41 rapes per 100,000 people in 1990.[55] It increased twenty-two of the twenty-six years from 1960 to 1986[56] and nearly tripled in ten major Florida universities in the last three years.[57] Recent Bureau of Justice statistics estimated that for each reported rape, there are actually twelve hundred rapes or attempted rapes that go unreported.

The 1991 Uniform Crime Report estimated that between 1973 and 1987 there were an average of 155,000 rapes per year.[58] Recently, an extensive longitudinal survey of completed forcible rapes of adult women estimated that 683,000 adult American women were forcibly raped during a twelve month period in 1989-1990.[59] Attempted rapes and rapes of children under eighteen, which comprise 60 percent of all rapes, were not even included in the survey. These figures mean that one out of eight adult women has been a victim of forcible rape some time in her *adult* lifetime (18 or older). Of the 12.1 million adult victims, 44 percent had experienced more than one rape.[60] Over 60 percent of the reported rapes occurred when the adult women were children under 18.[61]

Over 84 percent of all rape victims do not report to the police.[62] In addition, "official rape statistics do not reflect the number of deaths resulting from rape. These deaths are reported as murders. The 1984 FBI Uniform Crime Report, for example, estimated 22 percent of the murders committed were sexually related, representing a 160 percent increase in such murders between 1976 and 1984."[63]

Since more than 60 percent of rape victims are children or teen-agers and more than half have never been married,[64] the cost of psychological treatment is enormous. Because rape victims experience devastating mental health problems associated with sexual assault,[65] the stress that previous sexual abuse adds to marriage is staggering. Almost one third (31 percent), or 3.8 million American adult women, have had rape-related, post-traumatic stress disorder (RR-PTSD), with one in ten rape victims, or 1.3 million, still suffering from RR-PTSD at the present time.[66] According to the director of Project Help in Naples, Florida, the characteristics of "rape trauma syndrome" are

> an intense state of fear, the loss of self-esteem, an inability to trust, helplessness, guilt, shame, rage, substance abuse, mental confusion, sexual problems, suicidal ideas and a lack of trust in one's own judgment. . . . The feelings of low self-worth kick in. The victim tries to remember what she said, who she said it to. She's on a quest for an answer to why the rapist chose her.[67]

In more evidence of a direct link between pornography consumption and sexual crimes, researchers Silbert and Pines found that in a series of rape cases, about one quarter of the "male attackers appeared to be acting out a 'porn script.'[68] One told his victim: 'I seen it all in the movies. You love being beaten . . . you know you love it. Tell me you love it.'"[69]

Dr. Goldstein found that "55 percent of the studied rapists admitted to being 'excited to sex relations by pornography.'"[70] Dr. Marshall found that 86 percent of rapists admitted regular use of pornography, with 57 percent admitting actual imitation of pornography scenes in commission of sex crimes.[71] Dr. Malamuth found convicted rapists generally accepted rape myths and were highly aroused by rape depictions. He also found 35 percent of college students would rape if they knew they would not be caught. These students shared the characteristics of convicted rapists in regard to pornography as did Koss' sample of 2,972 men at thirty-two colleges who frequently used pornography and whose behavior met the legal definitions of rape.[72]

In light of this overwhelming evidence, should pornography be so readily available to youth as a first "educator" about sex? Considering its dire consequences for women in our society, we must agree with former Surgeon General C. Everett Koop:

> I am certain pornography that portrays sexual aggression as pleasurable for the victim is at the root of much of the rape that occurs today. Impressionable men—many of them still in adolescence—see this material and get the impression that women like to be hurt, to be humiliated, to be forced to do things that they do not want to do, or to pretend to be forced to do things that they really do want to do (the "rape myth"). It is a false and vicious stereotype that leads to much pain and even death for victimized women.[73]

Every woman has an interest in protecting her own home from the harms of pornography. There are two facets to this problem. One involves our children; the other the men in our lives.

Help your children receive a secure start in life. Be there for them as they develop their personalities and form their values. Gently guide them to view entertainment that contains strong family values, and discuss how other programs negatively influence those values.

When it comes to pornography, understand the nature of it yourself and pass that understanding on to your children, especially your sons. Make them aware that it is not harmless fun, but a potential danger, a grave threat to the future of any person who becomes involved in it. If your son brings a pornographic magazine home, deal with it immediately. Some people will tell you that looking at pornography to find out about sex is normal and harmless. Don't believe it. This could be the first step toward addiction. Most addicts say their problem began with a magazine like *Playboy* or an R-rated video.

Do not allow any pornography in your home. Be firm in this, and never waiver. Your son may be exposed elsewhere, but he will know it is not acceptable to his parents. If it is hidden in your house, your child will find it.

Don't overlook your son's instruction in sexual matters. Find materials that are instructive and in keeping with your value system. Tell him that the messages of pornography are false and, in the long run, will destroy his respect for women. Before he is tempted to turn to pornography to learn how sex is performed, make him aware that it presents a distorted picture that leads to dissatisfaction and frustration, not to euphoria. Women do not want to be forced and raped. They want tenderness, romance, gentleness, and affection.

Tell him that *"real men" don't use pornography:*

What makes a real man? Strength of character. A real man
keeps his word. If he marries, he is faithful to his wife—for
a lifetime. He is a role model for his children. He has strong
beliefs he would die for. A real man knows he will become
that which he dwells upon. He not only has self-respect, but
he has equally high regard for others. And a real man is not
a "Peeping Tom." (After all, what is pornography if not
commercialized voyeurism?) A real man chooses to think
the best of others, honoring their privacy and integrity. And
a real man knows who he is, so he doesn't have to seek
security by defiling and humiliating others. The mark of a
real man is the choices he makes. That's why *Real Men
Don't Use Porn.* ("Real Men" campaign launched in 1990 by
the Coalition Against Pornography in Kansas City)

If you see a problem you cannot control, seek professional help
for your son immediately.

Be concerned about children who have been victimized and
abused by consumers of pornography. Encourage therapy and
support groups for children who need rehabilitation. Encourage
value-laden sex education that teaches appropriate and inappropriate sexual behavior to help children understand how to resist
abuse.

In facing pornography's impact upon a relationship, learn the
true nature of pornography consumption and addiction. Realize
that the moment you discover his involvement with pornography,
you face a serious problem. If the interest is only casual, encourage
him to give it up. When romance is new, your chances of success
are probably higher than they will ever be again. Help him understand the false picture it presents and the progressive and addictive tendencies it can foster. Many men don't understand the
strong effect pornography can have until they are educated about
it. Help him understand how offensive and degrading it is to
women.

Look for clues in order to determine how serious his habit is. If
his interest is deep and you have not yet lost your heart to him,
you would do well to break the relationship altogether. Look for
someone whose ideas of sex and marriage have not been distorted
by the messages of pornography.

If you plan to proceed with the relationship, you should seek
counseling immediately. If he is not willing to admit his problem
or to seek help, you should reconsider.

If you are already married and a sexual problem is newly
developed, pornography is often the reason. Some doctors have

found that if a man is willing to give it up, normal marital relationships can be resumed in three or four months.

Discourage his bringing it into your home. Don't bring in cable channels that contain soft-core pornography or porn videos to put spice in your sex lives. The risk that the porn queens will replace you in your husband's fantasies is too great.

If this is a habit developed in childhood, the patterns of behavior are much more deeply ingrained and the problem is much more serious. If he has been a steady consumer for years, the problem will not get better in time unless it is faced head on. Chances are it will get worse, much worse.

Understand the futility of giving in to the next degrading act and realize that your partner will never be satisfied as long as his pornography habit is maintained. The common pattern in pornography obsession is a downward spiral into increasingly perverse desires and behavior. He will eventually tire of each new perversion and want to try another. The cycle must be broken and the degrading behavior stopped.

If you want to help your husband overcome pornography addiction, prepare for a long, hard battle. Find help for your husband quickly, before the problem escalates. If possible, discuss it with him and share what you have learned. Encourage him to read this book. Offer to support him in his struggle to regain control of his life. Assure him of your love and forgiveness for past wrongs. Get him out of isolation and help him realize his greatest need is not sex, but intimacy. Help him understand he is not a worthless person, that people care for him and want to help him; and they, like you, will stand by him and not let him down.

Find a counselor for him; find a counselor for yourself. Hold each other accountable. When he is tempted by lust, ask him to share it with you and face it together. As you become more open and honest, true intimacy and love will begin to build. Help him fill his mind with positive, uplifting thoughts and images that can replace the pornographic images. A meaningful faith in God and the support of a church or synagogue can make the difference between success or failure.

Support groups based on the Twelve Step Program of recovery from drugs, alcohol and sex addiction are helpful. Sex Anonymous Chapters and Overcomers are particularly effective support group systems designed to help people with such life-controlling problems. There are now Overcomers support groups around the country.

If he will not admit he has a problem, you will need outside help to confront him. Like a drug or alcohol intervention, it must be carefully planned: a record assembled of times the problem was out of control, exactly what he required that was beyond normal sex relations, how much he spent on pornographic materials, how his habit interfered with his job, with family relations, etc. Because he will be operating from a different, distorted sense of values, it is important to find others who agree with you to help in the confrontation. Perhaps members of his own family, who have seen the problem develop, can support your efforts.

Expect him to deny the problem, but remain firm. Explain to him that it is an addiction that must be overcome; or he will end up as other addicts, losing everything he values. Be supportive, and promise to see him through the ordeal. If he still will not deal with the problem, consider your own safety and that of your children.

Pornography and Family Values

Adultery and illicit sex, sometimes necessary plot material, must not be explicitly treated or justified, or presented attractively.

—The Motion Picture Code, 1930-1966

"HELL HAD TO BE BETTER"

He was what many women dreamed of: tall, physically fit, very handsome. He opened car doors, ordered the entree at expensive restaurants, sent me flowers for no reason. He knew how to treat women! At age twenty-five he owned a beautiful home in a family neighborhood, drove an Eldorado Cadillac, and had a small chain of clothing stores.

I was raised in small towns. My family was considered middle class with high morals. I was popular in high school and had lots of the "right" kind of friends. I hoped to become a high fashion model, but my heart's desire was to find my prince charming, get married, have four children and live in a beautiful home with a white picket fence laced with flowers.

At nineteen he introduced me to the "jet set," interesting men and women dressed to impress with lots of gold chains. Everyone owned their own business or had an important job. We dated six months, decided to live together and planned to marry. Two months later, I excitedly told him I was pregnant. When I refused to abort the baby, he reluctantly married me. He really did love me and didn't want to lose me.

93

On our wedding day, he got angry and called me horrible names. My parents pleaded with me not to go through with it, but I thought he was having a hard time with the new adjustment. When I was four months pregnant, he decided to have a party. He invited his friends and showed them stag movies. I watched a few minutes, felt sick, and left the room. He made me come back and sat me in a chair in the middle of the room and ridiculed me in front of all his friends who were drinking and smoking pot. Some of the women began to remove their tops and let the men feel their breasts. I threw up and went into our bedroom and locked the door.

Two days later, he sat me down and told me how inexperienced I was. He would educate me so I could satisfy him. He began bringing home *Playboy* magazines and other sex books. He set up the projector in our bedroom and made me watch for hours. He would lock the door so no one would know what I was doing since I was so embarrassed. I kept hoping when our baby came he would have a change of heart and be the perfect husband and father. I believed "til death due us part" and that I could help this man.

When my beautiful child was six weeks old, I was told to stop breast feeding. He drugged me and made me perform before a camera. He had a convincing manner and told me he would tell people lies about me and they would believe him. He began to physically harm me. It was easier to take the hitting than to hear the terrible things he said to me. I realized that he hated women. He called us "snakes." It was all Eve's fault for the downfall of man.

I was now in prison with no escape. I began to think that hell had to be better. During a five year period I attempted suicide three times. Each time I was found in the nick of time except the last time. I checked into a motel and drank over 100 tranquilizers with a bottle of red wine.

Three days later I woke up and felt terribly sick. I called the hospital. It was suggested that I admit myself to the local mental hospital. I did and after a week, they convinced me that I was all right. It was my husband who had the problem. . . .

It has been sixteen years and I am just now beginning to be able to talk about it to others. I used to think pornography was for those who wore trench coats and nothing under-

neath. During those five years I saw people from all walks
of life who were obsessed with sex in an ugly way—respectable businessmen, insurance salesmen, realtors, car deal-
ers, attorneys, doctors, even a judge. Pornography was
their way of life.

Stories like this, and there are multitudes of them in our
culture today, are the result of pornography's war on the family.
From its inception, *Playboy* magazine downgraded women and
marriage. The December 1953 issue presented a "factual" essay
about the horrors of marriage and warned young men that women
marry only for money. It was the beginning of Hugh Hefner's
campaign for "no-fault" divorce and the elimination of alimony.[1]
Marriage was continually modeled as repugnant while wives—
usually portrayed as fat and ugly—were commonly cartooned as
copulating with the family dog, "not only by *Playboy*, but by its
imitators *Penthouse* and *Hustler*."[2]

According to Dr. Dolf Zillmann, a leading researcher of the
effects of eroticized and violent media, the values in pornographic
entertainment are on a *collision course with family values*. He
considers the family "the most fundamental social institution in
society." Independent of any pleasure-seeking considerations, its
significance is in what it is capable of producing—healthy, intellectually and morally mature, as well as emotionally well-adjusted
offspring.[3]

It is no secret that parental commitment has notably deterio-
rated in recent years. Although getting married has lost little of its
popularity, and, despite the best intentions by those entering into
matrimony, unions do not last as long as they did in earlier times.[4]

Marriage seems to have become an arrangement of convenience that is readily abandoned.[5] The result is children raised by
single parents, a mixture of natural and step-parents, or a single
parent with live-in companion.[6] Under these conditions, parental
commitment is often deficient and children are neglected.[7] Increasingly, children are perceived as burdens, impairing careers
and preventing access to a multitude of immediate gratifications.[8]
Resentment toward children is replacing the inclination to care for
them. Recent assessments show the abuse of children in defunct
families to have reached staggering proportions.[9] Spouse abuse is
similarly rampant.[10]

Dr. Zillmann and Dr. Jennings Bryant initiated a search for
single factors capable of explaining this deterioration of parental
commitment. While factors like economic conditions, changing
sexual mores, and a new egocentricity (emphasis on the individual

as the center of everything) are undoubtedly part of the problem, they believed there was something more. They asked what could affect the desire to have and raise children, what single factor could influence attitudes toward sexuality, infidelity, and marriage as an institution.

Drs. Zillmann and Bryant decided to investigate how rape would affect existing sexual relationships and the trust between partners.[11] Because pornography's message is the exact opposite of the "freedom-curtailing" commitments required by marriage and child care, they thought it might prove capable of influencing people in these directions.

Pornographic sexuality is sexuality that has no interest in producing offspring. It is totally recreational—projecting fun to be had by anyone who cares to play.

> Pornography scripts dwell on sexual engagements of parties who have just met, who are in no way attached or committed to one another, and who will part shortly, never to meet again. Not by accident, the parties involved accept no curtailing rules for their social and sexual conduct, enjoy sexual stimulation for what it is, and do so at no social or emotional expense. Sexual gratification in pornography is not a function of emotional attachment, of kindness, of caring, and especially not of continuance of the relationship.[12]

Participants in the sex act yield to urges of sexual desire. There is no social relationship, neither are there responsibilities, curtailments, or costs.

Dr. Zillmann sees the hedonistic (pleasure-seeking) formula as containing two major elements: (1) instant access to the greatest joys in life (2) at no cost to the participants. This "gospel of pornography" has been confirmed by systematic analyses of the content of pornography:[13]

1) Pornography depicts sexual engagements among persons who have just met, have no interest in getting to know one another, and are unlikely to meet again.

2) Pornography regularly depicts a series of sexual engagements with different partners, further underscoring the impersonality of pornographic sex.

3) All sexual activities portrayed in pornography are shown to produce extreme euphoria in all persons who participate in them.

The message is threefold: 1) there is ready access to immediate sexual gratification; 2) the greatest sexual pleasures are fully attainable in transitory relationships; and 3) pleasures can be experienced without freedom-curtailing emotional involvement or commitment to other human beings.

If these values are adopted, committing oneself to an enduring, intimate, sexual relationship would be most undesirable. If sexual gratifications are expected to be as high, or higher, in impersonal relationships as in lasting ones, if the great joys of life can be obtained without any investment, what would compel anyone to make a commitment to marriage? For essentially the same reasons, it should be most undesirable to commit oneself to parenting.

Looking at societal changes (see chap. 1), Dr. Zillmann concluded that we seem to be moving in a direction consistent with the values of pornography rather than the values of the family. While the family was never perfect, it seems to be less perfect than ever before.

Because the values reflected in pornography are so anti-family, Drs. Zillmann and Bryant decided to conduct an investigation to determine if the consumption of pornography could have harmful effects on values concerning intimate relationships, marriage, family, and children.

To duplicate the normal consumption patterns as closely as possible, they recruited men and women from both a college student body and the adult population of a city. The subjects were shown commonly available, non-violent pornographic videos during one-hour sessions conducted over six consecutive weeks. A control group watched innocuous entertainment fare devoid of sexual content. In an ostensibly unrelated study one week later, they completed several questionnaires designed to assess their perceptions of the American family and aspects of personal happiness.

Their earlier work had shown that prolonged consumption of pornography made particular sexual practices seem much more popular than they actually were. The Value-of-Marriage Survey and the Inventory of Personal Happiness focused on attitudes having to do with living with sexual partners, marriage, family, divorce, and their desire to have children.

They found that the effects were the same for students and non-students. Surprisingly, women were as strongly affected as men. They concluded that the following perceptual changes were brought about by prolonged exposure to pornography:

• Both male and female promiscuity were deemed more natural, more acceptable, and less objectionable.

• There was a decline in expected faithfulness.

• There was a greater acceptance of sex before marriage and outside of marriage.

- Sexual intimacy with persons other than the committed partner was accepted to a much higher degree.
- They rejected the notion that sexual relationships be exclusive either for themselves or for their intimate partner.
- They accepted the myths that sexual restraint is unhealthy and that unrestrained sexuality is wholesome and healthy.

Simply stated, after heavy exposure to pornography, they believe it is natural to be promiscuous and that holding back sexuality constitutes a health risk. Unexpectedly, pornography did not instill distrust by increasing worry about possible infidelity. Instead, it promoted tolerance for infidelity and trivialized its consequences for intimate partners.

After seeing pornography, the percentage who considered marriage essential to society dropped monumentally. More than twice as many said they believed the institution of marriage would become obsolete and be abandoned by society. When asked whether they felt that the institution of marriage is essential to the well-functioning of society, 60 percent of the subjects who were not exposed to pornography said *yes* compared to only 38.8 percent of those exposed to pornography. Only 15 percent who had not seen pornography thought the institution of marriage would eventually become obsolete and be abandoned in modern society, compared to 36.2 percent of those who had been exposed to pornography. For men, women, students, and nonstudent adults, the percentage who saw marriage as obsolete more than doubled when they were exposed to pornography.

Perceptions relate to attitudes. Dispositions imply that the attitudes will be translated into actions. To determine dispositions toward dissolving marriage, subjects were asked their reactions to a list of potential grounds for divorce. There were marked differences between those who had consumed pornography and those who had not. For those exposed to pornography, occasional infidelity, frequent infidelity, unusual sexual requests, desire for additional lovers, and spouse having homosexual affairs all dropped between seventeen and twenty-nine points as a reason for divorce. A spouse's sexual disinterest, however, rose sixteen points as an acceptable reason for divorce.

For all subjects, exposure to pornography reduced the desire to have children. Desire for male offspring dropped 31 percent, and desire for female offspring dropped an astounding 61 percent. Male subjects expressed little desire for female offspring, and the desire of females for daughters shrank to one-third its normal strength.

Zillmann concluded that "prolonged consumption of pornography makes having children and raising a family appear an *unnecessary inconvenience.*"[14] This is understandable because pornography projects easy access to superlative sexual gratifications without emotional investment, economic obligation, or sacrifices in time and effort, but the dramatic decline in the desire of women to have female children was surprising. Dr. Zillmann believes there is something in the portrayal of women in pornography that is so demeaning that it becomes altogether undesirable to bring up a female child.

This point was dramatically confirmed recently by a very beautiful young woman whose husband was addicted to pornography. Under constant pressure, she had performed every deviancy he demanded in order to keep his affection.

> I was six month's pregnant and in perfect health when my doctor predicted I would have a baby girl. I became immediately ill. Blood started pouring out of me. I was hospitalized for a week and had to be given three pints of blood. I spent the rest of my pregnancy terrified that my husband would have sex with my child if it was a girl. I knew I would be so overprotective of her that it would destroy her. When my son was born, the fear left me and I have been able to enjoy him ever since. But I know I could never have enjoyed having a daughter!

Changing attitudes toward family issues in the United States are being noted by other social scientists. Dr. Thornton recently reviewed the evidence and found an important weakening of the normal imperative "to marry, to remain married, to have children," and "to restrict intimate relations to marriage."[15]

The Zillmann/Bryant investigation addressed "personal happiness: satisfaction with life in general and with sex in particular." Pornography was not shown to affect happiness outside the sexual realm, but it greatly diminished sexual satisfaction. Consumers became dissatisfied with their partners' physical appearance, sexual performance, and willingness to explore novel avenues of sexual gratification.

Dr. Zillmann explained this effect as the dilemma for pornography consumers: pornography is initially consumed because of curiosity and in hopes of finding greater sexual gratification. After consistently viewing healthy bodies doing athletic things and performing in ways that many are incapable of performing, they are more likely to become dissatisfied with what they have at home. It is this comparison of the consumer's own lot with the utopia of pornography that intensifies sexual dissatisfaction.

Those who are already somewhat dissatisfied are more strongly drawn to pornography than others. Initial sexual dissatisfaction leads to greater consumption. Dissatisfaction grows stronger, draws them still deeper into consumption, and makes them even more dissatisfied. Dr. Zillmann believes this explains some men's preference for masturbating to pornography's portrayal of women who are more attractive than their wives at home.

Some males find sexual situations embarrassing. It is easier for them to satisfy their sexual frustrations by looking at photographs and masturbating. When this is repeated, their desire for pictures replaces their interest in people. If this practice is established before marriage, the male's main sexual outlet may continue to be pornography, even after marriage to a beautiful woman. If he is used to being stimulated by pictures, he usually has difficulty relating with persons of the opposite sex. If it happens as a result of dissatisfaction in marriage, once he has become used to being stimulated by the beautiful women in pornography, sex with his wife may seem much less satisfying.[16]

The lesson to be learned is that it is hard to compete with the air-brushed bodies in pornography. Dissatisfaction with sexual partners will incite many men and women to look for conditions that promise more sexually gratifying experiences. "The somewhat unrealistic search for much better partners and much greater gratification is likely to fail more often than not, and dissatisfaction will prevail."[17]

At the same time, research has shown that sexual arousal[18] and accompanying excitedness[19] diminish with repeated exposure to sexual scenes. As exposure to commonly shown sexual activities leaves consumers relatively bored, they are likely to seek out pornography that features novel and potentially less common sexual acts. Such a shift toward a stronger interest in less common sexual practices was demonstrated by Drs. Zillmann and Bryant in their 1986 study of non-violent consenting sex pornography.[20]

They found that the consumer of common, non-violent erotic fare is likely to advance to harder material including violent pornography. This was demonstrated when the participants were left alone in a room with a wide range of videos from which to choose. While the group not exposed to pornography chose regular PG movies, a large number of participants who had been exposed to soft-core pornography chose hard-core tapes depicting such things as pain during sexual activity or intercourse with animals.

Common sense suggests that men who fill their minds with violent images are more likely to abuse their families than those who do not. Rather than teaching men to control their anger, pornography promotes a lack of discipline. At the same time, it implants a clear message that pain and violence heighten a man's sexual experience.

There is increasing evidence that pornography is a factor in domestic violence. Irene Diamond of Purdue University discovered in a study of police reports that wife batterers are frequently devotees of pornography.[21] Dr. James Bannon of the Detroit Police Department reported that in family violence cases, they often "find that the man is trying to enact a scene in some pornographic pictures."[22] Sergeant Don Smith of the Los Angeles Police Department has testified that many men show pornography to their wives then re-enact the scenes.

In a 1980 survey, Dr. Diana Russell found that 10 percent of women reported being asked or forced by their mates to imitate sex acts that came out of pornography. "Battering and other physical violence were involved in 45 percent of the marital rapes reported in a representative sample in Boston of married women with children aged six to fourteen."[23] Two studies reported that "10-14 percent of the married or formerly married women were raped or sexually assaulted by their current or former husbands."[24]

Dr. Edward Donnerstein explained that subjects "confuse the pleasurable reactions they had to the sexual portion of a pornographic film with the violent portion with the result that their feelings about violence can change in a more positive direction."[25]

The May 1984 issue of *Penthouse* carried an article about a man's sexual encounter with his young niece. He told of spanking her until "my hand was stinging so badly I couldn't continue." After oral and violent sex acts were described, the uncle stated, "I could sense she was enjoying her punishment and that her defiance and pleading were only an act. . . . She was moaning and crying with the intense feelings of pleasure and pain."[26]

Pornography helps build a defense system so men don't have to feel guilty about their aggressive behavior toward their families. Seeing aggression on film and in magazines legitimizes it, makes it acceptable. Forced sex *in pornography* always has a happy ending. The rapee starts to like it, so the rapist begins to believe it's all right to rape, especially his wife.

Such anti-family messages are as old as the first slick men's magazines. For nearly four decades, *Playboy* magazine has told men "that only orgasm is important and orgasm is far less costly than marriage." The very first issue of *Playboy* promoted the idea that women trick men into marriage in order to divorce them and get their money. It has been anti-family ever since.

March Bell, as quoted in *The High Cost of Indifference*, stated: "evidence shows that the popular and least offensive pornography has been the most effective in achieving the goals of the sexual revolution." Dr. Zillmann has clearly established that six weeks' exposure to pornography is capable of altering attitudes toward sexually intimate relationships. The conversion of attitudes into actions that lead to deterioration of relationships and eventual violence cannot be ethically demonstrated through scientific research. Neither can we adequately measure the influence of years of exposure during adolescence when values about sexuality are formed. However, research has established the potential influence of pornography on family attitudes and dispositions. As we witness over time these changing dispositions expressing themselves in action, Dr. Zillmann concludes that we can expect a continuing "erosion of the nuclear family in America."

It is usually accepted that women are the true victims of pornography. As detailed in chapter 6, children are victimized in many ways. Pornography is often responsible for the divorce of their parents and the break-up of their homes. They are victims of adult abuse resulting from pornography-fed appetites. Easily entrapped by pornography, they are victimized when it falls into their hands at an early age. Their value systems are distorted, and they are robbed of an innocent childhood and the desire and ability to enjoy family life as adults.

Pornography-damaged boys grow up to be emotionally-damaged men. Often, they are so addicted to pornography, they cannot function as normal adults (see chap. 9). These men are victims, too.

Dr. Zillmann believes that "we have a societal victimization." If it could be proved that pornography was directed against a minority like Native Americans or blacks or Jews, it would be censored in a minute, but the fact that it is directed against our entire population means only that the entire population must suffer and that family values will continue to decline as long as the problem is not solved.

The hundreds of testimonies that speak of the escalating appetite for pornography, the terrible loss of control, the loss of a sense of decency and respect for human life present a bleak outlook for the future of marriages in our country. But one man's testimony at the Commission on Pornography hearings ended on a higher note. After describing the progression of his "marriage destroying addiction," which led to acute marital problems, he told how husbands and wives can help each other by joining local support groups. "Wives," he said, "are filled with anger, hurt, frustration, and rejection. Husbands with tremendous guilt, anxiety, frustration." But through compassionate sharing, they can do a lot of "marriage rebuilding."

Johnny was introduced to the world of sex by his cousins at the age of seven. Pornography through his teen years fueled his sexual desires and deviant interests. His first marriage was filled with conflict. Only the children provided the friendship and closeness he desired. When their sexual games were exposed, divorce followed.

The discovery of sexual games with the step-children of his second marriage shocked his wife Carol to her core. When she recovered, she decided she could not hate her husband, she could not undo the past, but she could change the course of events for her family's future. Her pastor aided her in crisis intervention and John shared everything about the awfulness of his childhood. Carol was moved to compassion and agreed to help him.

During his jail term, Carol stuck by him. Weekly therapeutic counseling helped him develop new patterns of thinking and he is now back with his family. Through loyalty, open communication, and the restructuring of family activities, the family has been rebuilt, and he has been delivered from the desire to see pornography and perform dark deeds in secret. This family's courage and boldness to confront the truth and work toward wholeness has given hope to countless other families with problems. They have succeeded in restoring family harmony and genuine love and are now starting a support group to help other couples win their battle against pornography.

Often, the collision between strong family values and the "gospel of pornography" starts in the teen-age years. A renowned child psychologist described the problem:

Today's teenager is being compelled symbolically to walk alone down a long, dark corridor leading toward adulthood. On either side of this gloomy hall are many large doors, labeled alcohol, drugs, pornography, premarital sex, on and on. Every form of addictive behavior is represented by at least one door. As he approaches each portal, he can hear boisterous laughter and gaiety from within. His friends—or people he wants as friends—are already inside and they are obviously having a blast. . . . For a certain percentage of individuals who open one or more of these doors [such as pornography], a tragedy begins to unfold. . . . Some, but not all, will be held in its addictive power for the rest of their lives.[27]

Society and the media call it harmless entertainment. Actually, we are waging the "second great civil war" for the survival of the family. The war is over *ideas*—about family, morality, and values, the pillars of our democracy. The prize is the hearts and minds of the people; the victims are our children and families. The outcome is still in doubt.

Chapter 9

Pornography Addiction: Key to the Pornography Explosion

Pictures shall not infer that low forms of sex relationship are the accepted or common thing. . . . Sex perversion or any inference of it is forbidden.

—The Motion Picture Code, 1930-1966

Shame. It's an emotion we've all felt and tried desperately to avoid. In fact, the episodes I'm about to share were so private and shameful, at one time I very nearly killed to keep them a secret. Living alone with the shame of an escalating addiction to pornography, I paid a terrible price. I tell my story to keep others from paying a similar price.

I was twice molested at age nine and when I found my uncle's hidden stash of soft-core pornography, my emotional soil was so broken these seeds sank deep and grew quickly into a devastating force in my life.

I began to introduce other boys to pornography. When my uncle's material was no longer titillating, I began to frequent liquor stores that sold pornography. No one seemed to mind my looking at the magazines. I bought them when I could, or stole them and sold the pictures at school. I quickly learned that the more graphic and explicit the photos, the more money I made. I progressed from the "men's magazines" I had encountered at my uncle's to the hardest types of pornography. Other boys became my "buddies" in ever more risky attempts to steal pornography. The thrill of this risk was intoxicating to me.

105

After a while, even this thrill wasn't enough. The pictures in the magazines got old, and I began to look for more real and dangerous ways to satisfy my need. I began to experiment with voyeurism, watching girls undress through holes in the wall or windows, or sneaking into girls' showers when my sister's friends spent the night.

My pornography habit kept me totally alienated from any real relationship with girls. I found it difficult to relate to real girls who didn't behave like the girls in pornography. I didn't have girlfriends, because the girls I met or dated reacted with fear and disgust to my pornography-inspired advances. Pornography had taught me that the way to be accepted and loved was through sex. In reality, my obsession with sex brought me alienation and rejection.

My yearning for attention and recognition was so acute I took to partially exposing myself from a window. In *Playboy* fantasies, exhibitionism led to exciting encounters. But once again, I found people frightened and disgusted with me. The rejection in my life continued to be compounded, forcing me deeper into fantasy to find the acceptance I craved.

Through my high-school years, I moved into harder material and more risky episodes until finally a crucial experience at a church camp motivated me to recommit to the religious values I had casually accepted growing up as a preacher's kid. I dropped my pornography habit cold and enrolled in Bible college. Wanting to work in establishing new churches, I opened my own roofing business and married my wife Joni. I firmly believed I had turned my life around.

But I had never properly healed. I was like a man walking around on a badly-healed broken leg. The fundamental weakness needed only an unusual stress to cause another break. That stress occurred eighteen months after my marriage when my wife was pregnant with our first child. Because of her reaction to the pregnancy, our sexual relationship evaporated and stress began to build in our marriage. As I passed an adult bookstore one day, my sexual frustration drove me inside.

It's difficult to describe my reaction to my first visit to a hard-core bookstore. I was deeply shocked and disgusted at the material I saw. I was ashamed of myself and promised never to go again. But the sight of the hard-core material and my shame at being there was like a sudden injection of some incredible drug straight into my veins. In an awful way, it excited me tremendously. And in spite of my vow to myself, as my relationship with my wife worsened, I went back again and again.

Just as it had in high school, my pornography addiction began to consume more and more of my time. I found reasons and excuses to visit the store for more and more hours every day. My business and church responsibilities began to suffer as much as my marriage. I would hide money from my wife to spend on pornography. Even after I was forced into bankruptcy, my habit progressed.

We moved to California and things were better for a time. At each critical step, I felt I was being given chances to stop and turn myself around. But I didn't take them. For several months, I tried to commit myself to making a new start, but when business took me to an area where there were adult bookstores, I picked up where I had left off. It became an easy way out of all my feelings of rejection—feelings that I was inadequate and that no woman could accept and love me. In my pornographic fantasies, those needs for love and acceptance were met.

Gradually, I found a growing interest in sadistic pornography. In the ever-increasing violence of my fantasies, I found an outlet for my anger at all the rejection I had faced from women all my life—women who wouldn't love me or meet my needs. As my mental scenarios demanded more graphic expression, I gravitated to more and more twisted and horrible pornography, into material that once would have nauseated me.

I want to make clear, that pornography never FORCED me to make these choices. But at each stage, as pornography became more influential in my life, my ability to resist the compulsion for it grew less and less, until I was seemingly powerless to resist it.

I now found myself in a helpless situation. I would drive by a liquor store that sold pornography and force myself, with all of my willpower and every ounce of my mental strength to drive on past . . . only to find myself involuntarily turning around and returning to the store.

By this time, images on paper and film were no longer

satisfying me. Increasingly, I craved the "real thing." Just
as with the bookstore, my first visit to a strip-tease joint left
me shocked at myself. I left promising never to return
again, but I was soon back, spending hours and hours
watching the girls. From there I progressed to massage
parlors, and finally to using prostitutes. Just as at each
step before, what was at first shocking and repulsive became easier and easier to accept. In fact, it was the shock
and repulsion that gave me that "rush" I craved.

And I craved it more and more. I would arrange phony
business trips to cover my activities and even steal money
to cover the costs of my habits. I laid out elaborate plans to
keep myself from being suspected or caught. Even in my
own mind I lived a double life. I threw myself with everything I had into church and business activities. I became a
model of an upstanding, "spiritual" community member
and was a dedicated youth pastor at church. I was desperately trying to prove to myself that I really was "OK." I
realize now, reviewing the headlines of the last several
years, that some other men who seem to throw themselves
into making a spiritual "name" for themselves were probably doing the same thing—compensating for devastating
inner problems. Like some of these prominent men, my
public life was commendable, but the fruit of my private life
was bitterness and pain.

The pain only increased as I made futile attempts to draw
closer to my wife. As I put pressure on her to "perform" like
the women of my pornography fantasies, she naturally
responded with revulsion. My attempts at closeness only
ended in more alienation and anger.

As this anger was building, I found that even my visits to
prostitutes didn't dissipate the rage inside me. More and
more, I found myself fantasizing about satisfying myself
and venting my rage at the same time. I began to entertain
thoughts of raping a woman.

At first, it seemed only a game. I would make intricate
plans in my mind about how I would do it without being
caught. Then I began to do "trial runs" of a rape. I would
visit dark parking lots at night and follow women home.
But always something stopped me. It remained a game, but
an ever more serious game.

Finally, as I was getting out of my car at a racquetball club,
I saw a girl—who fit my mental scenario perfectly—walk-

ing to her car alone in the dark parking lot. Something inside me said, "she's yours," and my game became reality.

I followed her to her car and asked directions as I positioned myself in front of her open car door. Then I lunged at her and forced my way into her car, my hands on her throat. Terrified, she asked me what I was going to do to her. I told her. A look of pure fear came into her eyes, and that fear was like a slap in the face.

Suddenly, with my hands around her throat, I realized what was happening—how far I had come down a horrible road. I came to the sickening realization that I had intended to kill this woman, if necessary, to keep my terrible secret. Reeling from the shock of my awakening, I stumbled backwards, muttered something about having made "a mistake" and walked in a daze straight to my car. I need to emphasize that not until that moment, when I was a razor's edge away from killing someone, was I finally forced to admit that I had a terrible, uncontrollable problem. Up until that time, even though my will was being increasingly sapped by my addiction, I had still managed to lie to myself. Now the truth descended on me like an avalanche.

Once the truth was out, it pursued me relentlessly. Naturally, the woman had seen me walk to my car and taken my license number. As I was home beginning to open up my secret to my wife, the police came, and arrested me, and sent me to jail. My attorney pointed to a one-time occurrence and my sterling reputation in the community, so I was given a lenient sentence.

Let me warn you that there are thousands, if not millions, of men out there who are no different from me. Pornography isn't a $10 billion a year business without dedicated customers. We are only beginning to uncover the enormous numbers of men who are susceptible to this addiction. I've found the number of men with problems that have the potential to become full-scale addictions is astounding.

[We are deeply indebted to Gene McConnell for sharing his personal testimony. It has a happy ending. Through much counseling, repentance, and spiritual renewal, he now has a successful marriage and a productive business. He has also become active in anti-pornography education and victim assistance in California.]

For many years the terms *pornography addict* and *sex addict* have been bandied about, but, until recently, no one had clearly established from the clinical literature that pornography can become an addiction. In the past, scientists and clinicians thought people could be only addicted to a mood-altering substance. Now they acknowledge that sexual addictions occur without a drug being ingested. It is possible to be psychologically, as well as biologically, addicted to behaviors or experience, to memories of such things as pictures seen in pornography or to fantasies portrayed in or stimulated by pornography. Like drug ingestion, sexual behaviors and experiences can alter moods and cause internal chemical changes.

Sex addiction, in which pornography is the key and sometimes only ingredient, has many parallels to other, more commonly recognized forms of addiction.[1] First, it is *progressive*, building up a tolerance for pornography and its varied sexual experiences. Just like an alcoholic who must consume greater amounts of liquor to get high, a pornography/sex addict requires greater and greater stimulation to satisfy increasing cravings. The amounts and kinds of pornography consumed by the sex addict would leave most people aghast, yet they leave the sex addict unsatisfied. As pornography/sex needs escalate, this built-in dynamic drives the addict on to the next stage.

Second, pornography/sex addiction follows *obsessive-compulsive patterns*. Thoughts of pornography/sex grow, crowding everything else out of the addict's mind, until he must do something to try to satisfy his irrepressible urges.

The addict becomes powerless to change. Even harmful consequences like threat of disease, disruption of family life, public humiliation, criminal convictions, and jail are not powerful enough to extinguish the addiction without some outside help. "As the obsession turns to compulsion, sex addicts find themselves doing the things they don't want to do; things they have promised never to do again. It is as though they are standing outside themselves, pleading with themselves not to go on, but deaf to their own cries."[2] In the end, what the addict sought to control has come to control him.

Ex-addicts readily admit the loss of control over their lives:

> You enjoy looking at pornography and at first you think you have everything under control. It seems harmless but soon your mind is filled with strange desires, sexual fantasies you can't fulfill and before you know it, you're out of control.[3]

Third, a sex addict suffers *withdrawal symptoms*—like an alcoholic who gets the shakes without liquor—when he attempts to or is compelled to give up his drug (pornography) for any length of time. He "goes crazy" without it and is driven to binge anywhere, with anyone, regardless of the consequences.

Finally, like most addictions, his cravings force him into behavior that he himself abhors, producing *crushing shame* from which he cannot escape. To escape the burden of shame, he attempts to shift the blame to his wife, girlfriend, parents, even his work. Often the cycle ends in insanity, criminal conduct, or self-induced death.

A person can consume or experiment with pornography or have a stronger than normal sexual appetite and not be a pornography/sex addict.[4] While pornography and sex addiction are closely related and often interchangeable, a sex addict may not always use pornography; but sex will always be the motivating force for a pornography addict. A sex addict sometimes uses fantasy from past experiences and sexual affairs to fuel his sexual addiction rather than pornography, but exclusion of pornography appears rare. Thus, to help avoid confusion, we will use the terms interchangeably. Clinicians have identified nine characteristics of the pornography addict:

1. *Circular behavior*: Sexual activities are followed by a temporary mood change then an inevitable return to the original unpleasant condition.[5]

2. *Isolation*: While an addict is not necessarily physically alone, he is emotionally detached when he uses pornography, and/or engages in sexual fantasies or sexual activity.

3. *"Analgesic fix"*: Persons who engage in addictive behavior self-medicate or mask their emotional pain by some part of their sexual behavior pattern.[6]

4. *Secretive*: He develops a double life, practicing masturbation, using pornography, paying for prostitutes, and hiding what he is doing from others, in a sense, even from himself.

5. *Devoid of intimacy*: Completely self-focused, a pornography addict cannot achieve genuine intimacy. His self-obsession leaves no room for others.

6. *Devoid of relationship*: While the attitude of gratuitous sex is more clearly seen with pornography, fantasy, and masturbation, sex with a partner does not necessarily involve a relationship. To a pornography addict, the partner is not a real person, only an interchangeable part in an impersonal process.

7. *Victimizing*: The overwhelming obsession with self-gratification blinds the addict to the effect his behavior is having on others.

8. *Ends in despair and shame*: Rather than fulfilled as when married couples make love, addictive sex leaves the participants feeling guilty, empty, and ashamed. In these dark moments of despair, they want to stop, promise to stop, but cannot stop. Without help, they are incapable of changing their attitudes and behavior.

9. *Progressively damaging consequences*: The illness is nearly always *progressive*. Tolerance develops, and the body's own defense system is overridden. The addict gets into difficulty with himself or others. Most addicts do not seek help until this occurs.[7]

Symptoms described by pornography addicts include generalized and chronic anxiety, panic-attacks, a feeling of being "out of control" in relation to sex, and low grade depression with peaks of acute anxiety.[8] The activity that seeks relief from psychological stress leads instead to increased distress.

While no one knows how many individuals are so afflicted, in 1988 it was reported that there were five million sex addicts and over one hundred Sexaholics Anonymous groups in the country. This is 6 percent of the American population.[9] In 1985 there were about one thousand individuals in twenty chapters of Sex Addicts Anonymous in Minneapolis and St. Paul alone.[10]

The key to medically understanding pornography addiction is that the sexual response cycle causes significant changes in *body chemistry*.[11] Any activity such as rape fantasy or pornography that "causes intense excitement and pleasure can become compulsive."[12] It is noteworthy that the same endocrine and sex steroids activate both sex and aggression.[13]

When two research tracks finally converged, clinicians and researchers "recognized that sexual addiction is a clinically identifiable illness."[14] First practitioners observed that clients who engaged excessively with activities such as drinking, gambling, eating, drug use, and sexual behavior presented very similar descriptions of their disorders.[15] Second, researchers made amazing discoveries about the neurochemistry of the brain. In 1974 John Hughes and Hans Kosterlitz discovered enkephalins: pain-killing molecules that are produced naturally in the brain.

When that happened, the entire medical and scientific community had to rethink what caused addiction. Researchers discovered that the body can produce its own chemicals (at a higher level than normal) either to deal with painful feelings, or for purposes of gratification, or for both.

According to Dr. Douglas Reed, there are two neurochemical effects in the transmission of nerve impulses. One is the *arousal preference and response*. For people who prefer excitation and arousal, pornography supplies an enjoyable rush or high that is neurochemically equivalent to taking a drug.

The other is the *relaxation or inhibitory preference and response*. Sedation people, while enjoying the sensations of pleasure that pornography provides, do not enjoy a sustained high. They prefer the relaxed mood of viewing without risk, or the post-climax sedation. Being excited makes them uncomfortable so they try to avoid it.

People learn as children what rewards them and makes them feel good physiologically. They perpetuate that behavior when they need to cope with stress as adults or when they seek gratification. The pairing of the preferred mood state with pornography use is what makes it potentially addictive.[16]

Dr. Zillmann described these effects in terms of "sensation seekers" and "sensation minimizers and avoiders." The latter generally consume pornography in the privacy of their homes. Because the process is addicting and progressive, the danger lies in the constant need for the "quick fix," which tragically ruins the addict's life and his relationships with spouse, family, and friends.[17]

Those who look for excitement, "sensation seekers," use pornography as a turn on. As they become addicted to the turn on, they move progressively in the direction of becoming a social danger. When pornography no longer satisfies their need for a greater sexual high, they begin acting out their fantasies. Even acting out with their own wives is a problem. When the husband demands more and more, there comes a point where the wife cannot handle it. At first, he may be satisfied with relatively normal sex. Then he may want to tie her up. When symbolic bondage loses its thrill, he may want to inflict pain and draw blood. Now she has a problem she cannot handle.

A pastor who testified before the Attorney General's Commission on Pornography explained his earlier struggle with pornography, which had taught him that he was an authority on how to satisfy a woman. He said,

> Marriage came along and I began to lead my new wife in all my intellect of sex. I sought to fulfill all my lustful desire learned from pornography with her. She pleaded with me ... to get rid of the magazines because of her feelings of rejection. . . . My marriage bed was directed by most of this material, and I was always on the brink of doing something really deviant to my wife for a greater fulfillment for myself.[18]

Leading researchers dealing with addictive behavior now talk about sexual addiction as a pathological condition, a disordered condition, and an illness. Dr. Carnes defines it as "a pathological relationship with a mood altering experience."[19] Drs. Milkman and Sunderwirth defined an addiction biologically: "self-induced changes in neurotransmission that result in behavior problems."[20] Dr. Coleman also sees this behavior "as an illness" and as a "pathological psychosexual state or disorder."[21]

The definition is now considerably expanded by the National Council on Sexual Addiction:

> Sexual addiction is obsessive, compulsive sexual behavior which if left unattended, will cause severe distress and despair for both the individual and the family. The sexual addict is unable to control his or her sexual behavior and lives with constant pain, alienation, and fear of discovery. The addiction progresses until sex becomes more important than family, friends, or work.[22]

According to Drs. Donovan and Marlatt, "What sets this behavior pattern apart from others is the individual's overwhelmingly pathological involvement in or attachment to it, subjective compulsion to continue it, and reduced ability because of dependence to exert personal control over it."[23] When these renowned researchers and clinicians, who have been known for years in the alcohol and drug relapse prevention field, finally admitted that sexual behavior/pornography can be addictive, the research community began considering this as a fact.[24]

Alcoholics progress from sipping an occasional beer through "social drinking" to guzzling hard liquor straight from a bottle. A drug addict graduates from recreational marijuana to crack cocaine. Like other addictions, a pornography addict inevitably progresses from men's magazines to hard-core, more deviant pornography. He continues to escalate into new frontiers of the "forbidden fruit" looking for ways to act out his increasingly bizarre fantasies when pornography, fantasy, and masturbation no longer produce the desired "sexual high."

Every addict, whether to pornography, alcohol, or drugs, says that he escalates slowly at first, then more rapidly to where he is out of control and cannot regain control. Many addicts secretly live out stories like the one at the beginning of this chapter until they are exposed by sex crimes or suffer publicly humiliating consequences.

Understanding the steps in the cycle and its different stages or levels as the addict spirals downward can make it easier for those around him to identify the problem, choose to help him, and ultimately answer this question: How did a normal boy/man end up committing such heinous acts?

As not all users of marijuana or beer drinkers become drug addicts or alcoholics, not all users of pornography become pornography/sex addicts. However, a significant number do, and all who do become addicts eventually travel through these stages or levels if not stopped or helped.

Illustration I

Cline's Pornography Addiction Stages

1. Addiction: Powerfully drawn to and controlled by pornography.

2. Escalation: Over time, requires harder and more deviant material to reach the "sexual high."

3. Desensitization: People become sex objects; abnormal, deviant behavior becomes normal and acceptable.

4. Actualization: Fantasy needs to be acted out; molestation and rape becomes means to new sexual highs.

Arterburn's Sexual Addiction Levels

1. Pornography, Fantasy, Masturbation

2. Deviant and live pornography, fetishes, and affairs.

3. Minor Criminal offenses: Prostitution, Voyeurism, Exhibitionism.

4. Severe Legal Consequences: Molestation, Incest, Rape, Sexual Murder.

The Cycle of Sexual Addiction

Within each stage or level there is an Addiction Cycle occurring which drives the spiral downward. After repeated cycles at each level, the addict is driven to then next stage or level, final progressing to "acting out."

1. Obsession
Focus on personal pain. Emotional or sexual trigger (e.g. pornography). Mind becomes saturated with sexual thoughts.

2. The Hunt
Driven to look for something sexual: Pornography, Fantasy, Sexual Release/Masturbation, often highly ritualized.

3. Recruitment
Identifying and obtaining as "victim" through buying pornography or seducing a woman or child.

4. Gratification
Achieving orgasm by masturbation, fantasy fulfillment, pornography or perverse sexual behavior.

5. Return to Normal
Brief Interlude

6. Justification
"Everybody does it; I need/deserve it."

7. Blame
Seeks a scapegoat. Shirks personal responsibi for his actions.

8. Shame
Guilt and shame. Feels bad about what he h become. Bottom rung of society.

9. Despair
Feels hopeless to change. Turns to other compulsions. Contemplates suicide.

10. Promises
Never again. Promises trigger obsessive thin Cycle starts over again; sometimes at a differ stage or level.

Four Stages of Pornography Addiction

One clinical psychologist, Dr. Victor Cline, now professor of psychology at the University of Utah, has treated over 240 sex addicts and has pioneered a four stage syndrome of pornography addiction. He found these stages common to all his patients almost without exception.[25] Regardless of the sexual deviation (child molestation, voyeurism, exhibitionism, sadomasochism, fetishism, rape, etc.), pornography has been a contributor or facilitator in the acquisition of their sexual addiction.

1. *Addiction*—first, they get hooked on pornography. The sexual material provides a powerful sexual stimulant. The aphrodisiac effect is followed by sexual release, often through masturbation. Remembering the "high," they keep coming back for more.

2. *Escalation* follows, with the addicts requiring more explicit and more deviant sexual material to achieve the "high."

Willing sex partners do not solve the problem because addicts often prefer masturbating to the sexual imagery in their minds to having sexual intercourse. The fantasy is all-powerful—much to the disappointment of their partners. Their capacity to love and express affection is always diminished by the pornography addiction.

3. *Desensitization* occurs. Sexual scenes, which were originally shocking, abnormal, repulsive, or taboo breaking—though still sexually arousing—in time become commonplace, acceptable, and normal. Individuals in pornography become sex objects, and sexual activity, no matter how bizarre or deviant, becomes legitimized.

4. *Acting out*—finally, there is an increasing tendency to act out the sexual or violent behaviors repeatedly viewed in pornography, in spite of the negative consequences in their lives. The pornography legitimizes and fuels the sexual fantasies, which now captivate them. They are unable to change or reverse their direction.

Four Levels of Addiction

Stephen Arterburn, whose entire practice for many years has been counseling sex addicts, explains the downward spiral of sex addiction in a four level model.[26] It is strikingly similar to Dr. Cline's four stage model of pornography addiction.

Level 1: Pornography, Fantasy, and Masturbation

Anyone participating in this first level of sex addiction would have no trouble justifying his actions in light of our society's liberal, sexually promiscuous behavior. Using pornography, like men's magazines or X-rated videos, the addict can masturbate while fantasizing about sex with women not his wife or girlfriend, sex with children and teen-agers, sex that inflicts pain and violence, or sex with multiple partners.

While pornography, sexual fantasy and masturbation are considered harmless amusement by many in our society, "they form the gateway to deeper levels of enslavement."

Level 2: Hard-Core or Live Pornography and Illicit Affairs

After addiction sets in, escalation inevitably occurs, drawing the addict to harder and harder pornography. Sometimes, pornographic fantasies are acted out by attending nude dancing establishments, obtaining fetishes (items like the underclothing of a fantasized but real person) to enhance erotic feelings, touching sexually (such as "accidentally on purpose" brushing up against someone), or engaging in phone sex. While *Level One* involved sex on paper or in films, *Level Two* attempts to make contact with real people. However, even respected affairs do not provide enough thrills for very long. Perverse forms of sex involving bondage, masochism, sadism, or multiple partners of both sexes are often injected into the affair to sustain the "high." These deviant behaviors reflect: (1) the reduction of people to sex objects and (2) "the ever-diminishing satisfactions of addictive sex devoid of intimacy."

Level 3: Prostitution, Voyeurism, and Exhibitionism

This level relates to the "acting out" stage in Dr. Cline's model, but it involves only minor criminal offenses. Many sex addicts are unable to persuade normal people to perform in deviant ways or without attachment. They progress to prostitutes, many of whom have been sexually abused or are, themselves, addicts.

Voyeurism, as innocent, at first, as joggers who look in windows, might begin and progress to "peeping toms" hiding in bushes. Exhibitionism, as mild as undressing in front of open windows and having a fly unzipped in public, progresses to men flashing nude bodies to shocked women and children. While the criminal acts and consequences to victims are minor, the stage is set for more serious criminal behavior. All the bizarre and deviant behaviors presented in pornography as normal and taboo breaking are seen as acceptable sexual outlets in the eroticized, fantasy world of sex addicts. The step to *Level Four* is not far.

Level 4: Molestation, Incest, and Rape

For most addicts, the natural progression of sexual fantasy portrayed in pornography as normal, fun, and exciting eventually leads to criminal conduct. The consequences are severe for the

perpetrator—jail and humiliation if caught—and for the victim—
"often a life sentence of emotional turmoil and pain." Unfortunately, sex addicts will commit serial sex crimes because they are
now locked in the chains of sexual addiction and unable to stop.
Often jail provides the intervention necessary for them to receive
help. Unfortunately, prisons do not prevent prisoners from receiving hard-core pornography from the outside. In some cases, they
even provide it in their commissary.

Even without newly obtained pornography, treatment at this
point can be extremely difficult because the attitudes acquired
from pornography consumption have been cemented by repeated
"highs."

While independently discovered, Dr. Cline's four stages of
pornography addiction and Arterburn's four sex addiction levels
are very compatible. When combined, they begin to explain the
downward addictive spiral to destruction if professional help is not
sought.

Within each of the four levels of Arterburn and the four stages
of Dr. Cline, a ten step addiction cycle is occurring, often many
times before the addict progresses to the next level or stage.[27] The
following ten step cycle can occur many times at each stage before
the addict finally descends to the fourth and final level in the
downward spiral of pornography or sex addiction.

A Ten Step Cycle at Each Level/Stage

1. *Obsession*—The addiction begins with severe focus on self,
either of the "poor-me" variety or an obsession with past hurts.
The addict loses the ability to concentrate on daily life as his mind
becomes saturated with thoughts of how he will obtain relief. The
triggers of obsessive thinking can be anger, shame, pain, anxiety,
or some other momentary emotional upset. Or the trigger can be
sexual in nature: some form of pornography, an attractive individual glimpsed in passing, an innocent-looking picture in a magazine or on television that stirs up lust.

2. *The Hunt*—Eventually, the addict is driven to action. He
looks for something or someone with which to be sexual. He might
seek out a familiar bookstore or nightclub to obtain pornography.
He might go out in search of a sexual partner, perhaps in singles'
bars or on the street. Or, he might simply find a bathroom where
he can be alone with his fantasies and masturbate. Often, the hunt
is highly ritualized, built on years of practiced behavior and experience.

3. *Recruitment*—Identifying and obtaining a victim could be
as simple as purchasing a magazine or dropping quarters into a

peep show slot. Or it could be far more complex, as in enticing and seducing another unsuspecting person.

4. *Gratification*—On one hand, gratification is simply a matter of achieving orgasm, by means ranging from masturbation to intercourse. But it is not always so simple. Many addicts cannot achieve orgasm apart from elaborate—and ever-escalating—fantasy fulfillment. Finding the right kind of pornography, or the right kind of partner, or the right brand of perverse sexual behavior, is what fuels the addictive process from one level to the next.

5. *Return to Normal*—After the fantasy has been fulfilled and orgasm achieved, the obsession lifts and the addict once again feels "normal." Ted Bundy described a feeling of normalcy even after committing a murder. As with other addictions, this state of normalcy does not last. Reality intrudes again, pushing the cycle onward.

6. *Justification*—As the addict allows himself to become aware of what he has done, the need arises to justify his behavior. Addicts are accomplished mental gymnasts, going through colossal logical contortions to persuade themselves that it was really OK. No one was really hurt. Everyone does it.

7. *Blame*—When the addict can no longer believe his own rationalizations, he seeks a scapegoat onto whom he can project his problems. He looks for someone to blame for the dreadful feelings that always resurface when the euphoria of gratification wears off. He will blame his parents, society, even God, for making him what he is. He will blame almost anyone rather than accepting personal responsibility for his actions.

8. *Shame*—As the addict finds it increasingly difficult to project onto others what he has done, guilt and shame set in and eat away at his soul. He feels bad, less for what he has done than for what he has become. He sees himself as occupying the bottom rung of society.

9. *Despair*—Eventually the addict reaches a point where the pain is greater *after* than it was *before*. He feels hopeless to change. At this point, he might turn to drinking or might augment his sexual addiction with any of a dozen other compulsions, all in a desperate attempt to make the pain go away. Suicide becomes a distinct possibility.

10. *Promises*—The addict tells himself and others that it will never happen again. He will never go to that place again; he will never see that person again. But his promises serve only to refocus his obsessive thinking and trigger the addictive process once more.

As you can see from this downward spiral, the pornography addict is on a collision course with his family and personal integrity. Frequently, in his wake lie a trail of ruined relationships. The addict's victims feel needed—for a time—then simply used. Often their response to the addict's treatment of them will determine whether or not he will awaken to his problem and seek help before it is too late. After the first stage or level, intervention is usually required to stop his downward spiral. The addict cannot break out of the destructive addiction cycle without professional help.

Drs. Marshall, Reed, and others believe that pornography use can cause as well as maintain or increase addictive behavior. There are six major roots of compulsive/addictive patterns: (1) lack of intimacy; (2) family dysfunction; (3) abuse as a child; (4) conditioning; (5) shame-bound systems; and (6) neurochemistry and biological/genetic factors. How pornography becomes associated with any or all of these determines whether or not it is a causal factor.[28]

Dr. Reed stresses that "healthy sexuality needs to be learned." Dysfunctional families do not model healthy sexuality. Unfortunately, the media, which often act as substitute parents, fail to model healthy sexuality as well. They have, in fact, started many young children on the path to becoming sexual voyeurs and fetish users and have encouraged the creation of an appetite that requires more and more seductive material.

1. *Lack of Intimacy*: Lack of intimacy is a core issue with most sex addicts and is usually interrelated with other root causes. Problems with intimacy commonly result from a deprived or abused childhood. They are often coupled with self-obsession, usually in the realms of fear, anger, guilt, or shame.

2. *Family Dysfunction*: "Family dysfunction plays an important role in the origination and maintenance of compulsive/addictive behaviors," particularly "parental rejection, overprotection, overindulgence, perfectionism, encouragement of sibling rivalry, marital conflict, and excessively harsh or excessively lenient— that is, inconsistent—discipline."[29]

Drs. Marshall and Barbaree see inconsistent and harsh discipline in the absence of love as failing to instill constraints and social inhibitions against aggressive behavior. They might even facilitate the fusion of sex and aggression rather than separate them.[30] Coleman's clinical experience has lead him to believe that some type of historical family intimacy dysfunction or abuse has occurred in the backgrounds of all sex offenders.[31]

Much pornography feeds into that dysfunction, especially that which shows rape as pleasurable to the victim.[32] "Researchers at Golden Valley Institute for Behavioral Medicine identified a particularly dysfunctional family pattern that promoted sexually addictive behavior: 'rigid-disengaged.' 88 percent of the addicts treated there came from families who were 'disengaged'; 77 percent from those who were 'rigid'; and 68 percent from families who were both."[33]

Individuals from this style of dysfunctional family are the most susceptible to compulsive acting out. In such a family, the rules are very rigid and do not change. The father is in control and decides what everyone in the family should do. There is no discussion, and no one can change his mind. The value structure usually is that sex is bad and dirty, and it's wrong to feel good. Such a family structure leads to feelings of shame and externalization of control. Since behavior has always been controlled by someone else, the individual's control apparatus does not work, and he has difficulty learning self-control.

In research on family viewing patterns, Dr. Singer found a powerful combination of authoritarian parent, physical punishment, and heavy viewing of sexually oriented or action detective shows in the most aggressive children in the study. At home these five- to eight-year-old children were very dependent on the family style, but in school, they acted out their aggression, destroying property and hitting other children. Similarly, the individual from the opposite, a rigidly-disengaged family, might appear to follow the rules of the house, but, looking for the intimacy he has lacked in early life, he might develop a secret sex life, which is fueled and maintained by pornography. The suppressed anger of such a person might be expressed in a preference for violent pornography or in acting out violent patterns of behavior learned from rape myth or sadistic scenarios.[34]

3. *Child Sexual Abuse*: Child sexual abuse is very prominent in the backgrounds of people with sexual addictive disorders. At the Golden Valley Sexual Dependency Unit, fourteen hundred sexual addicts have been treated on an inpatient basis. Case reviews revealed that of those who later became addicts, 81 percent experienced sexual abuse and nearly all of them—97 percent—experienced emotional abuse.[35] In a recent Los Angeles Police Department study, over 80 percent of the molesters had been sexually abused in childhood.[36]

Because children are so vulnerable to sexual stimuli at young ages, exposing them to pornography during latency or early adolescence should be considered a form of child abuse. Such exposure explains how children from healthy families sometimes become entrapped by pornography in spite of an early nurturing environment.

It also accounts for the rapid addiction to dial-a-porn of otherwise healthy nine- to twelve-year-old children. Normally, they learn by imitation. They become aroused and, not knowing how to deal with the new information in any other way, experiment with a younger child in their own household or in their neighborhood. This, then, creates an even larger pool of children who become predisposed to pornography use and abuse in the future. Alarmingly, the research of Dr. Ann Burgess suggests that the vast majority of violent sex offenders and child molesters were abused as children and grew up to become abusers of others.[37]

The teen-age years (12-17), when pornography use is rampant, are the most harmful developmentally. When high hormonal arousal is paired with peak sexual stimuli such as pornography, the exhilarating emotional experience for adolescents is one they might never forget and will probably seek again.

4. *Conditioning or Reinforcement*: Puberty appears to be the critical period in the development of sexuality. "If at this time a young male is exposed to deviant sexual activity, pornographic stimuli, or the original development of deviant fantasy, and fantasizes or elaborates these themes in the context of masturbation, it will result in the development of deviant interests. If this continues, the likelihood is that the next sexual contact and most, if not all, subsequent contacts will also be deviant."[38]

5. *Shame-based Systems*: The shame that is so penetrating in addictive people is most often an originating cause of pornography addiction. Children in shame-based families think that they are the cause of the abuse, whether it is neglect, physical, psychological, sexual, or emotional abuse. They develop "feelings of unworthiness, and a feeling that somehow their personality is inherently defective." They are haunted by feelings of shame, low self-esteem, and loneliness.

In order to alleviate some of the guilt and shame and to avoid punishment, they become secretive about their sexual behavior. Once they engage in compulsive sexual behavior, shame increases and they experience even greater "interference in interpersonal relationships." Dr. Coleman concludes that children who grow up "in [shame-based] families with intimacy dysfunction, are at high risk for developing unhealthy and distorted attitudes, values and behaviors regarding sex, intimacy, and drugs."[39]

Dr. Reed summarized the four major beliefs common to children of shame-bound dysfunctional families.

1. "I am worthless; I never do anything right."

2. "If people really knew me, they probably wouldn't like me."

3. "I can't count on other people to help me meet my needs. I have to take care of my own needs."

4. "My greatest need is sex, since that makes me feel better."

6. *Neurochemistry and Biological Factors*: Scientists are learning more about pornography addiction by understanding and describing the chemical changes that occur in the body while looking at pornography. Many researchers now believe neurochemicals and genetics play a significant role in addiction.[40] While many complex factors still need to be studied further, it appears that epinephrine, an adrenaline-type chemical in the body, is produced when the body is stimulated by pornography. This chemical, along with a physical release for masturbation, powerfully imprints the pornographic fantasy onto the brain. Over time, the brain seeks harder and harder images that will trigger the pleasure and pain reduction emotions experienced when the chemicals are produced. Those images, which the brain seeks, are the contents of pornography.

The use of pornography can be both a cause and a symptom of behavior that serves to arouse or sedate individuals. Which of these two states results depends upon the individual's neurochemistry.[41]

The best research and scientific evidence to date suggests that all sexual deviations are *learned*; none are inherited.[42] By repeated conditioning with pornography, sexual deviations have, in fact, been created in live subjects in the laboratory 100 percent of the time.[43] Further, if a man repeatedly masturbates to vivid sexual fantasy (pornography) as his primary outlet, the pleasurable experience endows the deviant fantasy (rape, molestation, sexual violence, or incest) with increasing erotic value.[44] If pornography validates and promotes the deviant conduct as normal and acceptable, such deviant conduct is more likely to be acted out.[45]

There are nine major sexual deviations called paraphilias that generally occur in our society. Like sexually transmitted diseases, all nine are rapidly increasing. Recent content studies indicate that over one-third of all hard-core pornography on the market today is paraphilic or sexually deviant, which means it appeals to the various illnesses listed in Illustration II.

Because of the highly repetitive nature of paraphilic behavior, a large percentage of the population has been or will be victimized by people with paraphilias.[46] Paraphiliacs are getting younger and younger as whole generations of children are raised on more deviant pornography. The implications for the future are staggering. In a recent survey of *non-incarcerated* pedophiles, almost 54 percent of the offenders developed their deviant sex interest before age 18, had committed an average of about 7 offenses in juvenile years (mostly molestation and rape), and 380 sex offenses in their lifetimes.[47]

In short, for thirty years, we have saturated generations of our

Illustration II
Paraphilias and Pornography

Paraphilias	Typical Behavior
Voyeurism	The act of observing unsuspecting people, usually strangers, who are either naked, in the process of disrobing or engaging in sexual activity. Usually no sexual activity is sought with the person being viewed. Pornography portrays the stimulus desired by the voyeur. Looking at pornography constitutes voyeurism for some persons.
Exhibitionism	The exposure of one's genitals to a stranger, sometimes masturbating while exposing. Some men fantasize with pornography that they are getting the reaction they want from the person in the pornography.
Frotteurism	Touching (Toucherism) and rubbing (Frotteurism) against a unconsenting person. It is the touching, no the coerciv nature of the act, that is sexually exciting. Some men are stimulated by pornography to engage in this illegal behav ior.
Fetishism	The use of inanimate objects, such as bras, women's underpants, stockings, shoes, etc. Pornography magazines (pictures) have clinically been demonstrated to serve as a fetish.
Transvestic Fetishism	Cross-dressing, form occasional solitary wearing of female clothes to extensive involvement in a transvestic subculture. There is substantial pornography related to this disorder.
Sexual Masochism	The act of being humiliated, beaten, bound or otherwise made to suffer. Most people with this disorder increase the severity of the acts over time, or during stress. Such acts dominate a substantial portion of pornography.
Pedophilia	Sexual activity with a prepubescent child. Those attracted to girls usually prefer 8-12 years old. Those attracted to boys usually prefer slightly older children. Nothing is more important to pedophiles that their pornography collections.
Hebephilia	Sexual attraction to the activity with pubescent and post-pubescent children ages 12-17. Pornography required for seduction, stimulation and blackmail.
Sexual Sadism	Acts in which the psychological or physical suffering (including humiliation) of the victim is sexually exciting. Usually the severity of the sadistic acts increases over time. This illness is joked about by the media, but it is no jo to real victims. Pornography fuels this disorder.

here are numerous examples of other paraphilia which are encouraged by pornography. Here are a few:
. **Partialism:** Exclusive focus on part of the body, such as breast, buttocks, vaginas, etc. More than half of the commercial pornog hy objectifies and focuses on some part of the body. The graphic close-ups in hard-core pornography feeds this disorder.
. **Urophilia:** Focus on urinating, which pornography calls "wet sports".
. **Zoophilia or Bestiality:** Sex with animals.
. **Klismaphilia:** Enemas, preparatory to anal intercourse, or as an arousing act alone.
. **Telephone Scatalogia:** Phone lewdness. Dial-a-porn is the perpetration of this illness.
. **Infantilism:** The desire to be treated as a helpless infant and clothed in diapers. Media ads suggesting that one "baby oneself" ed this illness.
. **Hypoxyphilia, or autoerotic asphysixia:** Involves sexual arousal by oxygen deprivation. It was fostered by a pornographic agazine and is considered to have caused hundreds of death.

young with increasingly hard-core and deviant pornography and are now reaping the consequences. Many youth are becoming conditioned to believe that deviant and abnormal sex acts are normal and acceptable, that vaginal sex in marriage is dull and boring, and that when it comes to illicit sex and abnormal activity, "everybody does it." Thus, two generations, with a third on its way, have, at the very least, become desensitized to deviant and illegal sexual activity and through pornography's fantasies, have been encouraged to try it.

The pornography industry treats paraphilias in a cavalier manner, calling them in Adult Video News "clean fetish fun." They make cartoons and jokes of them, as Dr. Reisman routinely found, in even generally accepted men's magazines like *Playboy* and *Penthouse* (see chap. 4 and 7). But violent sex offenders are no joke, and our society needs to be more aggressive in removing from the marketplace the paraphilic pornography that encourages them. This is not an issue of free speech, but a matter of public health and safety.

The fact that paraphilic pornography caters to and perpetuates the "recurrent intense images" that drive deviant sexual patterns is *prima facie* evidence (sufficient to establish the fact in question unless rebutted) of its harm to our society. One test for obscenity is whether the material appeals to a prurient/unhealthy, shameful, or morbid interest in sex. Paraphilic pornography appeals, by definition, to persons who are clinically ill with sex disorders. Thus, many professionals believe that any pornography that encourages such disorders and illness should be illegal. According to Dr. Reed and others, these materials are obviously hurtful, regardless of whether or not they are judged obscene.[48]

Additionally, almost all the paraphilias initiate in childhood or adolescence when psychological and physiological changes are at their peak. This is the time when major harm from exposure to pornography can be expected, particularly in children who have grown up in shame-bound or dysfunctional families. Sadly, studies show that this is the age that is most frequently exposed to pornography.[49] Such hard-core pornography must be kept out of the hands of vulnerable children through passage and strict enforcement of strong harmful matter *per se* laws discussed in chapters 15 and 16.

At a minimum, pornography that is paraphilic—(1) sexually aggressive, (2) rape myth oriented, (3) containing pseudo-child images, (4) involving sex with animals, (5) excretory functions in sexual activities, and (6) foreign objects inserted in body cavities— should be illegal *per se* like child pornography. Our society should not give "budding pre-addicts" deviant material to feed upon to commit their later crimes[50] (see chap. 15).

According to the Department of Justice, four million child molesters are thought to exist in the United States, and only 15 percent of sex offenders are known or incarcerated. Since a primary motivator of crime and the most common characteristic of pedophiles/child molesters, rapists, and sexual murders is pornography, our society must face the harm it causes. Even if we ignore the scientific research and clinical studies, we cannot dismiss the children who are molested, the women who are raped, and the victims who are murdered, because men like Gary Bishop, Jeffrey Dahmer, and Ted Bundy were addicted to pornography.

Chapter 10

Media Violence—The Verdict Is In!

The technique of murder must be presented in a way that will not inspire imitation. Brutal killings are not to be presented in detail. Revenge in modern times shall not be justified. . . . The use of firearms should be restricted to essentials.

—The Motion Picture Code, 1930-1966

FBI Director William Sessions has declared violent crime the major national crime challenge of the 1990s.[1] From school to prison, the daily diet of violence on television and film is taking effect. Expelling students for increasingly serious and violent behavior, schools across the country grapple with how to cope with an increasingly hostile student body.[2] Judges face younger and younger criminals. From Los Angeles to Washington, DC, prison workers express fear of the new generation of criminals.[3] They have no moral compass, no concept of right and wrong, no concept of family. Life is not important to them. Television scenes played out in their own neighborhoods validate violence as the way to settle petty grievances and solve everyday problems.

Concern about the amount of violence in the media has been building since the early fifties. Researchers have undertaken and completed literally thousands of studies, consistently finding a connection between viewing violence and later aggressive behavior. According to Carol Lieberman, chairman of the liberal group, National Coalition on Television Violence, "There are close to one thousand studies on all kinds of entertainment . . . that show 95 percent causal link between violent entertainment and subsequent harmful behavior . . . the [only] studies that don't show this are funded mostly by TV networks."[4] Scientific debate now centers

127

on *how* and the *degree* to which media violence influences behavior.

By 1975, two government commissions (the 1969 President's Commission on the Causes and Prevention of Violence and the 1972 Surgeon General's Report on Media Violence) had gathered sufficient evidence of negative effects to call for programming free of violence and explicit sexuality between the hours of 7 and 9 P.M.[5] The Federal Communications Commission worked with the networks to establish the promising concept of "family viewing hours," but the courts judged such restrictions to violate the First Amendment.

Anecdotal evidence from the 1970s cited by Dr. Russell G. Geen, a leading researcher on violence in the mass media, documented that acts of violence are frequently committed just after viewing brutality on the screen[6]:

> On 2 October 1973 in Boston, a gang forced Evelyn Wagler to douse herself with gasoline. Just as in a television drama aired two nights earlier, they then set her on fire.

> On 22 April 1974 in Ogden, Utah, three people were forced to drink a caustic drain cleaner which killed them. The police could find no motive for the killings except that three times in a single day the murderers had seen the motion picture *Magnum Force* which showed a man killing a prostitute by making her drink drain cleaner.

> In September 1974 in St. Louis, a young man watched the movie *Open Season* about Vietnam veterans who annually kidnapped a young couple, set them free, and hunted them down and killed them. When he left the theater, he purchased ammunition for his gun and shortly thereafter murdered a couple in an isolated area outside the city.

In 1975, after conducting a comprehensive review of 146 articles representing fifty studies involving ten thousand children and adolescents, Dr. M. B. Rothenberg called for immediate remedial action on television programming.[7] All of these studies demonstrated that television violence, defined as "intentional injury to another," increased aggression.[8] The next year Dr. Somers, alarmed about violent death statistics, "identified violence among youth as a serious and complex health hazard" and blamed violence in entertainment as a contributing factor.[9] A California medical association study estimated 22 percent of all crimes committed by juveniles had been suggested by television programs.[10]

By 1977, Dr. George Gerbner had found that "three quarters of all television characters were involved in some form of violence

and nine of every ten programs sampled contained violence."
Television viewing was almost synonymous with violence viewing.[11] But in spite of all this concern and the growing body of
negative evidence, the quantity of violence consistently escalated
over the years.

In 1982, the National Institute of Mental Health Report on
Television and Behavior summarized the findings of twenty five
hundred studies and concluded that there is overwhelming scientific evidence that a "causal relationship [exists] between viewing
televised violence and later aggressive behavior." The report
stated that the tentative conclusions of the first two commissions
in the early 1970s "were significantly strengthened" by the research studies in the following decade.[12]

Summarizing important studies of all ages, from pre-schoolers
to teen-agers, the report found consistent evidence that children
were more aggressive after watching violent programs. Because
violence is so pervasive in our general entertainment, increased
aggression was found even after watching large amounts of general television. For instance, there was a significant increase in
both verbal and physical aggression after television was introduced to towns that had not had it previously. Two years after the
introduction of television into Notel, Canada, in 1973, physical
aggression among children increased by 160 percent.[13]

Because so much television programming is laced with violence, a large international study by leading media researchers
Drs. Jerome and Dorothy Singer concluded, "The sheer amount of
television was the best predictor of aggression."[14]

According to the National Institutes of Mental Health Report,
television was molding children's attitudes. Seeing violence on
television, they accepted it as normal behavior and believed there
was more violence in the real world.[15] They exhibited more fear,
apprehension, and mistrust.[16] Research found that even cartoons
are not harmless fantasy for younger children.[17] Pre-schoolers who
watched violent cartoons were the most aggressive.[18] The study's
conclusion of the potential impact of violence viewing on real life
behavior is both frightening and prophetic: when people become
accustomed and hardened to violence from seeing too much of it,
they could be less likely to respond to real violence.

In 1985, the American Psychological Association reaffirmed
their conclusion "that television violence has a causal effect on
aggressive behavior for children and adolescents."[19] Despite the
researchers' verdict of harm and call for social policy change, the
entertainment industry continued to escalate violent depictions
and the public continued to consume them:

During the 1970's depictions of aggressive and sexual behaviors became increasingly "graphic," especially in feature
movies shown in theaters. It is almost as though the audiences had become callous and, to give them excitement, the
films had to be made more and more powerful in their
arousal effects.[20]

Copycat crimes continued to provide convincing evidence of
the influence of viewing violence in films.

Seventeen-year-old Cathy Ann Petruso and her boyfriend saw
the movie *An Officer and a Gentleman* together several times.
Cathy and, a few weeks later, her ex-boyfriend hanged themselves
just like the character in the film following the break up of his
romance.

In 1984, twenty-eight people had killed themselves playing
Russian roulette after watching the movie *The Deerhunter* on
television.

Jeffrey Alan Cox murdered his grandfather and grandmother
in exactly the same way the main character of *The Executioner's
Song* committed a murder. Cox had just seen the movie on NBC.[21]

There is now a strong consensus among researchers that
viewing television violence increases aggression. Laboratory studies have made an important contribution to their understanding,
but because the episodes were brief and often less violent than
typical television fare today, results may have been underestimated.[22] According to Dr. Russell G. Geen, many of those findings
have now been replicated in good, high-quality, real-life studies,[23]
which use natural settings, measure everyday behavior, and cover
longer time periods.[24]

Three out of the four major longitudinal studies of aggression
under natural conditions undertaken in the 1980s found substantial harm. Many researchers agree that similar outcomes in the
fourth study were under reported.[25]

First, a study by Drs. Eron and Huesmann followed eight-
year-olds for twenty-two years and found "considerable consistency in aggressive behavior among these children over the years."[26]
"Among boys, the frequency of viewing television and liking violent programs at age eight were found to predict criminally anti-
social behavior twenty-two years later." The study concluded that
*extensive TV watching of violent programs at age eight was a good
predictor of criminal behavior at age thirty*. Moreover, the study
proved, it is not true that television violence affects only those
children predisposed to aggression or those with lower socioeco-
nomic status or lower I.Q.s.[27]

Second, Drs. Singer and Singer studied nursery school children for one year and found that the time spent by children

viewing "action-adventure" television with a high level of violence "significantly correlated" with later aggressive behavior for both boys and girls.[28]

Third, an international investigation, led by Drs. Huesmann and Eron, studied first through fifth grade children in the United States, Finland, Poland, Australia, and Israel.[29] Boys and girls who watched televised violence more frequently were rated more aggressive by their peers, and frequent viewing was found to predict future aggression. The more boys identified with aggressive television characters, the more aggressive they were perceived in real life.[30]

Finally, Dr. Milavsky and colleagues, researchers for the National Broadcasting Company (NBC), studied seven-to twelve-year-old boys and teen-age boys over a period of years.[31] Out of hundreds of tests of statistical significance, they found significant adverse effects, but since the number of effects was small, they concluded these must all have been due to chance. One important factor in the perplexing findings was that the most aggressive boys dropped out of the study so Dr. Milavsky was left with a much less aggressive group. Regardless of this shortcoming, many of the correlations confirmed other longitudinal studies.[32]

This study was reanalyzed by Dr. Thomas Cook, an expert in evaluation research. "He came to the conclusion that there *was* an effect in those data" and that Milavsky had "underestimated television's cumulative impact."[33] Many researchers believe it is more than coincidental that this study was funded by NBC.[34]

On the other side of the crime act, the risk of being murdered in America has doubled over the past thirty years.[35] In 1988 there were 8.4 murders per 100,000 Americans. Germany had only half that many, and Britain (2.0) and Japan (1.2) were lower still.[36]

The increase in juvenile crime is the most alarming. According to the FBI, arrests of those under eighteen from 1983 to 1987, when the adolescent population declined by 2 percent, jumped 22.2 percent for murder, 18.6 percent for aggravated assault, and 14.6 percent for rape.[37] In 1984, violent crimes involved 1.7 million teen-agers.[38] The rate of teen-age victims of violent crimes has risen from 60 out of 1,000 in 1984 to 67 out of every 1,000 in 1990.[39]

The juvenile crime rate was about half the present rate in the early 1960s. It peaked in the early 1980s, dropped in the mid-1980s, and has been rising steadily ever since. Serious crimes have risen an average of 5 percent each year since 1985 except for 1991 where it went up another 7.9 percent to a total of 35 million.[40] The average U.S. child sees 8,000 murders and 100,000 other acts of violence on TV by the time he or she leaves elementary school, according to the new report by the American Psychological Association.[41]

Two studies provide strong evidence that watching violence either reported or dramatized on television encourages people to commit violent acts. In 1986, Dr. Phillips studied news reports of television and other news media to see if there was a relationship between violence-related events and rises in aggressive acts immediately after the reports. He has successfully shown a positive relationship between violent human tragedies reported by news media and increases in murders and suicides.[42]

A very careful study, which took every possible variable into consideration, compared homicide rates in the United States and Canada to homicide rates in South Africa, a similar culture, which had no television until twenty-five years after it was introduced into the United States.[43] Dr. Brandon Centerwall found that from the introduction of television in 1945 to 1974, white homicide deaths increased by 93 percent in the United States and by 92 percent in Canada. During this same period in South Africa, they decreased by 7 percent.

For both the United States and Canada, homicide rates nearly doubled after a ten- to fifteen-year time lag during which children exposed to television had time to grow up. Eight years after television had been introduced into South Africa, the homicide rate had already increased by 56 percent.

Dr. Centerwall examined an array of factors that might have confused the issue and proved him wrong, but none "provided a viable alternative explanation for the observed homicide trends."[44] He concluded that "1) exposure of susceptible populations to television is followed by a major increase in rates of violence and 2) the timing of the introduction of television into the population predicts the timing of the subsequent increase in rates of violence."

Statistically, Dr. Centerwall estimated that exposure to television—which includes massive doses of violent programming—is causally related to roughly one half the twenty thousand yearly homicides in the United States. Data also indicate that it is causally related to half the rapes, assaults, and other forms of interpersonal violence in the United States as well.[45]

In addition to obvious criminal behavior, watching filmed violence increases serious social problems like family violence. One highly publicized domestic-violence murder occurred in October 1985:

> A televised domestic violence film *Burning Bed* based on a
> real life experience, told the story of a battered wife who
> poured gasoline on her husband while he was sleeping and
> set his mattress on fire. That same evening in Milwaukee,
> after watching the film, a troubled husband doused his wife
> with gasoline and set her on fire to die as a human torch.[46]

One fourth of all homicides involve domestic violence, but many more people are affected than appear in criminal records. Two million victims are beaten every year by their spouses and another 1,700,000 are assaulted by spouses with guns and knives.[47] Drs. Huesmann and Eron found that "childhood aggression predicted the amount of physical punishment that men and women used with their children and the amount of spouse abuse indulged in by men."[48] Since childhood aggression is increased by television viewing, family violence can be expected to continue to escalate unless something is done.

Such studies warn against placing a television set in a child's room where parents lose control over what is watched and how often. Both schools and city streets have become places of fear. "There are nearly three million incidents of school crime in kindergarten through high school annually . . . ranging from simple assault to robbery to homicide. . . . Teachers can't teach and students can't learn in an environment that's filled with fear."[49] "A U.S. Education Department survey reported that incidents of violent crime in public schools are rising. Here's what teachers are saying: 42 percent saw at least one serious fight; 20 percent were threatened at school, and 44 percent saw more disruptive behavior than five years ago."[50]

In 1987 the *New York Times* reported that four hundred thousand boys took guns to school.[50] A first of March 1992 issue of *Newsweek* stated, "Gun violence is on the rise in schools all over America, and the nation's children are trapped in its path." One in five students carries some sort of weapon and one in twenty, a gun. Even fourth and fifth graders are arming, and elementary and middle school teachers are more fearful than ever. Discussing gunfire on the school playground, a principal of a California school said, "There's so much violence on TV and in the community that many kids expected this kind of thing."[52]

New York City has had the "bloodiest" school year ever. "In all, 5 teachers, 1 cop, 2 parents and 16 students have been shot—6 of the kids fatally." Even in award-winning Jefferson High, spot checks over these months turned up 121 weapons.

Overall, according to the U.S. Bureau of Justice, four hundred thousand students between the ages of twelve and nineteen were victims of violent crime during 1991. An L.A. city councilwoman believes "gun violence continues at a level that can only suggest a national character flaw."[53]

In the 1940s the greatest school problems were throwing wads of paper, chewing gum, and talking in class. Today, outright rebellion, murder, and rape top the list. Lack of discipline at home and at school and loss of teaching values in schools must share the blame with the value system taught through our media. The *Newsweek* analysis of the problem concluded that "schools won't be safe unless they can find a way to instill basic values of right and wrong, and teach young people to respect themselves and others." Educators need a big assist from the media in showing young people nonviolent alternatives.

If the schools are unsafe, the streets are more so. An Associated Press release entitled "Trend didn't stop in '91: Many cities set murder records" declared:

> For many American cities, 1991 followed a tragic pattern: another year, another increase in violent deaths. At least three of the nation's ten largest cities set homicide records [as did] several smaller cities. . . .[54]

> The total number of murders in 1991 was 24,020, an increase of 580 over 1990.[55]

Senator Joseph Biden, Jr., summed up 1991 in this way: "A year which saw the rest of the world become safer for America saw this nation become less safe for its own citizens."[56] Increasing headlines of unexpected mass killings bear this out.

Speaking of the new "casual killing, killing for kicks, drive-by murders," columnist Anthony Lewis pointed out the media connection:

> Why should we be surprised at random killing when television gives us dozens, hundreds, of murders a day? Why when foul language and calls for violence are the common coin of youth culture?[57]

Today's movies encourage young people to think violence is the solution to everyday problems of boredom, frustration, anger, and lack. *Thelma and Louise* needed money so they took a gun and robbed a store. Next they took obvious pleasure in shooting up a gas truck and taking revenge on its terrorized driver. Having crossed over the line and become wanted criminals, they said they felt more alive than they ever had before. Motivated by that movie, two women who ran short of cash on vacation committed their own robbery. Two men robbed a 7-Eleven after watching *Goodfellas* because they thought it would be easy and "cool to be a gangster."

The multi-award winner *Dancing with Wolves* showed soldiers obviously enjoying the excessively brutal beating of a fellow cavalryman. The glamorization of violence for power and control, for shock value for some, for the sheer fun of it for others, goes well beyond what is needed for realistic portrayal and necessary story progression. Too often violence is glorified as the only method for conflict resolution, and mutilation and homicide are presented as recreation.[58]

The enjoyment of violence, feeling more alive by living dangerously, is reflected in the statements of those who have killed for "fun" or "to see what it feels like to kill." The teen-age boys who brutally beat up the Central Park jogger callously stated, "It was something to do. It was fun." An eighteen-year-old shot the first person who came around the corner after midnight because "he wanted to commit the first murder of the year 1992."

Columnist Mona Charen noted, "When a society is raising a significant number of youngsters so remote from any standard of morality that they kill for the sake of a statistic, that society is failing at the most basic level."[59]

A year earlier she had listed "callous, what the hell murders ... like the Detroit kid shot dead for his goose-down parka, the four Chicago boys killed for their warm-up jackets, and the sixty-four armed robberies in sixty days in Newark for athletic clothing. In March of this year, a 13-year-old crack dealer in New York attempted to burn alive an 11-year-old who refused to smoke crack."[60]

Canadian psychiatrist Dr. Philip G. Ney, an expert on child abuse, has studied adults who have been physically and verbally abused as children and has concluded that verbal abuse has a deep and enduring effect.[61]

Children who are humiliated, blamed, criticized, and denigrated use the same epithets upon themselves long after they stop being verbally assaulted by others. Because verbal abuse does not result in visible wounds, the abuser is often less restrained, less conscious of the effect he is having on his victim. Many believe that the language of today's media represents a verbal assault upon our children.

Verbal abuse is more likely to be transmitted than any other form of abuse. Children use the same words and actions to harm their children that were used on them. If children hear people abusing each other verbally on television and film, they are more likely to respond to others in similar fashion.

Children neglected before they were abused are more vulnerable, more severely affected, and tend to look for emotional nourishment from people who will use and abuse them. Television is such a source; and just as physical violence is imitated in aggressive behavior in children, verbal aggression is repeated and imitated. The media's use of profanity, gutter language, and violent verbal assault is changing the way young people talk to each other. Since most profanity is aggressive and insulting, it is likely to elicit an aggressive response.

Dr. Ney believes the media facilitates the neglect of children by parents who chose to indulge their own selfish desires and use the television set for baby-sitting. The child, left to fill his needs for stimulation and learning with an inanimate object that doesn't respond to questions or feelings, is more receptive to what they witness in the media.

Additionally, *if a child is "entertained," his real needs are seldom discerned.* Parents go about their business content that he is not demanding anything, therefore he must not need anything, while the child may be starving for parental attention. In this emotionally deprived state, he loses himself in the actions on the screen in front of him and is particularly vulnerable to the abusive language and violent solutions offered. The media see themselves as innocent bystanders, but Dr. Ney believes they must share responsibility for the distress of our children.

Challenges to the majority consensus by researchers like Milavsky and Freedman[62] led Drs. Wood, Wong, and Chachere of Texas A&M University to undertake a systematic review of all the social science studies relating media violence to aggressive behavior.[63] The aggression measure used "captured the subjects' decisions of whether and how often to behave aggressively."[64]

Their review of twenty-eight laboratory and field experiments found that "media violence enhances children's and adolescents' aggression in interactions with strangers, classmates, and friends." The size of the effect was in the small to moderate range, "but cumulated across multiple exposures and multiple social interactions the impact may be substantial." Having demonstrated the causal relation between media exposure and naturally occurring aggression, they suggested that the cumulative impact of a lifetime of media exposure would be even greater.[65]

According to Dr. Geen, researchers have proposed several theories that help us understand *how* filmed violence influences behavior.[66] The first, proposed by Dr. Huesman, is that images of violent scenes and judgments about them are recorded or encoded in the brain and later retrieved as models of appropriate behavior.

When children observe violence in the mass media, they learn complicated scripts for social behavior. Scripts are made up of events of short duration called vignettes. A vignette consists of two parts, an image of aggressive behavior, such as one person hitting another in anger, and judgments about the context in which it occurs. This includes such things as the motives of the actors, the ultimate goal of the act, and how it is going to affect the characters involved.

As children observe acts of violence, these short events are recorded or encoded in their memories. Over a period of time,

multiple events are encoded, many of which have similar characteristics. A series of similar events eventually becomes a general
script. Once a script has been learned, it may be retrieved at some
later time as a guide to behavior.

As a child develops, he may observe cases in which violence
has been used as a means of resolving interpersonal conflicts.
Such events are common in television programming. This information, once stored, can be retrieved when the child is involved in
a conflict situation. Retrievability will depend partly on the similarity between cues present at the time of encoding and those
present at the time of retrieval.

Any characteristic of observed violence that makes a scene
stand out and attract attention enhances the degree to which that
scene is encoded and stored in memory. Therefore, the more intense an act of violence, the more likely it is to be encoded. The
more realistic the violence and the more vivid the scene, the more
likely it will engage the attention of children and become part of a
script stored in their memories. Once stored, it is available to be
retrieved as a model response when a similar situation is faced in
real life. This may explain the increase in violent behavior in
recent years as the portrayal of violence has become both more
realistic and more graphic. What could be more vivid than today's
media scenes of spurting blood and mutilated flesh!

Another theory is referred to as "priming." As water poured
into a pump readys the pump to function, media violence absorbed
into a person's thoughts can prompt a person to react with aggressive emotions and behavior. Watching media violence can prime a
network of associations from the observed aggression to similar
but different aggressive ideas, to emotions related to violence, to
actual aggressive behavior.[67]

Dr. Geen, in his ongoing research with colleague Brad Bush-
man, has been testing the "priming hypothesis" and has established that observation of media violence *does* increase the number of aggressive thoughts that the person has during and just
after presentation of the violence. Specifically, Dr. Geen found
that persons exposed to violent television list a greater number of
aggressive thoughts immediately afterward and show an immediate emotional response to the films.

If past experiences and past learning are translated into models of aggression and all these eventually translate into future
action, one can readily see the importance of what is fed into the
mind of young children as their associative networks are developing.

A third group of new studies asks the question: Do "people
who are characteristically aggressive prefer violent programs on

television to nonviolent ones, and as a consequence of this preference, selectively watch such programs?" Several studies have found that individual differences influence viewing of television violence. One study found that male subjects who created aggressive fantasies in their minds later chose to view films more violent than those chosen by subjects who had formed nonaggressive fantasies. Further, males who had been allowed to carry out physical aggression selected more violent material for viewing than men who had not acted aggressively. Both fantasized and actual aggression led men to a preference for violent over nonviolent media fare.[68]

The data show that there is both a change in aggression associated with viewing and a change in viewing associated with aggression. There is a cycle in which more aggressive people seek out more violence, but, in turn, the violence stimulates them to be more aggressive. The phenomenon, therefore, cannot be attributed simply to a pre-existing personality characteristic. The material, itself, increases whatever aggressive tendencies already exist and creates new appetites for aggressive material, which further influences aggressive behavior.[69]

The very latest study on the "Effects of Prolonged Exposure to Gratuitous Media Violence" by Drs. Dolf Zillmann and James Weaver found significant differences in the way different personalities are affected by contemporary, excessively violent films.[70] Adult students were exposed to violent films starring Jean Claude Van Damme, Arnold Schwarzenegger, Bruce Willis, and Steven Seagal. They were given a general personality inventory and chosen from the low and high extremes on the scale of psychoticism.[71] People possessing this trait are known to be rather solitary, hostile, and lacking in empathy. They tend to disregard danger and prefer impersonal, noncaring sex.

Although much of the data are still being analyzed, the "findings make it clear that prolonged exposure to gratuitous fictional violence *does* influence perception and judgment of violent action as a means of conflict resolution in real life. They make it equally clear, however, that this effect is *not uniform*." Women remained relatively unaffected after viewing these films. Young men comparatively high in psychoticism showed greater acceptance of violent action while men low in this trait showed less acceptance. The findings suggest that exposure to media violence

> further sensitizes sensitive young men to violence and its
> consequences, making the violent resolution of social con
> flict less acceptable. But young men who are already callous
> . . . appear to adapt the values [of] contemporary violent

films; namely that violence works and that the violent person does not have to answer any higher authority.

This "gives legitimacy to violent actions and makes them" seem "morally right."

When John Warnock Hinckley, Jr., shot President Reagan in March 1981, "he demonstrated one of the most obvious yet least understood aspects of the media-violence controversy: that dramatized violence on film or television elicits widely varying responses from audiences."[72] Hinckley claimed he was motivated to shoot the president by seeing the movie *Taxi Driver*. Most people who saw the film were not motivated to behavioral imitation. But while everyone is not motivated to imitate the behavior of a particular movie, individuals consistently respond to violence with measurable but different levels of emotional arousal.

Research has shown that inner-city residents who experienced more violence in their daily lives were significantly more aroused by viewing dramatized violence in film clips than were college students. Inner city subjects who viewed more TV and attended movie theaters more often also gave higher approval ratings to violent films. Thus, those who were aroused more by violence found it more acceptable and watched more of it.[73] Many believe the violent reaction of Los Angeles inner city residents to the trial of Rodney King in May 1992, was, in part, related to increasing media violence (see chap. 16).

Attempts have been made to educate children to become more critical viewers of television. Media literacy classes try to teach children how to view violence and not be influenced by it. Some studies, however, have shown that knowing something has negative effects does not necessarily protect viewers from its influence.

Drs. Zillmann and Bryant have proposed that exposing angry people to media material that is interesting and absorbing, but not violent, will lead to reduced anger and reduce their likelihood of instigating aggressive behavior.[74] Dr. Eron has reviewed attempts to implant non-violent scripts in children by exposing them to films showing nonaggressive responses. This research has given us encouraging signs of success in reducing aggression.[75]

Intervention in the media-aggression cycle can occur both through more careful selection of what programs people watch and through training or education in nonaggressive alternatives of action.[76] This kind of training should occur naturally within the family. Parents must both intervene and stop young children from watching violent programs and direct them toward programming that promotes ideas and behaviors that are beneficial.

While parental intervention and the promotion of

nonaggressive programming with beneficial themes are necessary and important, it is not practical to think they alone will solve the problem. A general recognition of the dangers of violent programming by our society is needed and pressure brought to bear on media industries in order to stop the escalation of violence in media entertainment. We need to reverse the "can you top this" mentality.

The recent passage of the Television Violence Act gives the industry networks an unusual opportunity to face this problem. The bill gives television executives antitrust immunity for three years to discuss and adopt standards on television violence. If they can agree on where to set limits and then work within those limits, they will provide a great service to our society.

Self-regulation by the industry is essential if the violence portrayed by the media is to be curbed. A self-regulating body similar to that of the Physician's College that will maintain ethics and standards is a possibility. However, even the liberal *Washington Post* acknowledges the problem: "Asking the entertainment industry about the effects of violence on viewers is akin to asking the tobacco lobby if smoking can kill you." The *Post* writer answers this question by emphatically stating, "Movie violence will be the death of us" and "we are committing suicide."[77] Without some kind of self-regulation, Congress, the FCC, and the courts must take regulatory action.

Chapter 11

The Influence of Heavy Metal Music and MTV

Dances suggesting or representing sexual actions or inde-
cent passion are forbidden. Dances which emphasize inde-
cent movements are to be regarded as obscene.

—The Motion Picture Code, 1930-1966

"Music and singing have played an important role in the learning and memorization process for centuries."[1] The success of "Sesame Street" in combining music, words, and colorful images to make learning fun and easy illustrates that children do learn what they see role modeled before them, especially when it is set to music.[2]

Grade school children and adolescents today are exposed to role models vastly different from those offered by "Sesame Street." The music, words, and colorful images of rock music videos are influencing increasingly younger children in progressively destructive directions.

"The rock video is generating the beat for today's youth."[3] The rise of the youth culture over the past thirty years "has been one of the most dramatic aspects of a cultural change in American society since the adoption of motorized travel,"[4] and the music video as displayed on cable channel MTV has been extremely influential in shaping that culture. As radio was the "tribal drum" that sent the message to America's youth in the early days of rock music, the music videos of MTV proclaim the message to today's youth culture.

Music television burst into our living rooms in August 1981. Now "free" on most basic cable stations, it has over fifty-four million family subscribers.[5] A whole generation has been molded and influenced by it. Indeed, it has sparked fashion trends, saved the record industry from decline, and introduced the nation's children to a new vocabulary of profanity, sex, and violence.[6]

MTV is the cable channel most watched by college students.[7] Informal surveys show that it is also becoming the favorite of nine- to eleven-year-olds in grade school. It is particularly intriguing for pre-teens who aspire to leave childhood behind and become "teen- agers." Nothing introduces them to the worst elements of the "grown-up" world faster than heavy metal rock music.

When not listening to MTV, children listen to rock music on radio. Both children and teens spend an average of a little over three hours a day watching television, but they spend four to six hours a day listening to music. That is eleven thousand hours between the seventh and twelfth grades.[8] High volume and the use of head phones eliminate competing noises, enhancing the "impact of the music and its message."[9] Unlike parents, rock music stars are always available to offer unqualified acceptance to young people hungry for attention and understanding. They appear to meet their needs and understand their chaotic emotions better than their own parents.[10] Research has found that listening to heavy metal music correlates with increasing discomfort in family situations, a preference for friends over family, and poor academic performance.[11] Rock music has become one of the primary means of group identification with individuals in the youth culture.[12] "For many, the bonding agent of their friendship is music, mainly heavy metal."[13]

Although the effects of the lyrics are virtually untested, teen- agers have more sustained contact with heavy metal music than they have with either pornography or horror films.[14] This type of music has been accused not only of being indecent, but obscene, violent, and satanic. Dr. Paul King found it to be correlated with increased chemical dependence, violence, stealing, and sexual ac- tivity.[15] Reflecting hedonism (pleasure-seeking) and irresponsibil- ity,[16] rock music is symbolic of the clash of values between parents and their children. Described as "primitive"[17] and inciting "baser passions,"[18] it reflects youth "at odds with adult society."[19]

In 1989, the American Medical Association released a report that concluded that music is a greater influence in the life of a teen-ager than television. Those involved in the rock culture were more likely to be low achievers, involved in drugs, sexually active, and involved in satanic activities. Saying that the issue is too complicated to prove a one-on-one correlation, they nonetheless concluded that a fascination with heavy metal music was an indicator of adolescent alienation and possible emotional health problems. One study found that "seventh and tenth graders who watched an hour of rock videos were more likely to approve of premarital sex" than those who did not watch.[20] Because much of the material is too pornographic and violent to deliberately show children, such studies are scarce. If, however, one hour of milder material influences attitudes, certainly four hours every day of heavy metal rock produces even more dramatic results.

"Music has the power to form character," Aristotle said. According to Bob DeMoss, an expert on the popular culture who has studied the effect of rock music lyrics and images on children for many years, the early themes of rock music were "Drug abuse is okay," "Casual sex is fine," and "Violence is an acceptable form of behavior." In the last ten years, these themes have degenerated to such explicit and graphic images and words, they almost defy description.[21]

The name of heavy metal bands reflect their character, image, and message. Free Congress' report on rock music lists 238 of them.[22]

> .... There are at least 13 bands named after the male genitals, 6 after female genitals, 4 after sperm, 8 after abortion and one after a vaginal infection. . . . [There are also] at least 10 bands named after various sex acts, 8 including the F-word, and 24 referring unflatteringly to blacks, the disabled or homosexuals.[23]

The report comments that "heavy metal and rap music today contains an element of hatred and abuse of women of a degree never seen before." In addition to extraordinary sexism, they contain equally offensive racism, blasphemy, and bigotry. Citing CBS Records president Walter Yetnikoff's comment "when the issue is bigotry, there is a fine line of acceptable standards which no piece of music should cross." This principle of acceptable standards applies to much more than bigotry.[24]

In December 1984, *Life* magazine labeled heavy metal rock music a "sadomasochistic nightmare." The themes conveyed by images of wild expressions, painted faces, blood pouring from mouths, blood spurting from bodies, guns, knives, leather, chains, spikes, and ropes fall roughly into five overlapping categories:[25]

1. *Aggressive Rebellion*

> You don't need those people around and that includes your parents. (Gene Simmons from Kiss)

Rock stars openly encourage children to rebel against their parents; not the normal rebellion that helps a child separate from his parents emotionally, but a vicious and angry rebellion, full of hatred and violence.

In the video "We're Not Gonna Take It" by Twisted Sister, a father becomes angry at his young son for listening to rock music, and the boy hurls him through a plate glass window. This video inspired a young man in New Mexico to murder his father in similar fashion.[26]

Dr. King wrote that "marketing heavy metal musicians as glamour figures and their message of hate as mere rebellion is confusing to youngsters who are trying to decide who they should be and what kind of behavior is appropriate for them."[27]

2. *Abuse of Drugs and Alcohol*

> We've always been serious alcoholics . . . no kidding around.
> (Nicky Sixx of Motley Crue)

> I took LSD every day for years. I went through cocaine by the bagful. . . . I O.D.'d about a dozen times, I sampled heroin, too. (Ozzy Osborne)[28]

Heavy metal music affirms anti-social, drug-addictive behavior. Not surprisingly, nearly 60 percent of chemically dependent youngsters chose heavy metal music because they considered it the musical expression of forces at work in their lives—violence, promiscuous sex, drug use, and increasingly, satanism.[29]

Dr. King compared music preferences with participation in violent behavior for 470 adolescent patients over three years. Heavy metal music was the choice of 59 percent admitted for chemical dependency. Of those, 74 percent were involved in violence, 50 percent in stealing, and 71 percent in sexual activity.

Large numbers of disturbed adolescents with low self-worth draw inspiration from heavy metal because it makes them feel powerful and in charge. Providing simple answers to complex problems, it gives them a source of authority for what they feel and do.[30]

3. *Graphic Violence and Suicide*

> The blade of my knife, faced away from your heart
> Those last few nights, it turned and sliced you apart
> Laid out cold, now we're both alone
> But killing you helped me keep you home. ("Girls, Girls, Girls," Motley Crue)

> In goes my knife, pull out his life,
> Consider that bastard dead.
> ("Shout at the Devil," Motley Crue)

> No apparent motive, just kill and kill again,
> Survive my brutal slashing, I'll hunt you till the end.
> ("Hell Awaits," Slayer)

A baseball cap with the letters AC-DC embroidered on it and a knapsack of heavy metal video tapes were found at one of the murder sites of the Los Angeles Night Stalker who killed sixteen victims by slipping into their homes at night and shooting or stabbing them to death as they slept.[31]

> I'm your night prowler, I sleep in the day
> Yes, I'm your night prowler, get out of my way.
> ("Night Prowler" from AC-DC's *Highway to Hell*)

In a study of twelve hundred rock videos, the National Coalition on Television Violence found 45 percent of them violent in nature.[32] One researcher speculated that rock music should be understood as a metaphor, that "killing someone or practicing satanism might stand for power, while . . . self-destruction might stand for depression and a sense of isolation."[33] Meanwhile, more than "5,000 teenagers are committing suicide each year, double the rate of 25 years ago."[34] The mounting statistics on teen suicide are more than symbolic. They indicate young people take these messages literally.

Two fifteen-year-old girls left suicide notes that quoted lyrics from Pink Floyd's 1979 album, *The Wall*.[35] They wrote, "Goodbye cruel world, I'm leaving you now."

John McCullum's parents brought a suit against Ozzy Osbourne after their son committed suicide while listening to his song:[36]

> Where to hide, suicide is the only way out
> Don't you know what it's really about.
> ("Suicide Solution," Ozzy Osbourne)

4. *Fascination with the Occult*

> I am possessed by all that is evil, the death of your God I demand, I spit at the virgin you worship, and sit at Lord Satan's right hand . . . . ("Welcome to Hell," Venom)

> We are instruments of evil, we come straight out of hell. We're the legions of the demons, haunting for the kill. ("Demons," Rigor Mortis)

In North Port, NY, a devil-worshipping cult called The Knights of the Black Circle gathered at a park and performed rituals that killed Gary Lauwers, 17, stabbing him while forcing him to say "I love Satan," and later gouging out his eyes. They left the names of their favorite rock stars: Black Sabbath and Ozzy Osbourne, who sings of satanic possession and once bit off a dove's head during a performance.[37]

The following description of satanic involvement in rock videos was taken from the Congressional Record:

> The satanic message is clear, both in the album covers and in the lyrics, which are reaching impressionable young minds . . . . The symbolism is all there: the satanic pentagram, the upside-down cross, the blank eyes of the beast, the rebellion against Christianity, and again and again, the obsession with death. According to most groups, it's all done in fun. But according to police it's having an effect on many children, a growing subculture that mixes heavy metal music with drugs and the occult.

> *The police chief estimated that heavy metal music indicators were found at 35 to 40 percent of the investigations of crimes involving satanic worship.*[38] (emphasis added)

The police all around the country are taking this issue seriously:

> "Basically, the music teaches that you don't have to listen to your parents, and that you should live life the way you want and screw the world," said Darlyne Pettinicchio, a deputy Orange County [FL] probation officer. . . .

> [While such] music doesn't automatically lead to aberrant, criminal behavior . . . some rebellious teens take lyrics literally and begin to live them—including embracing Satan "as a symbol of power."

> Satanic messages and traces of the occult are becoming common enough at crime scenes that police officers are routinely taking special courses on how to recognize them.[39]

5. *Sexuality that is Graphic and Explicit*

> I f——k like a beast. ("The Torture Never Ends," W.A.S.P.)

> I know a girl named Nikki. I guess you could say she was a sex fiend, I met her in a hotel lobby masturbating with a magazine. ("Darling Nikki," Prince from *Purple Rain*)

While rock music has always been associated with sex, it has gone so far beyond innuendo there is nowhere left to go in graphic explicitness:

1) *Incest*: "Incest is everything it's said to be"—from the song "Sister" by Prince.

2) *Oral sex*: "Eat Me Alive" by Judas Priest is about forced oral sex at gun point.

3) *Cross dressing / transvestite*: Alice Cooper "rose to fame by giving his fans exhibitions of transvestitism, snakes, mutilating chickens and mock executions."[40]

4) *Bondage and torture*:

> Tie her down, she knows what's waiting for her.
> Nothing too cruel, so beat her 'til she's red and raw,
> Crack the whip, it hardly stings the bitch.
> ("She Likes It Rough," Thrasher)

> Forbidden techniques, it's just what they seek
> Fantasy lane, dominance, submission, handcuffs and chains,
> Bondage and pain . . .
> ("Dungeons of Pleasure," Nasty Savage)

There is hard-core pornography on record albums, posters, fan magazines, and concert stages. DeMoss says, "it is hard to distinguish between the two except the latter is legally available to children." The erotic costumes of hard-core pornography magazines like *Bizarre Bitches* have been copied by bands like Bitch in concert and pictured in teen fan magazines.[41]

Perhaps the most brutal is W.A.S.P.'s lead singer, Blackie Lawless, who has appeared on stage wearing a buzz-saw blade between his thighs. During "The Torture Never Stops," he pretends to beat a woman wearing only a G-string and a black hood. As blood pours out from her hood, he attacks her with the blade.[42]

Sut Jhally, an associate professor of communications at the University of Massachusetts, put together 165 scenes from rock videos to make "Dreamworlds: Desire/Sex/Power in Rock Video." It reveals the direct relationship between the presentation of women for male consumption in these videos and "the prevalence of date rape and sexual violence in this country." Juxtaposing a real rape scene between actual videos, he demonstrates the end result of presenting women as nymphomaniacs in a male adolescent dream world.[43]

Every parent and public policy maker should see one of the many good videos that have been produced to show how extreme the performances of heavy metal bands have become.[44] No amount of research or written description can have the cumulative impact of actually seeing it.

Hearing the hate messages of today's rap music can be equally unsettling. Just as the police are taking satanic rock music seriously, they are suddenly taking rap's messages of killing policemen seriously. According to *Newsweek*, "Police organizations around the country called for a boycott of Time Warner over a song called 'Cop Killer,' by the Warner Records rapper Ice-T." Lyrics include

> I'm bout to bust some shots off
> I'm bout to dust some cops off
> . . . Die, Die, Die Pig, Die.[45]

As South Florida's Sheriff Don Hunter tried to tell a deaf local media, "Murder is not art."

Newsweek speaks of rap's "ability to alienate," of "its imagery, sound and lyrics" being "pure confrontation." As rap music attempts to define black culture and racism, it educates us all on the "hell" of inner-city life—"its gangs, lack of self-esteem, crime, rage, murder"—and fills the heads of tuned-in children with rebellion, hate, and more raw sex. Like sex, "violence sells." Kids tune in because they like "that violent thing."[46]

Like rebellious heavy metal, rap has found its home on MTV. In it, MTV has found "a music equal to its visual jump-cutting rhythms." But our culture has not yet discovered how to deal with entertainment that spews forth sheer hatred. As the Supreme Court rules in favor of hateful speech, young blacks from the ghetto are free to advocate hate and murder to all troubled youths, who seem eager to absorb it.

According to the *New York Post*, Time Warner is soon to release a new rap album urging the assassination of President Bush. The album cover shows a "menacing, uzi-toting black man about to ambush the president in front of the U.S. Capitol." Police groups and the secret service are outraged because they believe "it will give someone the idea they can get on an album cover if they kill the president."[47]

Those born before the advent of TV process information by moving from one idea to the next in a logical manner. But the rock-and-roll generation responds to sense impressions that are dominated by feeling, mood, and emotion.[48] MTV has done away with transitions and connectors. It compresses time. It is characterized by a surrealistic appearance and discontinuity. A mishmash of gestures, actions, and intentions out of context make up the imagery that often has little to do with the meaning of the song.

The music video borrows its techniques from television advertising. Lasting no longer than four minutes, videos feature short shots that grab the viewer's attention, quick cuts, no transitions, music to create a sense impression, bands of light, and optical illusion. It creates "an excited state of expectation"[49] and leaves the viewer "decentered, perhaps confused, perhaps fixated on one particular image or image series, but most likely unsatisfied and eager for the next video" which may at last satisfy.[50] It sounds like a perfect formula for addiction (see chap. 9).

As in advertisements "impossible things happen . . . . Ostensibly unrelated images are edited together to create surprising associations."[51] Rock videos average twenty shots per minute, only slightly less than TV commercials. Through close-ups of body parts, they promote fragmentation and dehumanization. By impossible imagery and a myth-like quality from separation of time and space, they draw young viewers to a world of mystery and instinct.[52]

The rock video is little more than a marketing tool to reach the youth market, roughly from twelve to thirty-four years of age. Profit-oriented, it deliberately "creates an unreal environment" to motivate people to buy recordings.[53] Offbeat themes and startling images[54] result from the struggle to attract and maintain viewer's attention. The easiest way to accomplish that is excessive amounts of sex and violence.

> I'll either break her face or I'll take down her legs, get my ways at will. ("Too Fast for Love," Motley Crue)

> . . . heart ripped from the chest decapitated, a meal of vaginas and breasts. ("Predator," Genocide)

A 1986 content analysis of forty hours of music videos on three networks found that "music videos are violent, male-oriented and laden with sexual content."[55] Sex was linked to violence in 80 percent of the videos containing violence. A 1983 study revealed that in more than half of the videos females were either nude or wore highly seductive clothing or undergarments.[56]

Drs. Hansan and Hansan report music videos to be high in sex and violence and portraying "rebellion against parental and lawful authority, drunkenness, promiscuity, and derogation and devaluation of women, the work ethic and family values," presenting anti-social behavior in a favorable light and as desirable and commonplace.[57]

"That the use of such themes is controversial is beyond doubt."[58] Critics include the American Academy of Pediatricians, the American Medical Association, the National Council of Churches, and a host of community groups, parents, and schools. By June of 1991, TCA Management company, with fifty-three cable operations and 420,000 subscribers in six states, had had so many complaints, they refused to carry MTV in their basic cable package. Calling it "borderline pornography," they offered to make it an optional service. When MTV refused either to become a pay channel that would have to be invited into homes at the subscriber's request or free as a special service, they decided to drop the channel alto-gether. TCA said videos like Madonna's "Like A Virgin" and Cher's "If I Could Turn Back Time" elicited hundreds of subscriber com plaints.[59]

Even MTV itself has recognized that their videos have gone too far. In December of 1990, they made their own decision to ban the Madonna video "Justify My Love," which featured Madonna dressed in a bra and garter belt, chains, black leather, and cruci-fixes. It portrays fantasies of "bisexuality, voyeurism, group sex, cross-dressing and mild sadomasochism,"[60] giving credibility to TCA's claim that many music videos are "borderline pornogra-phy."

A causal link between viewing music videos and negative behaviors has not been established in the research literature. However, it is highly likely that their role as a socializing agent is more important than any measurable short term changes. Re-searchers have already found that television "plays a dispropor-tionate role in the cultivation of social concepts," communicating values, relationships, and beliefs about life and society.[61] Since MTV is the favorite channel of multitudes of children, it is clear that rock videos play a large part in the socialization process.

"The very stability and existence of any society depends in large measure on the degree to which that society is able to instill in youth the shared norms and values of existing adult society."[62] If the images of rock videos are different from the accepted norms of society, they threaten to change not only existing norms, but the expectations and character of those who view the videos.[63]

One researcher of rock music claims that MTV already has had an impact on the lifestyles of youth whether they listen to it or not. Cultural norms for our youth *are* changing. "Unlike any television phenomenon past, present and perhaps future, the 24-hour cable music channel has had a profound impact on music, television, and pop culture in America."[64]

One medical explanation of why so many adolescents are attracted to such chaotic music is that they have failed to adopt a clear set of guidelines and boundaries from their parents; there-fore, they grow up harboring unresolved anxiety and anger. They are now expected to manage frustration, deprivation, and depres-sion and to contain their sexuality. They are told to bottle up the feelings churning inside.

"They feel like they are in hell, and they listen to music that resonates from where they feel." The music is an externalization of their inner worlds. The loudness and shocking quality of the adolescent's world is an attempt to control the "uncontrolled chaos" within with the "controlled chaos" of rock music. Adolescents use the "outer noise" of heavy metal rock music to suppress the "inner noise" created by the turmoil inside them. In other words, they drown out their anxieties with loud noises and, moving with the heavy beat, express their frustrations in unison with the group.[65]

The questions that arise are how long will the chaotic world of heavy metal rock music be classified as "controlled" and at what point can it be recognized as out of control and in need of regulation?

In 1986, the University of Florida (Gainesville) surveyed the rock music preferences of 694 middle and high-school students. The survey found that 9 percent of middle school students, 17 percent of rural, and 24 percent of urban high-school students were fans of heavy metal rock and punk rock music, which promotes homicide, satanism, and suicide. The lyrics in the study defied "any reasonable adult standard concerning the value of human life and Judeo-Christian and humanistic beliefs." They were described as "alienated, negativistic, nihilistic, and pornographic . . . promoting sex, sadomasochism, rape, killing, satanic practices, and in some instances suicide."[66]

Heavy metal fans listened to rock music more than thirty hours per week, and they reported knowing the lyrics of "all" their favorite rock songs more than did fans of general rock music. Almost twice as many heavy metal fans as general rock fans felt that it was proper for young children to listen to destructive rock music and that they would not in any way be affected. That most adolescents know many or all of the lyrics has been reported by others as well. In this case, many heavy metal fans reported agreeing with the words. Adolescents in this study who were not heavy metal fans reported concern for the effects of the music on children, often as a result of seeing their own friends affected.

A recent follow-up study looked at the music preferences of 120 adolescent offenders in two youth detention centers. They found that 54 percent of them were heavy metal fans, compared to less than 20 percent in the earlier study. Among the delinquent youths, the number was three times as high. "This finding suggests a strong relationship between antisocial or destructive behavior and preference for rock music with destructive themes." Dr. Wass recommended that mental health professionals "consider adolescents' music-related behaviors and orientations as a useful indicator for psychological assessment."[67]

In a recent study on the "Influence of Sex and Violence on the Appeal of Rock Music Videos," a high level of sexual imagery was found to increase the appeal of both the music and the visual content, making the viewer feel more happy, less sad, less fearful, and more sexual than either low- or moderate-sex videos. Visual

violence had just the opposite effect. Increasing the level of violence decreased the appeal of both the music and the visuals. The
combination of sexual and violent imagery was particularly
unappealing.[68]

In a similar experiment, stronger R-rated sexual materials
produced less of an increase in appeal and had a detrimental effect
in women.[69] The researchers explain: "Beyond some point, more
explicit sexual material becomes intrusive and detracts from, rather
than enhances, appeal."[70]

They reached an interesting conclusion:

> The formula for producing the least enjoyable (yet most
> profitable) rock video was clear: Make it highly violent, add
> sex and then, arousing music. Because there is substantial
> evidence demonstrating a link between television violence
> and aggression,[71] the potential adverse effects of violence
> give more force to the findings of our research. In particu-
> lar, if media depictions of violence have the potential to
> produce antisocial consequences and the viewer, in fact,
> does not enjoy it, why is there violence in rock music videos
> at all?[72]

The answer now appears simple: sex and violence is enticing
and addictive. When empowered by music and visuals, children
are progressively trying to achieve the thrill or "high" obtained
from the previous heavy metal rock video. For the producers the
answer is likewise straightforward: it sells, and profit is the bottom line. But "research has indicated that nonsexual, upbeat
visuals are given significantly higher evaluations than high-sex
videos."[73] If, indeed, more wholesome videos with less violence and
sex are more enjoyable, then why are we allowing our children to
be exposed to such a constant barrage of sex and violence?

Professor Donna Marie Beck, professor of music therapy at
Duquesne University, said that music is a powerful medium. It
has the power to lift the mind and the heart or the power to bring
it down.[74] The type of music your child listens to is important.
Don't ignore this problem because it is so difficult and so unpleasant to deal with. The issues of loudness and style are much less
important than the content. According to rock music analyst Eric
Holmberg, the beat and the tension are not harmful, the power is
in the lyric. From the time your child first becomes interested in
listening, take a *very* active role in helping him or her choose
music with words and images that are uplifting and positive.

The music your teen-ager listens to should tell you something
about the state of his mind. If you aren't aware of his tastes, ask
him, look through his music collection, note rock trivia—T-shirts,

decals, etc.—talk to his best friend's parents. If you disagree with the words of the songs, discuss how they differ from your family values. Explain how the ideas in the songs can distort his views about himself, the girls he is or will be dating, and his future attitudes toward marriage and family life. Together work out a plan to help him stop listening to music that feeds depression, anxiety, despair; that glamorizes suicide, brutality, promiscuous and deviant sex; that encourages rebellion, drug abuse, and satanic involvement.

Help your child understand that what he listens to will affect who he is and who he will become. For example, if he listens only to angry music, he will become angry. Music has the power to open doors to a subculture where death and destruction reign or to lift the human spirit above the cares of every day life. However, merely understanding its potential danger is not enough:

> Simply recognizing the artificiality of something does not
> ensure immunity to that thing. Simply knowing that you're
> an object of propaganda is not enough in itself to arm one
> against the appeals of propaganda.[75]

It is impossible to "just listen" day in and day out and to remain unaffected. If your child or teen-ager has already established a taste for heavy metal rock, the problem is more difficult. You may want to look together at one of the videos on rock music listed earlier in endnote 45. After discussion and making sure your own listening and viewing habits set a good example, establish a rule that he may not bring such destructive, negative music into your house. Eric Holmberg recommends giving him a day to get it out of the house, then trashing anything that is left. Some parents have agreed to buy albums back from their children or to replace them with Christian rock or contemporary music that celebrates positive values. Persist and remain firm in your decision. Your child needs boundaries to keep him from being pulled into a world where no boundaries exist.

Dr. King's research has shown that "at the very least, heavy metal music promotes, approves, and supports unconventional attitudes toward drug abuse, sexual activity and violence." Whether or not it directly causes aberrant behavior, he believes it constitutes a public health problem "serious enough to warrant some type of control." He recommends that major record companies, with the help of physicians, set forth guidelines "to ensure that potentially harmful material is not sold to our young people packaged as entertainment."[76]

As both research and anecdotal evidence mounts to prove Dr. King's assertion, responsible music companies must adopt more responsible policies. If they do not, government regulation is inevitable. There is a ground swell of fear among adults that the subculture is already out of control and that soon we will all be threatened. Hatred, violence, and perversion are not less influential because they are set to music. They are in fact more powerful.

The industry has resisted even the labeling of X-rated records. Chances of rock stars taking responsibility without parental and governmental pressure are next to nothing. Therefore, parents must encourage the Federal Communications Commission to be more diligent in efforts to enforce the decency standard on broadcast radio and television and help them by sending in cases. Since MTV has become readily available to children on basic cable, this standard should be extended to cable in the form of a "harmful to minors" law (see chap. 66, 15, and 16). Removing MTV from basic cable and making it a separate subscription channel that parents could realistically keep from their homes is an even better solution.

Chapter 12

Understanding the Appeal of Horror Movies and Slasher Films

*Methods of crime should not be explicitly presented. . . .
There must be no suggestion, at any time, of excessive brutality . . . action showing the taking of human life, even in
the mystery stories, is to be cut to the minimum.*

—The Motion Picture Code, 1930-1966

Horror includes many different types of films—ghost stories, devil movies, weirdo horror films, slasher movies, cannibal, and living dead films—all created to thrill the viewers by frightening them through the use of special effects. According to expert horror critic Kim Newman, the "central thesis of horror in film and literature is that the world is a more frightening place than is generally assumed."[1]

Since one of the goals of good parenting is to help children develop a secure and trusting view of the world, the horror film would seem to be a parent's worst enemy. Some children and adults are frightened and disgusted by the graphic violence of horror films and avoid them completely. Others, according to researcher Dr. Ron Tamborini, "find something very rewarding" in being scared senseless.[2]

The general appeal of these films is explained in numerous ways: 1) that there is pleasure in the termination of the threat; 2) there is psychic relief in allowing destructive anti-social tendencies, which exist in all of us, to run free; 3) the jolt of horror is exhilarating, and the increased arousal created by fear can be experienced as pleasure; and 4) witnessing and identifying with pain and suffering in others increases arousal. Sound effects, music, and fast-paced editing techniques add to the stimulation.

155

All of this results in intense emotional reaction, which makes watching horror movies a pleasure for some.[3]

Some people enjoy these films because they want to see the forbidden. The virtual elimination of regulation has left very few taboos to be broken. The wedding of explicit sex and graphic violence, so common in this genre, shatters the last taboos we have as a society. Perhaps because everything sexual can now be freely shown, the new wave of horror is what Morris Dickstein calls "a hard-core pornography of violence." Horror movies stimulate erotic feelings. Exploiting the rage and anger within us, they take us beyond voyeurism and put us in the position of the murderer, so that we see what he sees and are tempted to feel what he feels. Horror appeals to our secret fascination with the grotesque and touches "on the basic fears that make us all vulnerable."[4]

Dickstein says the "fear of death is the ultimate attraction of all horror films." The young go seeking "thrills that can only be had through risk and danger." They try to neutralize their anxieties—the fear of the dark, fear of being alone, fear of enclosure, fear of the supernatural—by making them specific and dealing with them through the vicarious experience of the horror movie. Dickstein concludes, "Getting caught up emotionally, walking out drained and satisfied, waking up relieved to deal with more workaday problems—this is the secret of all horror films."[5]

The most common reaction to these films, however, is aversion and emotional distress. Dr. Tamborini found that 80 percent of all subjects exposed to different horror films found graphic violence unappealing.[6] He also found negative reaction in these people even stronger than the positive reaction in those who enjoyed horror films.

Others claim the content of horror films provides a "reaffirmation of social norms." They see the message of horror films as a warning that "terrible things happen to those who venture beyond societal boundaries into the taboo."[7] "Good triumphs over evil. Violation of the norm can lead to disaster, and those who violate the norm will be punished. This interpretation suggests that the content of these films serves to provide society with the assurance that its norms and beliefs are appropriate."[8] For example, "in the movie *Halloween*, the teenagers who are killed are those who are engaging in premarital sex, while the heroine who survives the killer's assaults has kept herself pure."

Dr. James Weaver is one researcher who accepts this theory and believes that horror films of the monster/psycho variety popularized by films like *Halloween*, *Friday the 13th*, and *Nightmare on Elm Street* are one of many agents of socialization that supplement and reinforce what children learn from other sources. What other socializing agents say quietly, horror films say much more graphically.[9]

According to Dr. Weaver, the message from these films, commonly called slasher films, is that "if you do something you shouldn't do, you will be punished." The crazed killer's victims are those who do something inappropriate by social standards. Normally socialized children come away believing that, in the struggle between good and evil, good always wins. Therefore, purity is the most effective defense against evil. For example, he believes such films may encourage the young girl who is being pressured to have sex to say no. Children also learn that they are most vulnerable at their weakest point. If they have one fault, one Achilles' heel, that is where they open themselves up to trouble. So they had better overcome that defect.

Dr. Weaver agrees, however, that these films may be problematic for the child who has been abused or traumatized. They may be problematic as well for the child who comes from a dysfunctional family. As we have stated before, many families, even with well-meaning and caring parents, are dysfunctional in some aspect. For some viewers, any graphically violent material could be harmful, particularly when the viewer cannot distinguish between reality and fantasy. Poorly socialized children might take away the wrong message and come to believe such violence is accepted and normal.

Still on our minds, killer Jeffrey Dahmer provides a prime example of how horror films can affect poorly socialized, wounded, or rejected children. He was sexually abused at eight, enjoyed horror films at nine, and was abandoned by his parents in his early teens. His grotesque crimes involved the dismemberment of his victims (a common theme in horror pictures), saving body parts to eat later.[10]

Another case, detailed by psychiatrist Dr. Andre Derdeyn, involved a thirteen-year-old boy.[11] Carl, shuttled between relatives from infancy, was finally settled at age nine with an aunt and uncle. He responded well until puberty when he became defiant and disruptive, even destroying his guardian's home with an ax. When questioned during psychotherapy, he resented not being allowed to watch horror movies and admitted he was addicted to them.

After agreeing to watch *A Nightmare on Elm Street IV* together, the psychotherapist uncovered Carl's anger at the loss of his mother and his desire for approval from his aunt and uncle. Carl had identified with Freddy's ugliness and anger, had envied his power and invulnerability, and had identified with Freddy's victims as well. The horror films were reverberating with his feelings of loss and rejection. Once he worked through his anger, he was able to allow his guardians to express their more tender feelings toward him. Eventually released to his guardians, he was functioning well and no longer felt compelled to watch horror movies.

Because more and more children are not well socialized, the exceptions overshadow the rule. These films present a potential problem for large numbers of children who may miss the prosocial message altogether.

Some experts on horror believe the formula of the slasher genre is so clear and the outcome so predictable that children do not become frightened. According to Newman, "the victims are invariably a parade of dumb American kids, marked for death by predilection for drink, soft drugs, stupid practical jokes and giggly making out."[12] They know these films are fake, that Freddy Krueger, for instance, is fantasy. Dr. Weaver believes the child watches to be entertained and is taken on "an audio-visual roller coaster ride," which is more satisfying than frightening. For some, however, a roller coaster ride is a traumatic experience.

An unsettling but recurring theme in films is that evil cannot be destroyed. Because the vanquished villain keeps coming back in the next film, the message that good triumphs over evil is blurred. The audience leaves the theater knowing the villain is still out there somewhere, awaiting his opportunity to kill again. Young children, left with this terror, may or may not express it openly, but it may be creating a chaos of confusion and insecurity inside them.

> An example of very young children, four- to five-years-old, being affected by seeing sexually sadistic horror films was recounted in the German magazine *Der Speigal*. The children played "Dare You," a game of who could watch movies of sexual violence the longest. Several weeks later, these children had to be committed to psychiatric treatment because of chronic bedwetting. They could no longer hold their water through the night.[13]

Dr. Singer compared this effect with the Meltz study, which found that infants exposed to pictures on television imitated them twenty-four hours later. Often, children do not show manifestations of discomfort during the watching of slasher pictures or imitate what they see right away, but the images are very powerful and stay in the mind. They might reappear later and trigger discomfort, fear, or actual behavior long after initial viewing.[14]

According to Dr. Dolf Zillmann, horror films offer young adolescent boys a socially approved way to display their entrance into manhood.[15] In past societies where men faced life-threatening situations, rites of passage were initiated to help adolescents overcome fear. Although no longer necessary, there is still pressure on young men not to show fear when confronted with danger. The horror film is one of the only means left for an adolescent male to test his courage and prove his fearlessness.[16] Watching "gross out" movies proves that he is strong. The more he watches, the more he can say, "I am tough. I watch all this stuff, and it doesn't bother me."

Dating couples seventeen-years-old and older make up a large portion of the twenty to thirty million theatergoers who watch these movies.[17] In addition to giving young men an opportunity to demonstrate their manhood to other young men, these movies give young males an opportunity to play hero and protector to a female who finds the films too frightening to watch.[18]

> According to Dr. Derdeyn, millions of thirteen- and four-teen-year-olds flood the theaters to experience a "melding of their own experiences and their own needs" with what is going on in these films. What you see in the film is lack of caring, down right hostility, parents not listening to their children. Unfortunately, that is the way so many adolescents experience their parents. There is also some projection involved (blaming parents for their own inadequacies) as children try to devalue parents in order to leave them psychologically.[19]

The fundamental appeal of movies such as *Friday the 13th*, *Halloween*, and *Prom Night* lies in their apparent ability to help the adolescent control deep-seated anxieties while obtaining pleasure and gratification from the process. These modern day fairy tales allow the adolescent to internalize the powerfully disruptive inner experiences of anxiety and impulse in the hope of gaining relief from inner pressures of becoming independent from parents.

As spectators, teen-age viewers see, at a safe distance, the world of sex and aggression and are "warned" about the dire consequences associated with full participation in the adult world, especially the world of adult sex.[20] With the camera focused through the eyes of the "madman," the teens quickly identify with the aggressor. In their imagination, they are the ones who wield the knife. The psychological lures include a shift from passive-victim to active-perpetrator, from seeing to enjoying the sexual "crime," witnessing yet surviving the punishment totally unscathed.[21]

While such explanation aids our understanding of why teenagers enjoy these films, it is a warning in itself. That our sons and daughters—even if only in their imaginations—become the "vil-

lain" and enjoy committing the "crime" suggests a potential problem for society of some magnitude. We know that at least 20
percent or 10.7 million of the children of this nation have recognized psychological disorders and that seven million of them are
sufficiently emotionally unstable to seek psychiatric treatment.
Many more have unrecognized problems and are likely to be
vulnerable to the violent messages of these films (see chap. 1).

Viewing of Problems with Adolescent Horror Movies

Problem 1. *The moral lesson is lost.* "The fundamental difference between the classic fairy-tale and the degraded fairy-tale
'slasher' movie is that, in the latter, the moral lesson is lost."[22] The
experience is so intense and stimulating there is no time to reflect
on a symbolic meaning. It serves more to increase internal chaos
and anxiety than to help the young person better understand and
overcome his inner turmoil. *In such an aroused and charged
emotional context, the average pre-teen or teen-age viewer simply
cannot learn from the story.*

Problem 2. *Mastery of teen-age problems is not achieved.* The
teen-ager is suddenly aware that his next few years are critical.
His choices are numerous; the dangers immense, and his vulner-
abilities great. He fears he is not up to the responsibilities he must
assume. He watches film after film vainly seeking mastery of his
own problems.[23]

> Carl worried about his worth to others, the inadequacies of
> his body, his sexual and aggressive impulses. He felt power-
> less and unable to meet the expectations of his guardians.
>
> He was attracted to horror movies because both the charac-
> ters in the films and the audience of his peers shared these
> concerns. Although he envied the monster's power and lack
> of remorse, he identified with the helpless victims of ter-
> rible danger, and especially with the one among them who
> refused to accept the position of impotence. This one teen-
> ager survived to fight and win. He shared in her victory
> over and over in a vain attempt to master his own miseries.
>
> As is so often the case, his longing to be accepted and cared
> for by his guardians was uncommunicated to them and
> complicated by the normal adolescent impulse to renounce
> dependency. He adopted a style of dress and a preference
> for music belonging to a peer group unacceptable to his
> guardians. When he turned to horror movies, he became
> even more rebellious. Eventually, his rebellion took the
> form of antisocial behavior.

Carl's "addiction" to horror movies was an unsuccessful attempt to master anxiety.[24]

Problem 3. *Horror movies desensitize both children and adults to violence and enhance callousness toward others.* There appears to be general agreement that these films are harmful to young children. The research, however, does not exist to tell us at what age these films stop creating undue anxiety in children. It would be unethical to deliberately expose children to anything so frightening. But there is evidence that these films encourage callousness in both adolescents and adults.

A 1984 study by Drs. Donnerstein and Linz concentrated on movies that victimized women. Films like *Texas Chainsaw Massacre* and *The Toolbox Murders* were found to desensitize viewers to female brutality and to increase callousness toward women. The subjects, after seeing the films, judged the rape victims as having less worth as individuals and as being less injured.[25]

According to Dr. Tamborini, these findings "are consistent with the concerns expressed by critics who object to the type of graphic horror films that contain 'scene after scene of terrified, half-dressed women, screaming with pain and horror as they are raped, stabbed, chopped at, and strangled.'"[26] Such critics believe these films play to a predominantly male audience, fifteen to twenty-five, who must "harbor hostility toward women" since they appear to "enjoy seeing women victimized."

Dr. Zillmann believes it is almost demanded by society that men, in particular, become reasonably callous.[27] Watching horror films together, they learn to subdue their fears and prove they can take it. However, they can "grow so callous that they are not disturbed by scenes showing the most preposterous forms of violence."[28]

While developing a small amount of callousness can be helpful in overcoming fear, coping with minor injuries to others, and keeping one from being overly empathic, horror movies train young people in the worst kind of callousness toward other people. They teach young viewers to be insensitive to inflicting injury on others, to outright mutilation of human beings, and to all manner of suffering.

Problem 4. *Horror movies create an appetite for violence.* Further, they encourage young people to *enjoy* growing callous. Parallel research with less extreme violence and related pornography has shown a "habituation" effect. The more violence a person sees, the less it disturbs him. Aggressive actions and monsters that seemed terrifying at first become less terrifying. In addition, once he has experienced the thrill of arousal to violence, he will want to see more. Just as with pornography, it will take stronger materials to produce the same thrill. An appetite for horror and, more terrifying, violence is created.[29]

The first film in a slasher series has original elements in the story line that create interest. It is designed to scare the audience rather than to "gross them out."

> In the first *Halloween*, suspense is the main element. The haunting fear that the bogeyman may be just around the corner predominates. While he kills his victims brutally, there is not much blood shown.

The sequels and copycat films rehash the same plot, not to tell a unique story, but simply to make money. The plot no longer holds the viewers' attention because they already know it. The audience is no longer shocked by killing. The shock now is in the manner of killing, the suspense in *how* the bogeyman will attack his next victim. More recent slashers depict increasingly bizarre ways of killing and dismantling bodies, with greater amounts of blood and gore.[30]

> Typical of earlier slasher films, a knife stab in the chest was sufficient in *Halloween I*. In later films, weapons like the pickax are substituted for the knife. Death is accomplished by jamming a flare down the victim's throat or by thrusting a screw driver through the victim's eye.

These films promote violence for violence's sake. The interest is in the kill. The audience awaits each violent act with anticipation, unaware that an appetite for violence is being created within them.

An advertisement for a horror video makes an appeal to just such an appetite. The video *Filmgore*, a collection of clips from R-rated slasher films consumed primarily by fifteen- and sixteen-year-olds is available at many local video stores. The promotional advertisement accurately describes the contents:

> See Blood Thirsty, Butcher Killer Drillers, Crazed Cannibals, Zonked Zombies, Mutilating Maniacs, Hemoglobin Horrors, Plasmatic Perverts, and Sadistic Slayers Slash, Strangle, Mangle, and Mutilate Bare Breasted Beauties in Bondage.[31]

Forensic psychologist Park Elliott Dietz, M.D., sees a relationship between these films and the growing violence in every day life:

> If a mad scientist wanted to find a way to raise a generation of sexual sadists in America, he could hardly do better, at our present state of knowledge, than to try to expose a

generation of teen-age boys to films showing women mutilated in the midst of a sexy scene.[32]

Problem 5. *Horror movies are addictive.* Just as Carl recognized that he had become "addicted" to horror movies, so are legions of teen-agers in our country. Once an appetite has been created, it must be satisfied. Young people return again and again to see a new version of what they found so stimulating in the film before. When the drive to see a horror movie becomes so strong that it becomes a controlling interest in life, it has become an addiction.

According to clinical psychologist Dr. Douglas Reed, the combination of sex and violence is even more addicting than either sexual or violent imagery separately.[33] Many research studies have found this to be the most harmful of all materials to individuals who watch it (see also chap. 6).

> Eugene Pyles, an Army veteran with a spotless past, brutally raped, stabbed, slashed a seventeen-year-old girl across the throat. Addicted to pornographic horror films, he had rented four videos about sexual torture and murder the day before the assault.[34]

Problem 6. *Horror movies can become models for real life horror.* A survey of one hundred children reported that Freddy of the *Nightmare on Elm Street* series and Jason of the *Friday the 13th* series were better known to ten- to thirteen-year-olds than famous Americans like Abraham Lincoln and George Washington. Eighty-nine percent of the children surveyed had seen at least one episode, and 62 percent had seen at least four episodes. Most of the children reveled in the brutality of the films, making statements like the following: "What I like about Freddy is that he kills people," and "I like it when Freddy does things with his fingernails. It was neat."[35]

Adults seem to be encouraging the elevating of these brutal characters into national heroes. Not long ago, it was reported that the mayor of Los Angeles proclaimed a special "Freddy Krueger Day" on Friday-the-thirteenth. In addition to a television series entitled *Freddy's Nightmares* which premiered in 1988, there is a Marvel Comics Freddy Krueger comic book series, and a "900 number that children can telephone to hear Freddy talking of the pleasures of sadism and killing." The young male killer of young women in the comic book teaches the nation's children,

> It is through sexual ecstasy derived from the exercise of absolute domination of the power over life and death. . . . Only through the infliction of pain comes pleasure.[36]

Increasingly, new reports refer to specific horror movie characters as models for teen-agers who commit violent crime.

A girl who said she loved what Freddy Krueger does in the *Nightmare on Elm Street* movies charged with attempted murder.[37]

A teenager, dressed like Freddy Krueger and carrying a sawed-off rifle committed a series of violent armed robberies and a murder in Los Angeles.[38]

After a nineteen-year-old horror movie fan of Jason, the killer from *Friday the 13th,* murdered an eighteen-year-old girl in Greenfield, Massachusetts, Town officials urged the local theater to stop showing horror movie *Halloween IV.*[39]

Unfortunately, civic officials only stop these movies from being shown after they have been imitated in real life, and then only for a short time. By the time the next in the series comes out, the incident appears to have been forgotten.

It might be more than coincidental that horror movies have become progressively more graphic and violent as our society has become progressively more violent (see chap. 10, for violent crime statistics). The rise of blood and gore in movies has also paralleled a period in our history where people have become increasingly insensitive to cries for help as crimes are being committed.

Alfred Hitchcock's *Psycho* was on the cutting edge in the sixties as the movie production code was breaking down. It was a violent movie, but the violence was more implied than graphically acted out. In the famous shower scene, the audience never saw the knife enter the woman's body. They saw the knife raised, then blood dripping into the shower drain. In contrast, the 1992 psychological slasher, *The Hand That Rocks the Cradle,* shows a human being literally shredded by thousands of pieces of glass from a broken greenhouse ceiling.

It is now normal for young children to watch films originally targeted for sixteen- to twenty-six-year-olds. Surveys find that seven- to twelve-year-olds name slasher films as their favorites and say they not only enjoy movie violence, but like looking at people's faces when they are dead; like to see people killed; enjoy watching pain, agony, and torture; and enjoy body counts.[40]

As the audience becomes younger, the subject matter is changing to that which relates to every day lives of children. For example *Child's Play* features a young boy whose best friend is a demon-possessed doll, and the villain of *The Hand That Rocks the Cradle* is the children's nanny who moves in and takes over their home.

Toys produced for four- and five-year-old children, which identify with killers and trading cards that feature serial killers, are clearly not products that make children feel secure about their world. If, as a society, we encourage them to look to mass murderers as their role models, we deserve an increasingly calloused generation.

Three separate studies have determined that sensation-seekers—those who look for environmental stimuli that produce "sensation" and "arousal"—are attracted to horror films.[41] The Machiavellian personality trait is an even stronger predictor of attraction to horror films. This includes the use of power, force, and flattery to achieve one's goals: deceit, immorality, and cynicism. Of the four dimensions that make up this personality, deceit is the one most closely associated with an attraction to horror. According to Dr. Tamborini, that is because deceit is related to "a desire to violate the norms of socially acceptable behavior, or to see them violated by others."[42]

Horror films commonly present graphic violence in otherwise eroticized circumstances.[43]

> An example of "eroticized violence" is the scene from *The Toolbox Murders* which shows a young woman bathing when a man forcefully enters her apartment and assaults her. Failing in several attempts to escape, the woman offers herself sexually to the attacker. He is disinterested, however, and instead brutally murders her.[44]

A 1987 study by Dr. Tamborini found that women, when given a choice among violent drama, prefer films with the least graphic portrayal of female victimization while men prefer the most graphic. "A surprisingly strong relationship was found for males between the enjoyment of pornography and a preference for graphic horror featuring female victims."[45]

These findings imply that horror films appeal to men who harbor hostile feelings toward women because they have been sexually frustrated and that these men receive gratification from seeing the graphic portrayal of pain and suffering of those who have caused their frustrations. These films are capable of "creating attitude changes in real life values concerning issues like rape"[46] (see chap. 6).

Movie critic Roger Ebert asked in 1981 when he saw *I Spit On Your Grave* if there is not a correlation between these hostile feelings of men toward women and the ascent of feminism. He described watching the film as a "terrible experience." Speaking of its "brutal directness of style" and "raw impact," he said, "the filmmakers simply pointed their camera at their actors and then

commanded them to perform unspeakable acts upon one another."[47]
He was distressed by the shouts and loud laughter of the audience
as a woman was "repeatedly cut up, raped and beaten." He was
particularly disturbed by the comments of the totally respectable-
looking man sitting beside him who screamed out, "Give it to her!
She's got that coming."

Realizing that there are many such films, he saw that a basic
change had taken place regarding women in danger: the sympa-
thies of the audience were no longer with the woman. "The new
horror films encouraged audience identification not with the victim but with the killer." The camera took the killer's point of view
and the audience followed. The movies were not about a character
who was a killer, they were about the lust to kill, and the lust was
placed in the audience. The audience was invited to become the
killer, and, like Ebert's neighbor in the theater, some gladly accepted the role.

Pointing out that the crime of the women victims served as
their independence, critic Gene Siskel said,

> I'm convinced that this has something to do with the growth
> in the women's movement in America in the last decade.
> These films are some sort of primordial response by very
> sick people saying, "Get back in your place women!" The
> women in these films are typically portrayed as indepen-
> dent, as sexual, as enjoying life. And the killer typically—
> not all the time but most often—is a man who is sexually
> frustrated with these new aggressive women, and so he
> strikes back at them. He throws knives at them. He can't
> deal with them. He cuts them up, he kills them.[48]

As with most problems, the best thing parents can do to
prepare their children to deal with horror is to provide them with a
secure childhood, positive parental relationships, and strong socialization. Young children should not see these films, and if they
do, only with their parents present.

By watching these films with their teen-agers, and becoming
familiar with media images their children find appealing, parents
might find clues to their adolescents' problems. Seeking opportunities to discuss that appeal, they should warn their children of
possible negative consequences of viewing these films.

Dr. Ashbach stated that there are "predisposing psychological
factors in most families of children who compulsively consume
violent and erotic imagery."[49] A family who is concerned about the
appeal of these films to their children would do well to examine
how their family problems might be related to such an attraction.

While understanding their appeal for teen-agers, both Dr.

Ashbach and Dr. Derdeyn made it clear that children do not gain mastery of their anxieties by watching horror movies. Additionally, research has shown that they encourage callousness, desensitization to violence and the suffering of others, and an appetite for more violence. They can become an addiction.

We must question how much of the symbolism of these movies the viewer is able to understand as he is gripped in their terror. The recent trend toward showing evil rather than good triumphant in the end makes a prosocial effect even more doubtful.[50]

Considering the growing number of poorly socialized children and the large number of children whose viewing is unsupervised, warnings before television showings and unenforced R-ratings in theaters are not enough. Even Dr. Derdeyn, who argued in favor of the use of the horror film in the therapeutic situation, agreed that outside of the controlled situation, such films can be harmful. He concluded, "seeing violence tends to make people more violent. If you see violence on the screen, you are likely to take it in as your own."[51]

It is time for our society to rethink the easy accessibility of children and disturbed adults to this type of material. Are these movies and their related products worth the risk of putting an entire "population of children at risk of becoming violent?"[52]

Chapter 13

Prosocial Programming— A Vision for the Future

Mankind has always recognized the importance of entertainment and its values in rebuilding the bodies and souls of human beings.

—The Motion Picture Code, 1930-1966

The American entertainment industry dominates the world market, controlling over 75 percent of the world's television, music, films, and radio programs. We are exporting more than democracy and free market economy to Eastern Europe, Russia, and Third World countries.

Recent meetings with the World Council of Churches in Geneva, the Ecumenical Patriarch of the Orthodox Church in Constantinople, and the Pope in Rome raised a disturbing question. "Is it possible to have democracy *without* moral degradation, true freedom *without* sexual exploitation of women and children? Will the sex and violence shown in American media now be acted out on the streets of Eastern Europe and the Russian Republics?" European authorities came to a sobering conclusion, "If the price of freedom and democracy is our children's lives and our families' safety, the price is too high."[1]

Americans face an even more poignant question at home: "Can democracy and freedom continue to exist *with* moral degradation and a destructive value system?" George Washington and Alex DeToqueville did not think so. In his farewell address, Washington declared that a basic morality was essential to political prosperity. A generation later DeToqueville said, "It is their mores, then, that make the Americans . . . capable of maintaining the rule of democracy."[2]

On a very basic level, American media are promoting ideas,

168

attitudes, and behaviors that either undergird or undermine democracy. There is a marked difference between license and responsible freedom, which would be better served by promoting the values on which this country was founded than by the current "anything goes" mentality. Said Ted Baehr,

> Film is not an enemy but a tool that can be used for good or evil. We must redeem the mass media so that through them we can communicate the good, the true and the beautiful to our children, American society and the world.[3]

Clearly, television, films, magazines, and music have become powerful influences in our culture. They do much more than entertain. They can change time-honored cultural attitudes and replace them with destructive attitudes, or they can re-enforce positive attitudes, cultural values, and moral behaviors. Most researchers agree that entertainment media have unlimited potential for good that is virtually untapped. In this chapter we will look at a variety of ways the media are helping to influence people in positive directions.

According to Ernest Allen, president of the National Center for Missing and Exploited Children (NCMEC), "The media can be the best friend the parents of a missing child can have."[4] The incredible power of the media can be harnessed in a matter of hours to capture the attention of the entire nation, find a missing child, expose a most-wanted criminal, or solve a mystery that has long stumped authorities. An emotionally presented television news piece can burn a child's smiling face into the consciences of the country and move people thousands of miles away to join the search for a child they will never know.

The media have helped to raise the level of awareness about the tragedy of child abduction and molestation to a height no advertising budget could match. Made-for-television movies about the disappearance of Etan Patz and the abduction and murder of Adam Walsh have touched the hearts of Americans nationwide. Each time *Adam* was rebroadcast, NBC presented a two-minute role-call of photographs of fifty missing children. A mere thirty seconds television exposure per child yielded seven thousand calls that located twenty children. The growth in awareness from media exposure has helped the NCMEC recover 17,300 of the 28,000 missing or sexually exploited children since 1984 and has resulted in over eighty successful prosecutions of child pornographers.

No medium can convey valuable information in a more attractive, entertaining way than television. The NCMEC and many other groups are now working directly with television networks to place valuable information in entertainment programs. An excellent example of prosocial programming that provided good family entertainment was *The Secret*, aired on CBS in April 1992. Touching the hearts of all who watched, this movie addressed adult illiteracy and sent special encouragement to those who had difficulty reading because of dyslexia.

The participants of the national research conference which served as a springboard for this book appeal to the producers, directors, and executives of media industries to broaden their view of their mission to include strengthening the concept of family in our culture.

It is chic today to redefine the family. The media has helped by promoting all manner of living arrangements outside of marriage. It has portrayed family pathology so graphically, family appears to be the problem, not the solution to the nation's problems. But strong families have always been the strength of civilizations. It is when family bonds are weakened that society unravels and declines.

If even a handful of media executives could recognize how much the American family needs help and catch the vision of how prosocial programming could be developed to strengthen family values, there is no end to what they could do toward influencing for good the attitudes of the coming generation. Most producers, writers, and TV executives strongly believe that television entertainment should be a major force for social reform.[5] With the increase in abnormal sex, blatant sexuality, and graphic violence during the past years, we must ask, reform in what direction, and what kind of society is their goal?

If money is the motive for the increase in sex and violence, even industry executives are recognizing it is time for a change. A 1991 *Forbes* magazine article by Norm Alster entitled "Crude Doesn't Sell" points out the enormous success basic cable is having with old-fashioned family programs. Basic cable's audience share is up 33 percent while the networks' share dropped another four points in 1990, for a total of 25 percent since 1980. Alster reports surveys by Turner Broadcasting that show viewers eighteen to fifty-four "are absolutely opposed to [sexually] explicit television programming."[6]

Family viewing hours, Saturday cartoons without ads and violence, and other approaches are presently being explored by Congress, the Federal Communications Commission, and media executives. Indications are that prosocial programming stressing pro-family values will be profitable for the industry as well as salutary for the culture.

Dr. Dorothy G. Singer, co-director of Yale University Family Television Research Center, believes the media, particularly television, could provide role models for adolescents and teach them coping skills for everyday problems. Her research reveals that children are less concerned with drugs and sensational issues than they are with everyday concerns like how to maintain a close, intimate relationship with a friend and what to do about such things as lying and cheating in school, peer pressure, and grades. She said students are saying "we're really worried about our day to day existence: who is my friend . . . how do I come across to other people?"[7]

In the past, the closeness of extended families provided the child with direct observation of their parents and other relatives in adult roles. Such opportunities are infrequent in today's more separated families. Television is now their "prime window on the world of adulthood."[8]

Researchers have found a direct relationship between stress-ful life events and delinquent behavior and substance abuse.[9] Adolescent males in mother-only households are more likely to make decisions without direct parental input and are more likely to exhibit deviant behavior.[10] Teen-agers' uncritical viewing of available programming puts them at risk of developing negative attitudes and imitating harmful behavior. Dr. Singer recommends the creation of more entertaining and thought-provoking shows designed to help teens think critically and develop problem-solving strategies.

In order to test how thoughtful programming would effect young people's attitudes and behaviors, Dr. Singer showed five programs from the PBS "Degrassi Junior High" series to fifth- to eighth-grade students. These programs were intended as an alternative to the situation comedies produced in Hollywood where precocious, "well-adjusted," witty young people are presented in designer clothing, living in beautiful surroundings, and parented by loving, understanding adults. The "Degrassi" series attempted to portray the complex experiences of early adolescence with insight, humor, compassion, and respect and to offer ideas and suggestions for long term improvement rather than artificial quick solutions.

The programs have continuing characters but no "star." Different characters confront a particular dilemma each week. The audience has an opportunity to identify with youths like themselves or someone they would like to be. The situations selected included alcoholism in the family, parent-child relationships, lying, dating, dealing with handicaps, shyness, jealousy, shoplifting, judgment, decision-making, peer pressure, and sexual harassment.

Dr. Singer's subjects found they liked the PBS series and

substantially increased their viewing of the "Degrassi" programs at home. One of the major discoveries of the experiment was the extremely positive effect of teacher-student discussions after viewing (see also chap. 3).

While four of the five episodes were well received, the one that made the children uncomfortable, confused, and disgusted was an experience of sexuality and adult-child intimacy, suggesting once again the negative effect on children of the large amount of sexual content in today's media.

The long success of "Little House on the Prairie" is an example of a program that put forth strong family values, provided good role models, and addressed issues relevant to today's world. A more recent program, "Beverly Hills 90210," deals with problems pertinent to today's teen-agers and is receiving top ratings with this age group. There is good reason to believe such programs can be a financial success and have a positive influence on families at the same time.

Showing children possible ways of coping with everyday problems should be one of the priorities of television in the future. There has been a great deal of research done on "prosocial programming." Broadly defined, this term has been applied to anything that benefits an individual or society at large.

Dr. J. Philippe Rushton reviewed thirty-five research studies of filmed prosocial behavior. He found that television influences behavior in the direction of the content of the program. An audience that sees friendliness and kindness modeled will accept it as appropriate, normative behavior. If, however, the audience frequently sees uncontrolled aggression and anti-social behaviors, it will come to accept this as the norm. He concluded, "Viewers learn from watching television and what they learn depends on what they watch."[11]

A particular way of responding can be learned by watching others on film and identifying with them as they experience a situation. For example, children who experienced strong emotional arousal as they watched an episode of Lassie's master risking his life to save Lassie's puppy, strongly responded when given an opportunity to help puppies in distress in a later experiment.

Dr. Rushton summarized fourteen separate studies that demonstrated the potential therapeutic value of television to reduce fear. Watching specially constructed films has reduced children's fears of dogs, snakes, hospital surgery, and social interaction. They have reduced the anxiety of high-school students in taking tests and the fear of dental treatment in adults.

Even children's self-control can be affected by what they watch on television. Studies of cheating on games, touching forbidden toys, and delaying gratification demonstrated that behavior could be influenced in either a positive or negative direction. Programs could be designed to help young people increase their resistance to temptation in a world that entices them with forbidden pleasures. There is substantial evidence that programs which strengthen children's internalized standards of right and wrong, rather than chipping away at them, could help restore our declining cultural standards.

Educational television has been a fruitful field for the study of the effects of prosocial programming. Children's Television Workshop programs "have demonstrated the potential of TV programming for children's social, intellectual and emotional development."[12]

"Sesame Street," the most watched educational television program in history, regularly holds 75 percent of two- to five-year-olds in rapt attention. Solid research evidence reveals increased pre-reading skills and positive social skills and attitudes, made even stronger with parental discussion and encouragement.[13]

"Feeling Good," a primetime PBS program designed to motivate viewers to take responsibility for improving their health, was successful in changing simple but strategic health behaviors.[14]

"3-2-1 Contact" achieved its first year goals of helping children to enjoy science and to participate in scientific activities.[15]

"Freestyle" successfully changed nine- to twelve-year-olds' perceptions of sex roles and career options[16] in a less traditional direction. Girls became more independent and athletic, boys more nurturing.[17]

"Over Easy," which sought to reverse negative images of aging by using positive role models, produced an important guideline: use upbeat programming focusing on preventive behaviors rather than crisis intervention.[18]

Viewers of "As We See It" became more accepting of desegregation than nonviewers and more readily accepted members of other ethnic groups as friends or co-workers.[19]

Modeling programs have successfully motivated consumers to conserve energy, refuse cigarettes, and resist advertising.[20]

"Mister Rogers' Neighborhood," which stresses children's social and emotional development, combines entertainment with education to emphasize themes like cooperation, sharing, sympathy, affection, friendship, understanding others' feelings, controlling aggression, and coping with frustration. A 1976 study found significant increases in social contacts and in giving positive attention to others for all children who watched the program. These

and other studies have demonstrated that watching friendly behavior on television increases friendly behavior in real life.[21]

In 1982 an important study found that prosocial programs
could influence children with behavior disorders. These children
normally chose to watch action and violent programs and acted
out much of what they saw. During the experiment, they were
shown programs containing at least twenty-nine prosocial acts
and less than three aggressive acts per hour. The children who
viewed the prosocial programs showed an increase in their concern for the interests of others while those children who watched
the action and violent programs showed a decrease in this regard.
*It also found that prosocial programming held children's attention
as well as violent programs.*[22]

Researchers like Dr. R. J. Harris have concluded that even
when statistical proof of immediate behavioral change is lacking,
prosocial programming lays the groundwork for later behavior
change. It stimulates conversation with family, friends, or a doctor
and opens the door for meaningful exchanges between parents and
teens during dinner table conversation.[23]

According to Dr. Harris, a commercial ad that affects 1 to 10
percent of consumers is considered extremely successful, and af-
fecting even a small percentage of a mass audience is a substantial
accomplishment.[24] Dr. Harris suggests targeting those most con-
ducive to attitude and behavior change in a positive direction,
rather than those least likely to change.[25] Therefore, prosocial
programming designed to uphold and strengthen family values
should be aimed at Americans who are unknowingly adopting the
attitudes of a hedonistic society rather than at pornography addicts who deliberately seek hard-core material. Prosocial programming can be most effective for children and teen-agers who are
trying to learn right from wrong and good from bad without the
benefit of moral teaching and models from family, school, and
church.

Prosocial television heightens awareness of a problem and
helps the viewer perceive it differently. Once made aware of a
problem by prosocial television, the viewer is more likely to pay
attention the next time he hears a similar message and to be
receptive to other influences in the same direction.[26]

To successfully drive home the message, Dr. Winett suggests
the use of multiple models, similar to the target audience but a bit
more competent, portrayed in a range of situations that show the
model being reinforced for the appropriate social behavior. Dramatic stories that show variations of the desired behavior and an
accurate portrayal of the obstacles that can be expected help

viewer identification. Discussion helps to insure that the message is not lost.[27]

The most dramatic scenes are the easiest to recall. Therefore, these are the best in which to imbed the intended message. "The drama must be so intimately related to the intended lesson that they cannot be understood apart from each other. More than that, the drama must be the lesson."[28]

Researchers have concluded that "Viewers can and do learn from educational television. . . . The evidence of success with children as the target audience appears to be overwhelming."[29] Similar achievements with teen-agers and adults are possible if educators, researchers, and television producers poll what they have learned. Working together, they can make effective stories that model desirable behavior for specific audiences.

For example, saying no can be modeled effectively. What a fourteen-year-old girl will do when pressured by a boy in the back seat of a car or what the young man will do if she is reluctant might depend on the television images that flash through their minds at that moment. Will there be twelve thousand images of sex outside of marriage from the past three years of television and movie viewing or will there be models of delayed gratification and unselfish caring?

In recommending prosocial programming to the television and film industry, we narrowly define it as programming that espouses family values—those values that strengthen the concept of marriage and child rearing as primary in maintaining a healthy society.

Prosocial programming so defined can be very entertaining. It can include great drama, deliriously funny comedy, and spine tingling mystery. It requires the development of a value scheme, a systematic set of parameters, and limitations that guide the writer and director in drawing the line. Without limiting the entertainment value of the work, social value is added. Rather than limiting appeal, it increases the appeal for much of the audience.

An overall social policy promoting marriage and healthy family life in institutions throughout the country is needed to bolster the faltering American family. No institution is better able to communicate that policy to children, adolescents, and adults than the enterprising and innovative American communications media; and no medium could do it better than television. Dr. Winett foreshadowed the conclusions of the National Family Foundation Media Workshop when he declared, "Television that models socially valued behaviors, responses, attitudes or beliefs . . . is television used to best advantage."[34]

Chapter 14

The Family Market—
A Constituency to Be Courted

If motion pictures consistently hold up for admiration high types of characters and present stories that will affect lives for the better, they can become the most powerful natural force for the improvement of mankind.

—the Motion Picture Code, 1930-1966

When expectations are violated frequently enough, a portion of the audience stops viewing. During the period from 1980 to 1985, "viewership of network fare during prime time . . . declined from about 78 percent to 70 percent, whereas viewership of alternatives (cable stations, pay TV, VCRs) . . . increased from about 22 percent to 30 percent."[1]

The trend continues. According to Brent Bozell of Media Research, network viewership declined 25 percent from 1980 to 1991, but family friendly cable stations like Disney Channel and the Family Channel have increased audience share another 13 percent in the past five years.[2]

Expressing dissatisfaction with present media trends, John Underwood, former senior editor for *Sports Illustrated*, wrote an article entitled "How Nasty Do We Wanna Be, Reflections on Censorship and a Civilized Society."[3] The article was originally published in the *Miami Herald* and later reprinted in major dailies and the January 1991 *Reader's Digest*. Shocked at the overwhelming public response, Underwood wrote:

> The volume of mail in response has been like nothing I have ever experienced in many years of writing for publication (the *Herald*, *Time*, Inc., etc.). From Idaho to Maine to Louisiana, from editors to retirees, from 90-year-olds to teenagers, the letters keep coming. Beverly Sills, the opera singer, even called to ask permission to use it in a speech. . . .

What stood out in all that heartfelt testimony was the thing that took me most by surprise: the hunger Americans have for such commentary. I thought I was a voice in the wilderness; it turned out I was nothing more than a member of the chorus. Americans are crying out for a war on the Philistines. "Keep it up!" they write. "How can we help?" they ask. "What can we do?" It is not the messenger they seek, lest you should think I have been beguiled. It is the message.[4]

What was his message? Mr. Underwood talked about

a society that is increasingly loathe to draw the line between right and wrong. A society that has all but gone blind to the crucial difference between liberty and license, and why that failing will constrict liberty, not perpetuate it. . . . Giving in to the lowest common denominator is not what freedom is all about. Freedom within a social order is not just about "doing and saying whatever I please," it is also about responsibilities and obligations to the common welfare. It is not about seeing how much sewage a people must wade through before they sink under the weight of their own depravities; it is, in fact, just the opposite of that. It is about being "free" from those things . . . exercising our right not to put up with them.

The industry would do well to remember the family market. It is a constituency that has been long forgotten but nonetheless is a large part of its potential audience. Networks and film producers could join in a partnership with media researchers to develop a product that is seldom offered: the latest and best techniques in entertainment combined with time-honored values such as loyalty, fidelity, honesty, a day's work for a day's pay—qualities that are worthy of imitation. Dr. Louis Sullivan, secretary of the Department of Health and Human Services, has called for programs that promote "the natural role of parents as the loving nurturers of their children."[5] President Bush has urged producers and the networks to employ "the power of TV as a force for positive change."[6]

In recent years, special advocacy groups have been achieving a degree of success in Hollywood. According to Kathryn Montgomery, a professor of film and television at the University of California, "Hollywood is always searching for script ideas with dramatic and ratings potential . . . Television is quick to embrace prosocial issues that would legitimize its activities and make it look good."[7]

Although Hollywood has indeed embraced environmental issues, hunger, the plight of minorities and homosexuals, it has yet to embrace the weakening family in America as a *cause celebre*.

Yet the individuals who make up the world of Hollywood are not entirely without concern. "We have families. We're not immune to what's happening out there."[8]

Gary David Goldberg, producer of "Brooklyn Bridge" and "Family Ties," recently decided,

> My wife and I have pulled the plug on our eight-year-old daughter. No TV without a grown-up present. Not allowed. Period. That way, even if there's something that violates our world view, it's an opportunity for discussion . . . [Kids] don't process information the same way adults do—and certainly not the same way as your average Hollywood writer or producer.[9]

According to Bruce Berman, president of Warner Brothers theatrical production, "Filmmakers are now embracing the concept of family films. It's no longer a dirty word." Yet Berman admitted that "Hollywood filmmakers may not understand Middle America. They're *not very well equipped to deal in that context*"[10] (emphasis added).

What is needed are advocacy groups to educate the entertainment world about how a traditional family acts and thinks.

Even Bill Cosby met resistance from media executives who were sure a show about the traditional family would be too boring for the American people. Yet, for eight years, his show was the most watched show in television history as well as one of the most profitable.

According to *New York Times* writer Bill Carter, "It restored the television image of the parent as loving authority figure, and it gave viewers, black and white, an unwaveringly positive look at family life."[11] Research revealed that people actually watched the show to learn how to be good parents. In addition to changing the image of black America and family life, the show encouraged other shows like "Family Ties" and "Growing Pains" to make positive changes as well. Certainly Cosby proved the existence of the family market and that everyday problems were of interest to vast numbers of viewers.

The Family Channel was the first basic cable network that has tried to meet the needs of the family market.[12] It has already begun to move in the direction of many of our recommendations. Carried on ten thousand cable systems, it is now available to 90 percent of cable TV households or 55 million homes. Begun in 1981 as a commercial network, it first became profitable in 1984. A continual rise in ratings and advertising revenues has marked its success as the nation's leading family entertainer and one of the most trusted cable television networks.

The channel openly embraces traditional family values and promises its viewers programming that all the family will enjoy watching together. Los Angeles author Jane Wollman wrote, "all the shows support the traditional family values of marriage, motherhood, and morality. No premarital sex here, no exploitative violence, no blue jokes or foul language." Even grandma can watch with the parents and kids and feel good about it afterward.[13]

Quiet and conservative in style, the Family Channel's goal is to "celebrate love and life" and to "talk about values between husbands and wives and children . . . children aren't smart alecks and the parents aren't buffoons."[14] Special blocks of time are set aside for children's programming every morning and every afternoon. It shuns sex, drugs, and excessive violence. The channel does not show slasher movies, teen-age comedies like *Porkies*, or ads for alcohol and R-rated movies.

Drawing the line on gratuitous violence, Paul Krimsier, vice-president of programming explains,

> When violence is exploited it can contribute to a sense of fear and stimulate unhealthy enjoyment. . . . We don't show a woman getting raped and killed. I would like viewers to feel good about the time they spend watching us rather than feeling they have to go clean up afterwards.[15]

Specific shows are aimed at helping children and families. Reviewed and approved by the American Pediatrics Association, "Healthy Kids" and "American Baby" give parents tips on raising healthy children. "Family Edition," a quarterly newsmagazine show in partnership with Hearst entertainment and the Hearst Magazine Group, combines print supplements with television to help parents guide their children toward health and teaches them about the environment, education, and personal finance. Unlike the talk shows of the major networks, guests interviewed are research scientists, physicians, educators, and experts who offer instruction for American families.

The Family Channel offers teaching manuals to use with many of their programs and encourages teachers to tape episodes for classroom use. For example, "Zorro in the Classroom" teaches skills needed for personal development and decision making. The student is asked to compare Zorro's statement, "I have no need to kill another man, not even you," to a student who thinks he must hurt others to prove himself strong. "Roots in the Classroom" helps teachers discuss such issues as how people can become slaves to smoking, drugs, etc.

The Family Channel's ad revenue is continually rising: from $54 million in 1988, to $68 million in 1989, to $80 million in 1990.

According to Dick Hammer, head of advertising sales, "Advertisers ultimately came to the realization that we deliver a media value that they need and want."[16] Seven years ago advertisers wouldn't even talk to Family Channel, but today major clients like Colgate-Palmolive and Chrysler are impressed with the opportunity it offers to reach the family market and are signing year-long contracts up to $3 million.[17]

Family Channel presents a mix of old movies, the best in reruns like "The Waltons," and original programming. "Bordertown" was the first original production. Others include the "Adventures of the Black Stallion," "Maniac Mansion," a canine game show "That's My Dog," the animated "The Legend of Prince Valiant," and "Backstage at the Zoo." They are now the leader in new original programming among all basic cable networks with twelve original series and numerous original specials and movies.

That a market for family entertainment exists is supported by comments from the film industry: "Ted Conley, film buyer for Dallas-based Cinemark, the nation's seventh largest exhibitor, said there is a constant demand for family films at the company's 645 screens located mainly in the South and Southwest." Edward Durwood, president of AMC, the country's third-largest theater chain with 1649 screens said the "ideal situation" would be to have enough G-rated films to occupy at least one screen at all times.[18]

Realizing the enormous need for programming that all the family can enjoy together, many outside of the established entertainment industry have begun to produce their own films or to start new production companies.

Family Vision Entertainment Corporation

Headed by producer Brad Carr, Family Vision Foundation is newly established "to encourage the development of family books, films and television series." The foundation has been instrumental in developing an eight book series, *The Days of Laura Ingalls Wilder*, written by best selling author T. L. Tedrow about life in the frontier hills of the Ozarks. The books focus on the adventures of the author of *Little House on the Prairie* as she campaigns for issues that we face today—conservation, environment, education, illiteracy, animal abuse, women's rights, the plight of the poor, and racism. With advance orders of over four million copies, they will be released in July of 1992 by Thomas Nelson Publishers. A twenty-six episode, one-hour television series based on the books will be filmed in Vancouver, Canada in the fall of 1992.

A second spin-off project for 1993 is already underway, a book series and sixty-five half-hour television programs entitled "The Younguns." Other book-to-film projects in the development stage are a family-adventure mountain series, "Kodiak Jack," and a turn-of-the-century family comedy series, "The Monroe Street Tigers." This series about a group of five street-smart and mischievous kids will confront problems relevant to our times—stealing, cheating, lying, racism, child abuse, and parental alcoholism. Using ingenuity and self-reliance to get in and out of unforgettably funny situations with a mix of traditional moral values and street-smart sense, they are expected to capture the imaginations of American families.

Family Vision has identified important trends and an "economic barometer" that highlight the need for family and children's entertainment programming:

> Even though overall economic growth has stalled, spending by children aged four to twelve and spending by parents/relatives on these children has jumped to approximately one hundred billion dollars in 1991, more than double the market of only three years ago.

> More babies were born in 1990 than in any previous twelve month period in the last thirty years. This assures a huge family and children audience in the 1990's and beyond.

> The explosion of new broadcast and cable channels worldwide, as well as new satellites and transmission technologies, are creating an international demand for new programming, with the international market clamoring for family fare. . . .

> The KIDVID LAW, passed in November 1990, is forcing broadcasters to address the educational needs of children in their programming or face possible license revocation by the FCC. This has created a renewed interest in the development and broadcasting of children and family programming. . . .[19]

"With these market trends in mind, Family Vision Foundation is working with writers, producers, networks and studios to encourage the development of family entertainment to meet this demand." For more information, contact Brad Carr, Producer/Family Vision Entertainment Corporation/1000 Universal Studios Plaza/Building 22/Orlando, FL 32829/Phone: (407) 363-8449.

Feature Films for Families

Organized in 1988 in Utah by former news reporter Don Judd,

and in full operation since early 1990, Feature Films for Families began by distributing old movies on video. They created a new distribution system, which they hope will encourage the production of new films that promote traditional values. They have, in fact, produced two new films of their own and plan to produce four more in the coming year. Their most ambitious film to date, *The Butter Cream Gang*, was released early in 1992. It is a moving story of a group of teen-age boys who strive to bring their friend back to his former values after he becomes influenced by big city gangs.

After identifying families who were likely prospects, they began calling one family at a time. By mid-1992, they had made one and a half million telephone calls to homes to offer monthly specials on movies the whole family could enjoy together. They now report a support base of 600,000 families and have sold 1.75 million videos at $11.95 each plus shipping. The market appears to be the seven out of ten families contacted who said "they had a difficult time finding appropriate family entertainment." Too often, families have had only the films they rejected at the movie theater to choose from at the video stores.

Family Films claim to be the fastest growing distributor of motion pictures in the country with thirty to forty thousand new customers each month. They permit no profanity, nudity, or sexual innuendo and very little violence in their films. Even airline-edited versions do not meet their standards. For information, contact Michael Clapier, Public Information Director, Feature Films for Families/5280 South 320 West, #E240/Murray, UT 84107/ Phone: (801) 263-0117.

New Generation Entertainment

Actor Richard Kiel has formed New Generation Entertainment and has twelve family-oriented films in development. He claims that his first completed production, *The Giant of Thunder Mountain*, in which he starred, received a "fantastic response" from theater owners in its 1991 screening. Presently distributing their films themselves, they sent out a mailing to fourteen thousand theater owners nationwide and reported that the "phone was ringing off the hook" from buyers and managers who wanted to book the film. Kiel has no objection to PG-rated films but is bothered by extreme violence, explicit sex acts, and the anti-police, anti-parent, and anti-teacher attitudes of Hollywood.[20]

Challenger Films: The Winning Edge

A thirteen-week television series, under development for seven years, has been designed to inspire the best qualities in young people rather than inciting and reinforcing the worst. "The Winning Edge," produced by Challenger Films, will feature young people who have overcome great difficulties, being interviewed by well-known persons from sports, entertainment, and other fields. Expected to provide wholesome role models and the kinds of heroes children so desperately need, the first episodes will run August 6 and 10, 1992, on ESPN at 3 P.M. EST. Letters to Mr. C. Woodward/ESPN/Box 5,100/Bristol, CT 06010 requesting more such programming will determine whether or not the rest of the series will be aired. For information, write Dr. Diane Preston Reilly/2951 Flowers Road S./Oxford Building, Suite 243/Atlanta, Georgia 3034 or call (404) 458-6777.

The Dove Foundation

Brad Curl's Dove Foundation has been organized to rally consumer demand for more superior family-scripted films from Hollywood. Working within the established marketplace, it will offer videos of first-rate new films in edited family versions for distribution through regular video stores and direct mail order.

Presently they have awarded the Dove Seal to seven hundred existing titles, many of which are already available in video stores. An example of a recent award is to Republic Picture Home Video for *Sarah Plain and Tall*, a Hallmark Hall of Fame television production, which will now be available on home video.

The founders of the Dove Foundation have taken a pragmatic approach to the problem by making a reasonable bridge between filmmakers and the Christian community. They are not acting as censors but are proposing to make an edited version available along with the industry's uncut version, thus serving the long-neglected family market without narrowing the choices of those who want racier fare. Foretelling the coming strength of the family market, a studio manager told Dove Executives that one possible obstacle to getting Dove-edited versions from studios was their fear that the demand for the edited version could outstrip the demand for the studio version. They will also serve as an important resource for independent producers entering the family film market.

Working in conjunction with the MMPA Rating system and the Screen Writers' Guild, the foundation will recommend changes in new releases of the best PG, PG-13, and R-rated films and award the Dove Seal to those that meet the standards. The Dove Foundation is currently working with Blockbuster Video and several major Hollywood studios to develop a test of several new releases in selected markets like Florida and California.

A consumer group called the Dove Family Video Association is offering memberships that include discounts on family-approved videos and a guide listing the Dove-approved videos. They have a membership of over two thousand, which is growing rapidly. Write for details to Dick Rolfe, Managing Director/Dove Services/4521 Broadmoor SE/Grand Rapids, MI 49512 or call (616) 698-6553.

Dominion Satellite

Direct broadcast satellites are now operating over Japan and Europe. The race is on in the United States for this latest and most powerful means of broadcasting. Bypassing local TV stations and cable systems, it will bring hundreds of TV and radio channels to every home in North America.

Dominion Satellite has been working feverishly to provide a competitive electronic media alternative that is Christian-oriented to the present offerings of the media industry. They hope to secure a permanent place in space for delivering family-oriented television and radio directly to the home, office, church, and school.

Dominion is licensed for frequencies that can provide up to eighty digital video television and digital stereo radio channels. It will broadcast children's programs, family entertainment, science, travel, nature, wildlife, cultural and arts programming, vocational-technical-rehabilitative programs, up-to-the-minute headline news, local, state and regional weather, stock market and business reports, commodity, farm and agricultural reports, plus a great deal more. It will have interactive capability for polling and testing and multilingual audio and captioning for the deaf.

Unlike existing satellites, DBS signals are so powerful that only a twelve- to fourteen-inch receiving antenna is needed for each home to receive programming. Contracts have been signed with a major satellite contractor, and November 1994 is the projected launch date. What is needed now to get this potentially powerful project off the ground is thousands of families to become "Charter Home Affiliates." For more information, write Robert W. Johnson, President/Dominion DBS Network/P. O. Box 7609/Naples, FL 33941 or call (813) 566-3050.

Decency codes continue to breakdown: television lowered its standards in 1991 to allow six more "forbidden" words to be freely broadcast; nudity is becoming the "in-thing" in advertising, and porn movies are receiving the respectable NC-17 rating and appearing in legitimate theaters. Nevertheless, there are encouraging signs that both the family market and the harm done by most of today's entertainment media are being recognized:

• ABC has just rejected an R-rated network TV series, stating that is not the answer for network television in competing with cable's "adult" fare. An executive from CBS agreed that people sitting at home don't want nudity, excessive violence, or strong language.[21]

• The number of G-rated (suitable for general audiences) films per year released by the Motion Picture Association is beginning to increase: from six in 1989 and eight in 1990 to fourteen in 1991.

• Paramount pictures has announced they will make at least three family films in the coming year.

• In March of 1992, advertising took an important step to regulate itself fearing that if it did not, "government would do the job instead." ABC's proposed dumping of advertising restrictions was met with pressure from advertisers and industry groups alike. A few months later it "quietly issued guidelines that are as strict as any of the old rules—and are even tougher, in some cases."[22]

• Morton Kondracke, senior editor of the *New Republic* and a certified liberal, has joined the chorus of alarm from pro-family and religious organizations. He recently stated that because

> sexual liberation has gone way too far, . . . all kinds of
> people are suffering . . .the media, the churches, schools, the
> government, and other influential grown-ups ought to en-
> courage old-fashioned virtues—like self-discipline and the
> postponement of gratification—instead of encouraging young
> people (as much of the media certainly do) to screw their
> brains out.[23]

Mr. Kondracke made the connection between what the media encourages and the alarming statistics on out-of-wedlock pregnancies, venereal diseases, AIDS, and the breakdown of moral virtues.

In a recent column, Ellen Goodman noted that "the sexual messages of movies and TV and MTV are locked in a media time warp where sex is rarely safe." She quoted one child as saying, "When I grow up, I'm not going to have sex because I don't want to die."[24]

It is encouraging that more and more people are seeing the connection and acknowledging that media messages are indeed impacting the culture in a very dangerous direction. It is encouraging that the family market for entertainment without explicit sex and violence is being identified and organized. It is encouraging that so many new production companies are eager to provide constructive alternatives for families. However, if we, the consumers, do not help them succeed by buying pro-family entertainment and by shunning sexually explicit, graphically violent, or anti-family programming, then we will get what we deserve—trash. Unfortunately, if they do not succeed, our children and families will lose what they deserve—a future and a hope.

Chapter 15

Research, Public Policy, and Law: Combination for Change

Law, natural or human, shall not be ridiculed, nor shall sympathy be created for its violation.

—The Motion Picture Code, 1930-1966

Rarely are the results of scientific research understood well enough to directly influence law and public policy on controversial social issues. But in the area of pornography, sexual exploitation, and violence in the media, research has affected public opinion and brought about changes in law.

Scientific research was used by the 1970 Commission on Pornography to justify their recommendation to legalize all pornography and violence in the media.[1] Research allegedly found that such material had either *no adverse effects* or a *cathartic impact* on attitudes and behavior.[2] No major study since the 1970 Commission, however, has found the catharsis theory valid.

Although the report was overwhelmingly rejected by Congress and the president, the media publicized its conclusion that pornography was a "victimless crime," and law enforcement came to a standstill. By the late 1970s and early 1980s, however, sections of the scientific community were questioning that finding.[3] In 1986, a new Pornography Commission concluded:

> In both clinical and experimental settings, exposure to sexually violent materials has indicated an increase in the likelihood of aggression. More specifically, the research . . . shows a causal relationship between exposure to material of this type and aggressive behavior towards women.[4]

Later, the U.S. surgeon general gathered two dozen leading researchers, including critics of the Pornography Report like Pro-

187

fessors Malamuth and Donnerstein, to discuss the research. They reached five "consensus" conclusions, which found that pornography harms women and children[5] (see chap. 5).

Finally, virtually every research study in the 1970s and 1980s has underscored the finding that media violence dramatically impacts viewer's attitudes and behavior, especially in the young, immature, and unstable. Unfortunately, real life stories of violence in the news mirror the violent depictions in the media with devastating real life consequences.

These research conclusions finding harm, so different from those of 1970, have greatly affected public policy and law in the 1980s and can be expected to continue to impact the distribution of pornography, violent, and sexually violent material in the 90s. There are basically three categories of evidence that have significant value and impact on law and public policy: (1) general data; (2) law enforcement data; and (3) scientific research (field, laboratory, or clinical).

A dramatic change in the *content of pornography* over the last twenty years was illustrated by both the 1986 Commission and a 1982 Harvard Medical School content analysis (see chap. 4). This revealed that "mainstream" pornography, freely available on the open market in the 1980s, was virtually unavailable in 1970.[6] In 1970, the vast majority of "hard-core" pornography featured a nude woman posing alone. Only a small percentage today contains such imagery and less than 10 percent depicts vaginal intercourse between one man and one woman.[7] The most prevalent themes in hard-core pornographic material today focus on sexually deviant or violent behavior. Exploitation, degradation, victimization, and humiliation—especially of women and children—pervade current hard-core, illegal pornography.[8]

Second, because research established that the largest age category of pornography consumers is twelve to seventeen,[9] all three major studies agreed that pornography could have serious, harmful, and lasting adverse effects on the attitudes and behaviors of children.[10]

Third, illegal pornography in the U.S. has become a large and profitable commercial enterprise. Annual revenues from its production, distribution, and sale are now estimated between $8-10 billion, with organized criminal networks controlling the vast majority of its profits.[11] The dramatic increase in distribution, accompanied by the exploitative, violent, and deviant changes in content, appear to parallel the unprecedented increase in rape (526 percent increase since 1960) and child molestation (175 percent increase since 1980).[12] Conversely, when pornography is removed from the open market, rape rates significantly decrease even when they are increasing in surrounding areas. Oklahoma City, for example, experienced a 26 percent decrease in rapes after removing over one hundred hard-core pornography outlets while the state experienced a 21 percent increase in rape during the same period.[13] States that sell the highest number of pornography magazines also have the highest per capita incidence of rape.[14]

Fourth, many public health officials now find pornography consumption to be a public health problem because it encourages anonymous sexual activity in adult bookstores and promotes unsafe sex practices. According to Dr. James Mason, assistant secretary for health,

> I can't help but believe that an indulgent society that permits pornography in the media—that is seen casually by youth and adults—is a significant contributor to the epidemic of sexually transmitted diseases in our country.[15]

Fifth, heart-rending real life stories from victims highlight the connection between pornography and rape, child molestation, murder, family violence, and divorce. Similar strong connections have been shown between media violence and real life episodes. They are now widely reported in books, newspapers, television, and radio.[16]

Law enforcement agencies have collected extensive data showing that people convicted of serial murders, sex crimes, and child molestation often used pornography. For example, a recent FBI study of thirty-six serial murders revealed that 81 percent reported significant pornography consumption, making pornography one of the most common profile characteristics of serial murders and rapists.[17] A Michigan state police survey of forty two thousand sex crimes discovered that 42 percent of all sex crimes involve pornography either immediately prior to or during the commission of the act.[18] The rates of child molestation have dramatically increased over the last few years, and according to present crime trends, one in three females and one in seven males will be sexually molested before the age of eighteen.[19] Sex crimes are frequent in neighborhoods with pornography businesses.

According to the U.S. Department of Justice, law enforcement statistics have reported that "pornography's clientele have a frightening, but not surprising, degree of overlap with the police blotter's list of sex criminals and violent assaults." Connections between pornography and violent sex-related crimes, including rape of women and molestation of children have been proved by scientific research and hard data. They are no longer supposition.[20]

A recent review of existing research on pornography found consistent harmful effects in 82 to 88 percent of the studies[21] (see chap. 5). If researchers could ethically expose subjects who are most vulnerable and most affected—children, teen-agers, and sexual deviants—to the hardest kinds of pornography, it is highly likely that scientific studies would substantiate even greater harm.

Even critics Linz, Donnerstein, and Penrod found in their 1987 studies that

> The 1986 Commission maintained that there was a causal relationship between exposure to sexually violent pornography and negative changes in certain attitudes towards and perceptions of women as well as increased aggression towards women. THIS IS AN ACCURATE STATEMENT as long as we are referring to the results of laboratory studies examining sexually violent images.[22]

Research indicates that if factors sometimes present in real life pornography consumption—months or years of prolonged exposure for teen-agers and sexually deviant males or consumption of hard-core pornography accompanied by masturbation—the *negative impact* would be even greater.

The hearings for the 1986 Commission on Pornography and its Final Report contributed both to growing public awareness and to the federal government's decision to launch a major initiative against illegal pornography and child exploitation. The National Obscenity Enforcement Task Force (now called Child Exploitation and Obscenity Section) initiated a national law center; federal, state and local training; legislative assistance; and "how to publications" for prosecutors and investigators. Its creation led to a dramatic increase in federal prosecutions of obscenity and child pornography and comprehensive changes to the federal and state laws (see Table 1).

TABLE I
Federal Prosecutions from 1983 through 1989

	1983	1986	1987	1988	1989
Obscenity	0	10	78	37	120
Child Exploitation	3	147	249	150	255

Recently, President Bush echoed the Department of Justice's determination that obscenity and child pornography will be two of the top criminal justice priorities in the Justice Department. In his October 1991 White House address, he called the prosecution of obscenity and child pornography "top priorities of his administration."[23]

Prior to 1982, child pornography was judged under the strict three-part obscenity definition, which made prosecution of this material difficult. Among other things, research led both the U.S. Supreme Court in 1982 and later Congress in 1984 to conclude that child pornography must be a separate, distinct criminal offense with a lower standard of proof because of its harm to the child victim. "The prevention of sexual exploitation and abuse of children constitute a government objective of surpassing importance."[24]

Recently, in a U.S. Supreme Court decision concerning whether the criminalization of the mere private possession of child pornography was constitutional, the court held in *Osborne v. Ohio*[25] that the harm to children from pornography far outweighed any minimal privilege, which a possessor might have. A key brief filed with the court contained the following summary of argument:

> Scientific research and law enforcement studies further reveal an indisputable link between child pornography and child exploitation, as well as a severe harm suffered by children from child pornography. Evidence overwhelmingly supports the conclusion that child pornography primarily exists for the use and consumption by pedophiles and child molesters. Removal of all incentive for the production and distribution of child pornography, which is the ability to sell or distribute the pornography to a customer or possessor, is essential to dry up the circular chain of child pornography. Therefore, criminalizing possession of child pornography is paramount to curtail the harm to children, to break the cycle of child victimization and to dry up the market for child pornography.[26]

Research was also utilized in a recent Supreme Court case, *Maryland v. Craig*,[27] which allowed videotaped or closed circuit testimony of the child abuse victim in a molestation case because of the significant harm that might be experienced in the courtroom.

Law enforcement data concerning the connection between pornography and sexual crimes, as well as control of the industry by organized crime, led to extending RICO laws to include obscenity (1986) and child pornography (1988). These powerful racketeering laws, passed in the early 1980s to increase penalties against organized crime, permit asset forfeiture and increased jail terms for those who sell obscene pornography.[28] Two Supreme Court cases, *Fort Wayne Books* and recently *Pryba*, found that it is fully constitutional to make obscenity a basic offense in proving that an organization is involved in criminal racketeering.

Public opinion about the secondary effects of pornography establishments has led to a multitude of local regulations of sexually oriented businesses such as laws for zoning and licensing, public nuisance, removal of peep show booths, sex supermarket ordinances. The U.S. Supreme Court in at least two cases, *Renton* and *Arcara Books*[29] has recently found that secondary effects and evidence of harm were sufficient reasons to zone adult establishments, permit removal of peep show booths, and close pornography outlets.

Finally, investigative techniques on child molesters have been significantly altered because research found that pedophiles and molesters often consume and use child and adult pornography in the commission of their criminal behavior against children. Thus, questions such as "Did the molester show you any videos or pictures or did he take pictures of you?" are often asked of the abused child. Further, search warrants prior to or accompanying arrest are generally issued if there is probable cause to believe that pornography exists in the home of the molester. When pornography is found, it constitutes powerful evidence in difficult child molestation trials, which otherwise rely on child testimony.[30]

The 1980s have seen a dramatic shift in public policy, law enforcement techniques, and laws concerning the regulation of pornography. Because research about the adverse effects and harms of pornography has been uncovered and publicized, the 1990s may show an even more dramatic trend.

Legislators, prosecutors, the American public, city officials, and the courts want to know whether "pornography and media violence harm real victims" or are "a victimless crime involving harmless entertainment." If the research continues to show that pornography and media violence have both short-term and long-term harmful effects on real victims, public policy and law will continue to evolve toward media regulation. The trends in the 1980s lead to some natural predictions in the 1990s if research, public policy, and law continue to be integrated in the area of pornography and sexual exploitation. There are strong indications that there will be major changes in at least eight critical areas.

1) *Broadcasting and cable will be more closely regulated*. Research has established the harm of sexually explicit and violent material to children and the presence of children in the audience at all times of the day. Already the FCC has proposed a 24-hour ban on broadcast indecency. The main reasons are: (a) large numbers of children in the late night audience, (b) harm to children from indecent broadcasting, and (c) new technology making regulation to prevent child access difficult if not impossible.[31] Indecent material is defined as material that "depicts or describes in terms patently offensive, as measured by contemporary community stan-

dards for the broadcast medium, sexual or excretory activities or organs."

"Safe-harbor" periods are indefensible in light of broadcast data showing large numbers of children in late night broadcast audiences. They are further discredited by evidence showing a higher ratio of children to adults in the broadcast audience during late night and early morning hours. Suggested "time channeling" alternatives endorsed by broadcasters would in fact "narrowcast indecent programming to the very audience in need of protection—children."

2) *Telephone pornography, called dial-a-porn, will be virtually eliminated because of harm to children.* Evidence that children imitate sex acts learned from dial-a-porn in committing sex crimes against other children is overwhelming. Obscene dial-a-porn has been banned under the Child Protection and Obscenity Enforcement Act of 1988 and upheld under the recent U.S. Supreme Court decision, *Sable v. F.C.C.*[32] In July of 1990, the presentation of research proving harm to children led to severe restrictions on indecent telephone communication by the FCC.[33] The FCC received many comments highlighting recent cases of child sexual molestation by other children who listen to dial-a-porn. Many legal commentators believe research could eventually persuade the high court to uphold the strict regulation of indecent dial-a-porn and broadcasting.[34]

3) *Adult bookstores and X-rated theaters could virtually disappear.* While at one time there were more pornography outlets than McDonalds' restaurants in America, local regulations against pornography might drive the distribution centers of hard-core pornography (i.e., adult bookstores and X-rated theaters) out of business. By the year 1995, adult bookstores and X-rated theaters might be an ancient relic representing the old way to distribute pornography.

4) *"Violence for violence's sake" in movies and videos could be regulated under harmful to minors laws.* In response to increasing amounts of violence in the media and studies showing children who view graphic visual violence grow up to be violent, two states have attempted to include excessive violence in their harmful to minors laws.[35] If research continues to show that graphic violence alone has a negative impact on children and that it can lead to negative changes in attitudes and behavior—including the commission of violent crimes—other states and the FCC might examine the problem in the 1990s. Missouri and Tennessee are presently undergoing court challenges that will determine whether such statutes are constitutional.

5) *Pornography victims legislation, both federal and state, will*

aid rape and child molestation victims. If there is proof that pornography has been a catalyst or primary incitement to commit such crimes, victims will be compensated.[36]

6) *Sex Offender Registration Laws will sweep the country.* Research will expose both the serial nature of sex crimes and the high rate of repeat offenses and identify the "at risk" population.

7) *Harmful matter per se laws will be passed to prevent pornography from being distributed or shown to minors.* Formerly only material that 1) appeals to the pruient interest of minors, 2) depicts sexual content that is patently offensive in regard to minors, and 3) lacks literary, artistic, political, or scientific value for minors would have to be removed from the sight and reach of minors in the marketplace. The "variable obscenity" standard for minors would become objective, making all sexually explicit or violent material, which is excessively graphic, unavailable to minors without having to prove the formerly difficult to establish subjective tests.

The harm of pornography and violent materials to minors is widely accepted. While the harmful matter *per se* standard will not make such non-obscene material illegal for adults, if these laws are passed and enforced, the teen-age market will be eliminated. Therefore, a portion of the material will disappear from the market.

8) *Hard-core videos available in "family" video and convenience stores would be less prevalent.* They would be drastically reduced by harmful matter *per se* laws, economic boycotts, people buying from stores that don't offer pornography, and increased prosecution under obscenity laws.

9) *Finally*, one of the most notable changes that could occur in the 1990s is *the extension of the obscene per se standard, which presently applies to child pornography*. This standard, rather than the three-part *Miller* test for obscenity discussed above, could apply to all hard-core pornography or to some of the most deviant categories of adult pornography.

The court ruled in *New York v. Ferber* and again in *Osborne v. Ohio* that child pornography was obscene *per se*, harmful in itself, without regard to community standards.[37] Other forms of pornography similarly harm victims and society. If the research is well-publicized, public opinion might influence legislators and courts to conclude that other categories of pornography should also be declared obscene *per se*.[38]

Legislatures, courts, and the public will ask two primary questions concerning whether to make such pornography obscene *per se*: (1) how serious are the negative effects of such pornography, and (2) does such pornography produce any positive results.

As the harm from pornography is discovered, and the need to stop the market that promotes and incites child molestation and rape becomes more evident, *possession* of all illegal pornography could become a criminal offense. Almost all hard-core videos would disappear under the obscene *per se* standard.

Pornography and sexual exploitation are no longer solely moral or religious issues, they have become matters of public health and safety. Research can provide the evidence necessary to influence law and public policy in the nineties. Researchers have proposed studies to further clarify how serious and long-term are the negative effects of pornography and media violence. Recently, in private meetings with top researchers, the following approaches were suggested:

1) Update the systematic review of pornography research (see chap. 5) to include post 1986 studies, non-experimental studies, and good studies that were not published in peer-reviewed journals. The systematic review provides an overview of a research field and identifies the trends that the studies are showing. It makes no judgment about how good the studies are scientifically.

2) Undertake a meta-analysis of all pornography and all media violence research. A meta-analysis weighs the studies according to the scientific correctness of the methods employed and how well they were implemented in the research. Such a study could compare the results of systematic review both of peer-reviewed and non peer-reviewed studies and of experimental and nonexperimental studies. Comprehensive meta-analyses should shed added light on the issues of how harmful pornography and media violence are by giving us an even truer picture of what science is saying.

3) Survey clinicians throughout the country regarding a) victims of rape and child molestation and b) consumers of hard-core pornography to determine how many sex addicts and rape and molestation victims there are in this country. In addition to accurate figures of pornography-related victims, we could determine how many U. S. citizens are at risk of pornography-related sexual violence.

4) Undertake credible law enforcement studies to try to determine the connection between pornography and sex crimes and media violence and violent crimes. Most investigators or prosecutors do not look for or document the use or availability of pornography in sex crimes. A two- or five-year study employing standardized forms with "pornography connection" questions for all sex crimes would authoritatively establish the connection and, in turn, impact policies, prosecutors, and law enforcement agencies all across the United States.

5) Obtain a clear picture of the profile of a rapist by an extensive interview study of rapists and rape victims. Such a study would focus on date rape, juvenile rapists, and serial rapists. It would reveal the role of pornography in that profile and help us understand why sex offenders are progressively getting younger.

6) Study the secondary effects of pornography, like the secondary effects of smoking, to better understand the characteristics of and effects on the spouses and children of pornography addicts.

7) Study how pornography shapes values, attitudes, and behaviors of young people. Consumption of hard-core pornography by both male and female teen-agers has risen since the advent of VCRs, unrestricted pornrack magazines, pornography rock, and telephone sex (dial-a-porn).

8) Explore the connection between missing and exploited children and pornography, emphasizing the exploding runaway population, juvenile prostitution rates, and massive child sex abuse.

9) Review effects from theoretical learning forms other than social learning. There are three primary forms of learning: a) classical conditioning—pairing a stimulus and response such as pornography and sexual gratification; b) operant conditioning—acting out what has been reinforced (if the behavior we experience leads to rewarding conditions, we are more likely to repeat it); and c) social learning—imitating what we see others do (when we see others engage in behavior that is labeled "fun," we are more likely to try it). Almost all studies to date have taken a social learning perspective. Because many learning theorists view learning by conditioning as more effective, pornography should be studied from these learning perspectives. For example, future research should study pedophile and molester reports of using pornography to seduce children (operant conditioning) and the effect of masturbating while consuming hard-core pornography (classical conditioning). Research using conditional methods of learning might unlock answers to the degree of harm caused by pornography and media violence and the type of individuals most at risk.

Other research studies are already being discussed in meetings with Department of Health and Human Services and Department of Justice officials. Pornography-related questions will be asked for the first time in national incidence studies on child sexual abuse, domestic violence, divorce, rape, and sexual violence. Law enforcement is exploring making mandatory the inclusion of pornography-related questions in investigations and profiles on sex offenses, sexual murders, and rape. Sex offenses should begin to be tracked on the national crime index. Studies of the presence of sexually transmitted diseases in peep show booths and bath houses should be instituted to determine if they are public health hazards and how severe the hazard is. Finally, longitudinal and retrospective studies should review the long-term effects of pornography, the populations at risk from consuming pornography, and the relationship of the amount of exposure to the amount of harm done.

Three longitudinal and numerous other research studies have outlined extensive problems with media violence, especially for children and teen-agers. Two national commissions, the recent definitive systematic study, and public concern about their results have public health and law enforcement officials taking a second look at needed pornography research. While such research will be helpful, it is already clear that present research has uncovered negative effects of pornography use which are only the "tip of the iceberg."

Successful research effectively explained drove changes in public opinion, which affected public policy and law in the 1980s. It will continue to do so in the 1990s. The great challenge for researchers, lawyers, and policy makers is to integrate research, public policy, and law to protect America's most precious resources— our children and families—for the next century.

Chapter 16

Consensus and Recommendations for the 1990s

So, correct entertainment raises the whole standard of a nation. Wrong entertainment lowers the whole living condition and moral ideals of a race.

—The Motion Picture Code, 1930-1966

The twenty-five researchers, mental health professionals, and public policy makers who attended the National Family Foundation Media Workshop ended their three-day conference in unusual agreement. Given the diversity of participants, the strong consensus was surprising. Concurring that values in much of the mass media are on a collision course with family values, they agreed that the media are sending the wrong message to the nation's children and families.

They concluded that children must be protected from seeing excessively violent and sexually explicit material. A strong appeal must be made to the media to exercise responsibility and restraint. At the same time, new regulations to protect children must be considered. As a society, we cannot afford to expose a large percentage of the nation's children to certain emotional damage. Strong supporters of the First Amendment, the participants found the harm to children, women, and families to be of such great consequence, it outweighs other considerations. They favored regulation that would restrict the further distribution of hard-core pornographic materials in the marketplace.

Because of the generally aggressive nature of television content, excessive viewing, in itself, has negative effects and is associated with increased aggressive behavior. Excessive viewing by parents sets similar habits for children and can be passed from one

198

generation to another. Too much television viewing by children indicates there is a "gap" in parent-child relationships—a lack of contact, of interaction, and of emotional relating with parents.

Dysfunctional families are the seed-bed for later addictions. Individuals who have grown up in pathological families are more likely to be influenced by violent and sexual material and to become addicted to it than those who have grown up in healthy families. Deep concern was expressed about increasing amounts of pathology interjected into homes through television and video.

Recognizing that most families are deficient in some areas, the media, particularly television, have an unusual opportunity to contribute to a healthier society by offering prosocial programming that encourages strong family values. Such programs could be highly entertaining while illustrating how people who have grown up in disturbed families can break the cycle of pathology and pass on more positive ways of relating to their children.

The research on the effects of media violence overwhelmingly points to a causal relationship between the amount and intensity of violence viewed and real life aggressive and violent behavior. Cumulative research and the rising concern of the public encouraged Congress to pass the Television Program Improvement Act in December of 1991, exempting major studios from anti-trust laws for three years. This opportunity to work out guidelines for reducing filmed violence, if honored, could bring an end to the "Can you top this?" spiral.

The National Family Foundation conference participants urge the studios to make good use of this opportunity and encourage them to look for novelty in a prosocial direction. A re-exploration of voluntary "family viewing hours," agreed upon by all studios, broadcast, and cable networks, would remove much media sex and violence at times when most children are in the audience. If this move fails, children must be protected through harmful matter *per se* laws, which would prevent access to graphically violent material by minors yet provide an avenue for adults who choose to see it. Such laws would apply to all media, including television, radio, video, and convenience stores where children have unrestricted access to harmful materials.

When it comes to sexually explicit material, the solution is much more complex. It involves the pornography industry, which operates outside the mainstream of American culture. Largely controlled by organized crime, it is often involved in criminal distribution of obscenity. The media have made the subculture increasingly visible, until abnormal and harmful lifestyles and actions rejected by a large segment of the population appear to be normal. The harmful philosophy of instant gratification and "anything goes" has reached far beyond the subculture and has, in fact, permeated the entire, legitimate entertainment industry. An example is the vulgar, sadistic film *Basic Instincts,* which, missing only the footage of the male sex organ before penetration, would have gathered an X-rating. This film received an R-rating and is appearing in theaters all over the country.

If the trend of showing soft-core pornography in neighborhood theaters is not rejected by the people, Dr. Dolf Zillmann believes hard-core pornography will not only be accepted in erotic mainstream entertainment, it will come to be expected.

We challenge researchers, lawyers, and policy makers to integrate research, public policy, and law to protect our children and our families from such harmful media influences. As described in chapter 15, this was started in the 1980s and can be carried even further in the 1990s. Recommendations for new laws in chapters 6 and 15 must be explored if we are to stop the avalanche of harms that media pornography is causing to children and families.

What is needed is an education program that is as effective in turning around the thinking of the country as the recent campaigns against smoking and driving while drinking. Because the country has accepted that these activities produce harm, it has accepted restrictions on individuals who consume them and on industries that produce them.

There is more similarity than anyone has yet admitted between advertising messages to youth (promoting smoking and drinking) and lengthy dramatizations that relentlessly promote violence and sexual promiscuity. The sex and violence message comes, not in thirty second clips to promote a brand name, but in all lengths and forms, from short news clips to half-hour sitcoms, hour-long talk shows, and full-length movies.

The messages are just as powerful: "Use violence to solve your problems!" "The promiscuous lifestyle is the most rewarding!" Sex and violence are glamorized while the negative consequences of long jail sentences, unwanted pregnancies, divorces, sexual addictions, sexual diseases, death by AIDS, lost opportunities, and shattered hopes and dreams are as underplayed as advertising coverage of cancer from smoking or driving accidents from alcohol.

As a nation we are "ripping off our kids." We are deliberately deceiving them about how to live their lives. In constantly glamorizing destructive lifestyles, we are robbing them of their options for the future and for family.

With deviant pornography being mainstreamed and normalized, this country is threatened with the collapse, not only of national morality, but of national health. An education program against pornography's promotion of sexually transmitted diseases and deviant lifestyles, similar to those against smoking and drunk driving, is desperately needed. The authors hope this book will launch such an effort.

Education campaigns such as "Enough is Enough" by the Women's Leadership Task Force of the National Coalition Against Pornography must succeed if public opinion is to be changed and the myth dispelled that pornography is a victimless crime or harmless fun entertainment (see chap. 7). Children and adults alike must understand the toxic nature of pornography and the dangers of its progressive use. Education programs should be aimed at individuals who have an interest in the potential victim rather than at the potential victim or addict. Public service announcements for seat belts had little success until the slogan: "Make sure the ones you love buckle up." We must educate the women of the country on the potential harms of pornography not just to themselves but to their husbands, sons, and daughters.

The media industry must take seriously both a tidal wave of parental concern and the accumulation of research showing harm from media materials. As one of the media's major constituencies, the family deserves better treatment than it is presently receiving.

Considering the success of the highly profitable "Cosby Show," it is time for industry executives to realize how out of touch they are with the heartbeat of America. Bill Cosby said it

> . . . started and ended with the idea of a man who looked at TV and saw parents losing. I tried to give power back to parents. I tried to show that parents have more sense and experience than children.[1]

Bill Cosby proved the existence of the family market. Yet today, looking at television, we still see parents losing. We see children losing, families losing, the nation losing. We see the entertainment media occupying most of the nation's free time. We see it encroaching on children's study time and stealing their options for higher education and challenging careers. We see it robbing American business of qualified employees who can read and write. We see it eating up quality time for families, often replacing family relationships altogether. We see a set of values— projected in our theaters, cablecast, videoed, and broadcast throughout the country—that is the opposite of what families want and need.

Dr. Kubey warned that the public good concept cannot be lost to commercial interests.[2] Dr. Huston reminded us that the Communications Act, which governs public broadcasting in this country, "specifies the media obligation to operate in the public interest."[3] Though the media have an obligation to serve the public, in fact, they serve financial interests of advertisers and Hollywood producers. The media create, for the benefit of advertisers, the greatest possible audience in order to charge the highest possible rates for advertising. The public is of little concern until it is successful in convincing advertisers to withdraw from sponsoring particular programs.

We encourage the media to offer greater balance to viewers. Sex sells, but must it all be explicit, degrading, or violent? If the media want reality, they should contrast the physical and emotional problems connected with sex outside marriage with the deep satisfactions and joys of sex within marriage. Young people need this message, and no one could portray it better than today's filmmakers.

Every religious study finds that people in this country have a high regard for the influence of religious faith in their lives. The media, if they want truly to reflect the whole of society, should balance portrayals of rebellious and underground elements with programs that show religion as a positive force in the lives of its characters.

A separate channel or specific programs to help parents with child-rearing would be a great service to struggling families. Such a channel could be a mix of interviews, courses, comedies, and dramas that illustrate *good* parenting skills. It could provide prenatal courses, postnatal courses, mothers sharing their problems and solutions at different developmental stages, child psychiatrists counseling parents about their children's successes and failures. It could have evening programs for dads, impressing them with how essential they are to the proper development of their children's health.

Instead of celebrating single parenthood, such a program could offer advice to single parents and still emphasize the enormous need for every child to have the benefit of two parents. Primetime programs for teen-agers could send a message that, even though early sex is accepted in our society, delaying sex could provide lasting benefits and satisfactions. Judging from the number of troubled relationships, premarital advice and marriage counseling are greatly needed.

A channel offering such fare could be advertised by some of Hollywood's most happily married couples or celebrities who have struggled with drugs and promiscuous sex and wish they could do it over. Many political, entertainment, and sports celebrities say media sex and violence have gone too far. It would be easy to enlist them in promoting pro-family programming. There are millions of desperate parents in the culture who are looking for help for troubled children who have already listened to the media's destructive messages.

Having witnessed marriages failing for two decades, a growing group of young people want to do it better. These two groups make up a ready market for advertisers of materials and products used by families who could support such a channel. It could be a grand experiment, the vision of one person or a cooperative effort of broadcasting and Hollywood to give something valuable back to society.

The suggestion was made that the government fund a public television network just for children, ten hours a day. Such a channel should include representatives on its advisory board from among the most successful child psychologists, educators, and parents in the country. It should not be a forum for the politically correct ideas of the moment. Its orientation should be toward building character based on the time-honored values espoused since the beginning of our country. Rather than representing every bizarre type of family in existence today, it could present families who possess qualities that aid in survival and give strength. An alternative to government funding would be the cooperative effort of major foundations.

A bill designed to serve the needs of children has already been passed: the Children's Television Act of 1990. Peggy Charren thinks this bill will "begin to make commercial television feel a little more like PBS." Stations are now required to provide information and education for children or lose their broadcast license. "The act gives parents, educators, pediatricians—anyone who cares about young people—the muscle needed to get broadcasters to pay attention to children."[4] The new law has already resulted in the creation of a news program to educate young audiences. "Not Just News," created by Tom Hurwitz, general manager of WTTG, the Fox affiliate in Washington, is designed to meet the needs of the market created by the bill.

We request that the television industry analyze the familial impact of the programs it brings into our living rooms. Dr. Andreasen suggested the industry start with funding the evaluation of programs for their most likely effects on a family-oriented perspective.[5] Working with social science researchers, they could fund studies like that of Dr. Bryant on changes in teen-agers' moral judgments and how family rules influence the television experience.

A television-news service could explain all aspects of the television, film, and video industry without hype and glamour. It would provide families and consumers with the type of information they need to be more literate about television and movie viewing. It would include such things as an analysis of production costs, techniques, and appeal strategies of prime time and children's commercials, producer's goals for individual programs, audience targeting strategies, the agenda setting of news organizations, the accuracy of politician's charges and commercial claims, and the authenticity of portrayals of family life and behavior.

We also recommend changing the rating system to reflect the amount of potential harm to children, to make age ranges smaller, and to be more descriptive of what is in the film so parents know what to expect.

In addition to the public interest, it is in the best economic interest of the television industry to volunteer to take R-rated commercials off the air during times children are likely to be watching. For example, scenes from the movie *The Patriots* depicting graphic sex and killing were advertised at 1 P.M. and several times between 5 and 6:30 P.M. with the suggestion that the book was an ideal gift to buy fathers for Father's Day. Such ads disturb parents and could become the impetus for regulation and economic boycott.

Dr. Singer recommended that programs aimed at children or young teen-agers, like the "DeGrassi" series described in chapter 13, devote the last five minutes to a group of children discussing what happened during the program with a teacher. They could anticipate some of the expected responses and confusions, so that children viewing at home alone could have an opportunity to think through the meaning of the show and have their questions answered.[6]

We recommend more programs that help children deal with the problems they must cope with in the course of a normal day. Parents also need such help.

We urge the media to promote healthy messages about the family—more stories of families who spend time with their children and give them the loving nurture necessary for the development of healthy personalities. We need to see characters who exercise self control and who enjoy pleasurable and meaningful relationships with family members, friends, and business acquaintances without sexual overtones. We encourage all mass media technologies to help us move from an overpermissive and self-gratifying culture to a society that transmits healthy, value-laden messages to citizens, families, and particularly to youth.

Since the problem, like drugs, is one of supply and demand, we must, through new laws and law enforcement, prevent children under 18 from viewing pornography and excessive violence. It must be difficult to obtain all hard-core pornography and completely eliminate all child pornography. Pornographers should be required to pay for the ultimate harms done to women and children by the users and sexual offenders who are stimulated by pornography to commit sexual crimes.

While some of our recommendations have been outlined in chapters 6 and 15, the following is a summary of our suggestions:

1. We urge the president and governors to stop the distribution of pornography into federal and state prisons where sex offenders and addicts abound. Since prisoners do not possess the same constitutional privileges as others, this regulation could ban all sexually explicit and graphically violent material from prisons. Similar measures could be utilized to keep hard-core pornography off military bases. North Carolina military bases, for example, have utilized such measures and have successfully survived all constitutional challenges.

2. We urge government legislators and law enforcement personnel to use every means at their disposal to stop the flow of media materials that incite men to commit crimes. In order to better determine how many crimes are motivated by media portrayals of sex and violence, we recommend a law enforcement protocol which requires documentation, investigation, and, if evidence for court, the automatic collection of any kind of pornographic material—pictures, magazines, videos, films, computer data, etc., and any kind of violent material, horror films, magazines featuring violence, etc., found at the site of the crime or in the home or place of work of the victimizer or suspect.

Suspects of sexual and violent crimes should routinely be asked what kind of media materials they prefer and have viewed during the past six months. Knowing which media had influenced sexual or violent crime would help the American public understand what is happening in our society. Such data collection is critical for the formulation of public policy, for encouraging the enforcement of existing obscenity laws, and for considering new laws to help check the increase in violent sexual crime.

3. We urge the government to bring greater pressure on media to better serve the public interest. If television and cable cannot be persuaded to do this voluntarily, we recommend the banning of commercials for R-rated movies and dial-a-porn services (during the day and during primetime, if not twenty-four hours a day). Parents' surveys have shown that thirty-second teasers of frightening movies have often been cited as the programming that most upset their children.

For instance, a teaser about young babysitters being terrified was shown in the middle of Saturday morning children's programs and all day long as a preview. Thirteen-year-old girls would not have chosen to see this material, and their parents would never have chosen to expose them to it. If the industry cannot be persuaded to assume responsibility for keeping such teasers off the air when children are most likely to see them, they should be required to do so.

4. Immediate congressional attention must be given to the indecency standard for broadcast. As intended in its original mandate from Congress, the Federal Communications Commission proposed a twenty-four hour ban on indecency that was supported by the majority of the American people. When the Supreme Court refused to look at a federal court ruling that such a ban is unconstitutional, it opened the window for indecent broadcast from 8 P.M. to 6 A.M.

There is no question that millions of children are in the audience in the early evening and early morning hours. Arbitron and Nielson ratings have revealed that though the overall audience shrinks in the late night hours, more children per capita (up to seventeen years) are in the audience than adults after midnight. Concerned parents should write to the Federal Communications Commission and request that it reduce the window of indecency to be as narrow as possible, not longer than from 2 A.M. to 6 A.M. The evidence of harm, the law, and audience statistics amply support such a limitation.

Congress should address the broader issue of television indecency and, like dial-a-porn, require the FCC to devise a way that would protect children but allow adults to see indecent programming. One possible mechanism would be to segregate all "adult" programming from quality entertainment by removing indecent programming from basic cable and satellite television and creating special "adult" pay-per-view channels.

In the meantime, the FCC could take a more active role in fining stations than it has in the past. From April 1987, through June 1990, the FCC received 44,110 complaints about offensive programming. It fined ten radio stations, clearly a step in the right direction, but television continues to break standards without penalty. Parents and concerned citizens should learn from pro-family groups how to file a proper complaint with the FCC, include a taping of the offensive program, the name of the station, time of day shown, and signature of the complainant.

5. "Harmful to minors" laws have already been used to put soft-core pornography behind the counter, out of sight and out of reach of minors, to prevent teen-agers from entering R-rated movies unaccompanied by an adult, and from purchasing or renting X-rated videos. These laws need to be strictly enforced. We recommend the tightening of controls to prevent children from renting or buying R-rated and sexually explicit unrated films. Blockbuster Video has

provided a model for video stores. They rate all unrated films themselves and require parent's permission to allow minors to rent anything R-rated.

We urge the enforcement of the prohibition against children buying a ticket to a G-or PG-rated film and slipping into an R-rated film in multi-screen theaters. This is one of the most poorly enforced laws in the nation. We urge the recognition of the NC-17 film for what it is, an X-rated film by another name, and the banning of such films from legitimate theaters.

The often repeated complaint about harmful to minor and obscenity laws is that they are too subjective or vague to be certain what is illegal. Legally, the definitions are clear, but in practice, they can be misunderstood.

6. Therefore, in order to establish a more objective standard, harmful matter *per se* laws should be pioneered. In short, harmful matter *per se* laws would put off-limits all sexually explicit depictions—intercourse, masturbation, sexual violence, or lewd exhibition of the genitals—for viewing of minors without written parental permission. Therefore, *Playboy*, *Penthouse*, and all X- and many R-rated movies would not be sold, rented, or shown to minors.

Harmful matter *per se* laws should be extended to include sexually explicit and graphically violent materials on broadcast radio and television, basic cable, dial-a-porn, and music recordings.

7. We must create an objective obscenity *per se* standard similar to those that made child pornography illegal *per se* for materials that are paraphilic, sexually aggressive, rape-myth oriented, or which promote unsafe sex practices as outlined in chapter 9.

8. We also urge both state and federal governments to pass Pornography Victim's Compensation Acts. As with "dram shop acts" against excessive serving of alcohol, pornography victims should be able to bring a civil suit against pornographers for the crimes their lucrative, destructive products cause.

9. Child sex offenders have the biggest recidivist rates of all crimes. Sex offender registration laws must be passed to require them to notify law enforcement of their whereabouts—almost like lifetime probation. A national registry with mandatory state reporting of child sex offenders would enable all organizations who provide child care and children's programs to effectively screen their volunteers and employees for convicted child sex offenders.

10. New child protection laws would define children as "under 18," make all child sex offenses a felony, and make possession of child pornography an offense. If states were encouraged to pass

such minimal child protection laws through withholding federal criminal justice funds until accomplished, such laws would spread like wildfire through the nation. As 55-mph speed limits were promoted by withholding federal transportation monies until passed, child protection laws eliminating child pornography and dramatically reducing child molestation would be promoted.

11. Finally, we must call upon our government leaders to declare prosecution of illegal pornography and sexual exploitation a high priority and implement measures to prove it. The federal investigative agencies (FBI, IRS, Postal Inspector Service, and Customs) must create special strike forces with its best and brightest agents to complement the Justice Department's Child Exploitation and Obscenity Section created in 1987. A national clearing house of investigative, prosecutive, and legislative information must be created, fully funded, and accessible to all levels of government to combat the well-funded pornography defense attorneys and lobby. Federal-state task forces, which have proved to be successful in the past, should be re-emphasized with local, state, and federal officials participating in joint training programs and sharing intelligence information.

We urge our society to rethink its fierce defense of individualism and to reconsider the need to limit the pleasures of adults for the greater good of protecting innocent children, women, and families. As a society, we must exercise greater restraint if we are to preserve individual freedom. Our society is dangerously close to the moral decay that caused the fall of great civilizations of the past and the anarchy and lawlessness that results when everyone does his own thing.

We must address the problem of excessive commercialization of the media in this country. Is the making of money the only criteria for what is fed into our homes and shown on movie screens across the country?

The lucrative pornography industry exists for the sole purpose of making vast amounts of profit on material that appeals to the basest instincts of mankind. The increase in sexual addicts in the last decade indicates we are on a path to slavery to our own lusts. The rising terror of AIDS, other sexual disease epidemics, pregnancies out of wedlock, abortions, and rising divorce rates confirm the destructive influence of this material on our culture. Our right to see and read anything we want in any medium must bow to the greater good of our society.

To expand our consensus and help this become a national priority, we recommend undertaking additional research as detailed in chapter 15 and convening a National Consensus Conference, which would bring together top researchers, mental health professionals, public policy makers, and legislators. Carefully planned and directed, such a conference could be an important step in correcting media abuses.

It has become popular among special interest groups to lobby Hollywood, television executives, Congress, state legislators, and policymakers to present the views of their constituents in the most favorable light. Environmental groups, animal right groups, pro-abortion activists, gay rights advocates, minorities, and radical feminists all have lobbyists who educate people in authority to further their interests. Many of them have opened offices in Hollywood and Washington, DC, and are called upon as consultants to the industry and Congress.

Only recently have pro-family and religious groups begun to lobby for a return to high moral standards. The Religious Alliance Against Pornography, which represents all mainline denominations and almost 150 million people, has been particularly effective on limited measures in Congress and in the executive branch in Washington, DC. Such broad-based coalitions are needed in every state and major city in America.

There are basically three ways that could bring about the reform of the media:

1. The industry could reform itself by accepting an updated version of a voluntary code.

2. Government could regulate the industry by passing strict national standards.

3. A combination of laws against blatant media excesses and strong public opinion could move the industry toward voluntary standards.

Given the present media mindset, the third is the most realistic and should eventually encourage the industry to adopt the first method.

The silent majority who value strong families must learn a lesson from special interest groups who work within the industry and who daily rub elbows with those in the power structure in Washington. When a slur is made in a film against a lesbian or a gay, for example, they go directly to the source and demand that the script be re-written. If they fail, they pour huge amounts of money into expressing their opinions and support well-paid lobbyists to see that it does not happen again.

The cable industry is a special business interest that works 365 days a year for their advantage. In addition to wining and dining Washington, they have multiple high paying lobbyists in every state capital in the country.

Individuals working within the grass roots should encourage the creation of a pro-family coalition, which would become the lobbying arm of the majority of people in this country. That means, at the very least, pulling resources to put a full time lobbyist in Hollywood and Washington. Flying in once or twice a year will not do the job. Such a lobbyist should have had years of experience and be someone who is respected by industry and government officials.

Concerned families need a spokesperson who represents vast numbers of people. The organizations that make up the coalition must lay aside personalities and their needs for raising funds for their own organizations, and unite in fighting for the values that make this country strong.

These lobbyists can take the research reviewed in this book, the research that will proceed from its recommendations in the future, and use it to help media executives, people in Congress, the White House, the Federal Communications Commission, Health and Human Services, and state legislators to understand the depth of the problem and the desperate need for reform.

The economic boycott is another powerful weapon in the war for values. Targets for boycotts must be chosen very carefully. They must be well focused on a problem that is recognized as harmful by large numbers of people. Participants must be motivated enough to be willing to sacrifice convenience to uphold the boycott.

As audiences at the box office dwindle, Cardinal Roger Mahony, the archbishop of Los Angeles, has won attention by calling for voluntary standards. He has challenged the film industry to consider that during the "Golden Age" of Hollywood, 1930 to 1966, the Motion Picture Code of America guided all feature films. "Today," he says,

> the motion picture and television industries too often contribute to the assault against the values held by the vast majority of people in American society. . . . As a result of that assault, we are suffering a breakdown of social morality, public health and public safety in the United States, especially among our young people.[7]

Cardinal Mahony spoke out about the "blurring of the distinction between pornography and what is now considered mainstream entertainment." He pointed out that "adolescents, particularly vulnerable and easily exploited, have come to accept promiscuity as a norm." He has challenged the entertainment industries to accept their responsibilities for the "tragic results" of sex and violence and to "recognize that the time has come for voluntary reform," that the issue is one of "human rights and dignity" rather than "freedom of expression." The basis for the voluntary code, which he recommends, is: "evil must not be glamorized; violence is not the way to solve problems; and there are serious consequences to sexual activity."

Believing that Hollywood could be revitalized by returning to the values on which the country was founded, Theodore Baehr of the Christian Film Commission of Atlanta, Georgia, has joined Cardinal Mahony in calling for a new, voluntary industry code. He promotes a two-pronged strategy: "helping the entertainment industry appreciate the concerns of Christians and helping Christians develop discernment in their viewing habits."[8]

The old code was purely voluntary and had nothing to do with government censorship. The new code suggested by Dr. Baehr is also voluntary and is meant to be used as a guide to Hollywood screen writers and directors who do not understand the family market. It offers moral guidelines to help Hollywood meet the concerns of American families. Without the force of law, it in no way conflicts with a free society.

Dr. Baehr argues that Hollywood has changed homosexual programs at the insistence of 2.5 percent of the population. It is not unreasonable for the 86.5 percent of American people who think of themselves as Christian to ask for equal sensitivity to their concerns. Since 91.5 percent of the Hollywood filmmakers do not attend church or synagogue, they need help in understanding the values of such a large potential audience.[9]

Jack Valenti's reaction that a new code would "torment the Constitution"[10] echoes the cry of censorship by the ACLU in past decades. It strikes fear that the next step after reasonable standards is a totalitarian state because people do not know where to stop once they start making rules.

On the contrary, Hollywood has not known where to stop in breaking down and trampling the rules that served our society well for its first two hundred years. At no time was our country threatened by becoming a totalitarian state when the old code was honored. There is no reason why a more lenient, revised code—which is voluntary—would cause any more of a threat.

While everyone would not agree on where the line should be drawn, a consensus is forming that it must be drawn somewhere. Even some of Hollywood's own would welcome a return to some standards:

> I wish we could go back to the innocent days of television. Looking at some of the current shows, I wonder: how far can we go before the audience is offended and turns off?[11] (David Gerber, CEO of MGM/UA Television Production Group)

When Hollywood was guided by the old motion picture code,

"movie producers recognized the high trust and confidence which was placed in them by the people of the world . . . they recognized their responsibility to the public."[12] Today, to hold their dwindling audiences, movies and television rely on shock, sex, and violence rather than value.

They seem not to have noticed that shock is no longer working and that people are tired of the bleak realism that has dominated media entertainment in recent years. The idealism of fifties entertainment has been derided by many, but there is nothing wrong with entertainment that demonstrates the best of humankind, the best of family life, etc., if it inspires the next generation to higher levels of achievement. The better-than-life women in pornography who have better-than-life responses to men's unsolicited sexual advances, however, create a harmful expectation that encourages men to take what they want by force.

If you believe the present generation is at risk from sexually explicit and violent entertainment, there are, at least, four things you can do to help curb the growing media problem: 1) take control of that dial and implement our suggestions in your own home, 2) let the media know at every opportunity the kind of programming you want and expect, 3) speak with your pocketbook to broadcast and cable networks, video stores, and convenience stores by refusing to do business with them until they remove harmful pornographic material, and 4) share this information with as many other people as possible. We encourage you to take this book to your legislator, a policy maker, a law enforcement officer, a pastor, or a school official. Lend or give it to someone you know in a position of power, to someone who can do something about it in your city or state. Perhaps together we can encourage producers to try to rebuild the trust and confidence that the American people once had in their programming and to once again produce shows that would be welcome in any home at any time.[13]

Notes

Chapter 1 The American Family—At Risk in the 1990s

1. Onalee McGraw (Paper delivered to Eagle Council, St. Louis, Mo., September, 1992).

2. Margaret S. Andreasen, "Patterns of Family Life and Television Consumption from 1945 to 1990",(Paper delivered at the National Family Foundation Media Workshop, Pittsburgh, PA, November, 1990.)

3. T. Hine, *Populuxe*, (New York: Alfred A. Knopf, Inc.) as cited in Andreasen, "Patterns of Family Life."

4. Andreasen, "Patterns of Family Life."

5. Yankovich, Skelly and White, Inc., *The General Mills American Family Report 1976-77: Raising Children in a Changing Society* (Minneapolis: General Mills, Inc., 1977) as cited in Andreasen, "Patterns of Family Life."

6. Andreasen, "Patterns of Family Life."

7. Hine, *Populuxe*, 177.

8. Andreasen, "Patterns of Family Life."

9. *Children's Well-Being: An International Comparison* U.S. Department of Commerce, Bureau of the Census (November 1989).

10. Lori Darvas, "The Aids Tale," *Naples Daily News*, 4 June 1992.

11. Norvel Glenn, *Retreat from Marriage*, Rockford Institute.

12. Deborah A. Dawson, "Family Structure and Children's Health and Well-Being," *Journal of Marriage and the Family*, 53 (August 1991): 573-584.

13. N. Zill & C. Schoenborn, "Developmental, Learning, and Emotional Problems, Health of our Nation's Children," National Center for Health Statistics, Advance Data, Number 190 (16 November 1990):1-9.

14. Ibid.

15. Ibid.

16. U.S. Bureau of the Census, Marital Status and Living Arrangements: March 1990, Current Population Reports, Series P. 20, No. 450.

17. Zill & Schoenborn, "Health of our Nation's Children."

18. Patrick S. Fagan, "Family Policy, Media and the Formation of Character" (Paper delivered at the National Family Foundation Media Workshop, Pittsburgh, PA, November 1990).

19. *Washington Watch*, Family Research Council, Washington, D.C., February 1991.

20. AP, *Washington Times*, 13 January 1991, A-3 as reported in *Eagle Forum News and Notes*, 1 February 1991.

21. *Washington Watch*, Family Research Council, Washington, D.C., February 1991.

22. Barbara Vobejda, *Washington Post* 20 January 1991 as reported in *Eagle Forum News and Notes*, 1 February 1991.

23. National Center for Home Schoolers, Washington, D. C.

24. Dolf Zillmann, "Erotica and Family Values." (Paper delivered at the NFF Media Workshop, Pittsburgh, PA, November 1990).

25. L. White, "Freedom Versus Constraint," *Journal of Family Issues*, 8,

pp. 468-470, as cited in Zillmann, "Erotica and Family Values."

26. Zillmann, "Erotica and Family Values."

27. *U.S.A. Today* (29 July 1987).

28. Zillmann, "Erotica and Family Values."

29. Donald B. Rinsley, "25 Years—What's Happened to America," (Paper delivered to National Family Foundation, 9 November 1987.

30. Ibid.

31. Ibid.

32. The comments on child development in this section and the next two sections were taken from the initial Core Group meetings of the National Family Foundation. Many of the thoughts came from the late Donald B. Rinsley, M.D. and Dr. Charles Ashbach.

33. Chuck Colson, Address entitled "Ethics" presented to the Harvard Business School (4 April 1991).

34. Ann Rule *The Stranger Beside Me*, (New American Library, 1980).

Chapter 2 Right Media, Wrong Message

1. Media Comparisons, Bruskin Associates, 1990.

2. Television Brings It All Home, a brochure of the Television Bureau of Advertising, Inc., New York.

3. Quoted in the February 1991 issue of *World Monitor* in a letter to the editor by William P. Weber.

4. Larry Woiwode, "Television: The Cyclops That Eats Books," *Imprimis* Vol. 21, No. 2 (Hillsdale College, Michigan, February 1992).

5. J. Philippe Rushton, "Effects of Prosocial Television and Film Material on the Behavior of Viewers." In L. Berkowitz (Ed.), *Advances in Experimental Social Psychology*, vol 12., (New York: Academic Press, Inc., 1979).

6. Ibid.

7. Ibid.

8. "Why We Use Television," The American Association of Advertising Agencies brochure.

9. *Broadcasting* Washington, D. C., 4 July 1988.

10. "Why We Use Television."

11. Ibid.

12. Ibid.

13. Robert Kubey," Media Use and its Implications for the Quality of Family Life" (Paper delivered at the NFF Media Workshop, November 1990).

14. James Quello, "The Public Outcry: A Plea or a Warning? (Paper delivered at the Morality in Media Annual Rally, Naples, FL, 20 January 1992).

15. R. W. Winett, "Prosocial Television: Effective Elements, Barriers to Broadcasting." *Information and Behavior; Systems of Influence*_(Hillsdale, N.J.: Lawrence Erlbaum Associates, Inc., 1986).

16. Brad Curl, Press Release (11 March, 1992).

17. Discussion, NFF Media Workshop (1990).

18. James Brooks Interview by *The Door*.

19. Discussion, NFF Media Workshop (1990).

20. Ibid.

21. Kubey, "Media Use."

22. David B. Larson, M.D., M.S.P.H. and John S. Lyons, "Religion In Media and Academia: Similarities and Differences" (Paper delivered at NFF Media Workshop, November 1990). Data from psychiatrists published in the *American Journal of Psychiatry*.

23. Michael Medved, *Hollywood vs. America, Popular Culture and the War on Traditional Values* (Harper Collins and Zondervan, in press).

24. Ibid.

25. Michael Medved (Paper delivered at Eagle Council, St. Louis, MO, 28 September 1991.

26. Richard Grenier, "Hollywood's Foreign Policy," *The National Interest* (Summer 1991):67-77.

27. Linda S. Lichter, Robert Lichter, and Stanley Rothman's 1982 Study of the Attitudes of Hollywood's TV Elite as summarized in *AFA Journal*, (February 1989):11.

28. James Brooks Interview by *The Door*.

29. Statistical Abstract of the United States, No. 1002 (1980): 590.

30. Radio Advertising Bureau Radio Facts for Advertisers (1989-90).

31. Fall 1991 Neilson Television Information, *Media News*, January 1992.

32. "Wired Bedroom" 1; P. Christenson and P. De Benedittis, "Eavesdropping on the FM Band," 36, Journal of Commerce (Spring, 1986):27,30.

33. Salem Comments, 70.

34. Nielson Television Information, *Broadcasting*, February 1992.

35. Marie Winn, "The VCR, A New and Important Baby Sitter?" *The New York Times* Vol. 6 (27 August, 1989): 29.

36. *Report*, 5 FCC Red. at 5305, para. 64.

37. From a 36-page concurring opinion by Circuit Judge Baldock to Wilkinson V. Community Television, No. 85-2157, 10th Circuit Court of Appeals (8 September 1986).

38. Steve Kuykendall column, *Arkansas Democrat Gazette* November 1991.

39. Douglas Reed, Summary presentation at the NFF Workshop (November 1990).

40. Harold Voth, "The Effects of Media on Family Values," (Paper delivered at the NFF Media Workshop, November 1990).

41. Ibid.

42. Thomas Skill, "Family Images and Family Actions as Presented in the Media: Where We've been and What We've Found" (Paper delivered at the NFF Media Workshop, Nov. 1990).

43. Richard Zoglin, "Home Is Where the Venom Is," *Time* magazine, (16 April 1990).

44. Larson and Lyons, "Religion In Media."

45. "Big World, Small Screen: The Role of Television in American Society," *American Psychological Association Report* (University of Nebraska Press, 25 February 1992).

Chapter 3 Media Effects on Personality, Perceptions, and Judgment

1. Andrew N. Meltzoff "Imitation of Televised Models by Infants," *Child Development*, Number 5 (1988): 1121-1229.

2. Lyle & Huffan study (1982) as cited in Meltzoff above.

3. Harold Voth, M.D., "The Effects of Media on Family Values," (Paper delivered at the National Family Foundation Media Workshop, Pittsburgh, PA, November 1990).

4. Ibid.

5. Steiner, 1963, as cited in Meltzoff, "Imitation of Televised Models."

6. Charles Ashbach, " The Inner Image and the Outer World: Media Influences and Personality Development" (Paper delivered at the NFF Media

Workshop, Pittsburgh, PA, November, 1990). The ideas in this section were taken from this paper.

7. Ashbach, "The Inner Image." The ideas on the development of inner images and personality were all taken from Dr. Ashbach's paper unless otherwise noted.

8. Ismond Rosen, M.D., *Sexual Deviation* (Oxford: Oxford University Press, 1979).

9. Andre Derdeyn, M.D., Discussion, NFF Media Workshop (1990).

10. Ashbach, The Inner Image." The ideas in this section are taken from this paper unless otherwise noted.

11. B. Ginsburg and S. Oppen, *Piaget's Theory of Intellectual Development* (2nd ed. New Jersey: Prentice-Hall, 1979).

12. Hayton, "The Effects of Indecent Broadcast Programming on Children," (Paper delivered to the NFF Media Workshop, Pittsburgh, PA, November 1990). All the ideas in this section are taken from this paper.

13. Morison and Gardner, "Dragons and dinosaurs: The child's capacity to differentiate fantasy from reality," *Child Development* 49 (1978):642-648.

14. C. Lewis, "Disturbed Attitudes Reinforced," *Dallas Morning News*, (5 May, 1988).

15. Ashbach, "The Inner Image," The ideas in this section are taken from this paper unless otherwise noted.

16. Hayton, "Effects of Indecent Broadcast."

17. Ibid.

18. Ashbach, "The Inner Image."

19. Ibid.

20. Melvin Anchell, M.D., *Sex and Insanity* (Portland Oregon: Halcyon House, 1983),128-129.

21. Ashbach, "The Inner Image."

22. Andre Derdeyn, M.D. and Jeffrey M. Turley, M.D, "Television, Films and the Emotional Life of Children" (Paper delivered at the NFF Media Workshop, Pittsburgh, PA, November, 1990).

23. Ashbach, "The Inner Image."

24. Hayton, "Effects of Indecent Broadcast."

25. Charles Ashbach, "Public Images and Private Resentments: Advertising, Envy and Self-esteem" (Paper delivered at the NFF Media Workshop, Pittsburgh, PA, November 1990) The ideas in the section on fantasy-based advertising were taken from Dr. Ashbach's paper unless otherwise noted.

26. Ibid.

Chapter 4 Sexual Trends in the Media

1. Robert Kubey. "Media Use and Its Implications for the Quality of Family Life" (Paper delivered at the NFF Media Workshop. Nov. 1990).

2. Ibid.

3. E.J. Roberts, "Television and Sexual Learning in Childhood." in D. Pearl, L. Bouthiler, and J. Lazar (eds.), Television and Behavior: Then Years of Scientific Progress and Implications for the Eighties, (Washington, D.C.: U.S. Government Printing Office, 1982).

4. Bradley S. Greenberg, "Content Trends In Media Sex" (Paper delivered at the National Family Foundation Media Workshop, Pittsburgh, PA, November 1990).

5. Bradley S. Greenberg et al., "Sex Content on soaps and primetime television series most viewed by adolescents" Report No. 2 (East Lansing: Michigan State University, Department of Telecommunication, 1986).

6. Ibid., Content "Trends In Media Sex."

7. Ibid.

8. Ibid.

9. J. Reisman, "Images of Children, Crime and Violence in Playboy, Penthouse and Hustler Magazines," Executive Summary 8 (1987) (Available at the Office of Juvenile Justice and Delinquency Prevention, U.S. Department of Justice.)

10. N. M. Malamuth and B. Spinner, "A longitudinal content analysis of sexual violence in the best-selling erotic magazines," *Sex Research* 16(3) (1980):226-237.

11. J. E. Scott, "An updated longitudinal content analysis of sex references in mass circulation magazines" *Journal of Sex Research.* 22(3) (1986):385-392.

12. Bradley S. Greenberg et al., "Sex content in R-rated films viewed by adolescents," Report No. 3 (East Lansing: Michigan State University, Department of Telecommunication, 1986).

13. Ibid.

14. Ibid.

15. Greenberg, Discussion, NFF Media Workshop (Pittsburgh, November, 1990). Hereafter Discussion.

16. Greenberg, "Content Trends in Media Sex."

17. R. L. Baxter et al., "A Content Analysis of Music Videos," *Journal of Broadcasting and Electronic Media,* 29 (3) (1985):333-340. "31 percent of the videos with sex content featured provocative clothing, 31 percent showed embraces, 27 percent contained dance movements that were sexually suggestive, 21 percent nondance movements that were sexually suggestive, 15 percent dating or courting, 11 percent kissing, 11 percent a male chasing a female or the opposite, and in 8 percent someone used a musical instrument, typically a guitar, in a sexual manner."

18. B. L. Sherman and J. R. Dominick, "Violence and sex in music videos: TV and rock 'n' roll," *Journal of Communication* 36(1) (1986):79-93.

19. Ibid.

20. Greenberg, Discussion.

21. Greenberg, Press Release, 8 November 1990.

22. J. Massey, *Report on Presidential Commission on Obscenity and Pornography* (1970).

23. D. D. Smith, "The social content of pornography," *Journal of Communication,* 26 (1) (1976):16-24.

24. G. Cowan et al., "Dominance and inequality in X-rated videocassettes," *Psychology of Women Quarterly,* 12 (1988):299-311.

25. Ibid.

26. T.S. Palys, "Testing the common wisdom: The social content of video pornography," *Canadian Psychology,* 27 (1) (1986):22-35.

27. Ibid.

28. Attorney General's Organized Crime Report in California, 7 (1986).

29. Ibid.

30. *AGCOP Final Report,* 73-76; Minnery, *Pornography: A Human Tragedy* (1986):34-35, P. Dietz & A. Sears, "*Pornography and Obscenity Sold in "Adult Bookstores",* Journal of Law Reform* (1988):21.

31. C. A. Winick, "A Study of Consumers of Explicitly Sexual Materials," *Technical Reports of the Commission on Obscenity and Pornography,* Vol. 4 (Washington, D. C.: United States Government Printing Office, 1971):225-262.

32. B. J. Lebeque, "Paraphilias in Pornography," *Australian Journal of Sex, Marriage and Family* 6(1) (1985):33-36.

33. Greenberg, "Content Trends in Media Sex,"

34. Judith Reisman, Discussion.

35. Ibid.

36. Jennings Bryant, Discussion.

37. Greenberg, Discussion.

38. George Will, "America's Slide Into the Sewer," *Newsweek,* 30 july 1990.

39. Stuart Elliott, "Has Madison Avenue Gone Too Far?" *New York Times,* 15 December 1991: Section 3,1.

40. Ibid.

41. Ibid.

42. Melvin Anchell, M.D., *Sex and Insanity* (Portland Oregon: Halcyon House, 1983),79.

Chapter 5 Pornography—A Research Case for Harm

1. Report of the Commission on Obscenity and Pornography, (1970):239-240 (Available at U.S. Government Printing Office, Work Order).

2. *Report of Attorney General's Commission on Pornography* (Rutledge Hill Press, 1986) 40-47.

3. E. Kanim, *Date Rapist,* 14 Archives of Sexual Behavior (1985):219-231.

4. Dr. James Mason, Assistant Secretary of Health, Address to the Religious Alliance Against Pornography (26 October 1989) (hereafter Dr. Mason's Speech).

5. Pornography and Public Health, Surgeon General's 1986 Workshop (republished conclusions, its findings (15 December 1989). All five conclusions are taken directly from this document and Dr. Mason's speech, which is the introduction in this 1989 republication. See also D. Byrne and K. Kelly, "Psychological Research and Public Policy" in E.P. Mulvery's Report of the Surgeon General's Workshop on Pornography and Public Health (Washington, D.C. 1986).

6. Ibid., 2.

7. See American Psychological Association, *Psychlit Data Base on Sex and Violence in the Media* (June 1990); Gang & Gang, "Sex and Violence in Adult Videos," 40(2) *Journal of Commerce* (1990):28-42; D. Zillmann and J. Bryant, *Pornography: Research Advances and Policy Considerations,* (Hillsdale, New Jersey: Lawrence Erlbaum Associates, 1989).

8. J. Weaver, "Pornography and Men's Sexual Callousness Toward Women," *Pornography: Research Advances and Policy Considerations* (Hillsdale, New Jersey: Lawrence Erlbaum Associates, 1989):95-125.

9. Report of Surgeon General (1989 republication):3.

10. Surveys, content reviews, and studies with unspecified stimuli were excluded because they were interested primarily in the scientifically valid data about cause effects.

11. J. Lyons and D. Larson, "A Systematic Analysis of the Social Science Research on the Effects of Violent and Non-Violent Pornography" (in publication 1992) (Paper delivered at the National Family Foundation Media Workshop, Pittsburgh, PA, November 1990).

12. Ibid.

13. Ibid.

14 See D. Galin, "Educating Both Halves of the Brain," 53 *Childhood Education* (1976):17. (Visual data, whether good or bad, true or false, appears to be processed as "truth" immediately, forcefully and with some degree of permanence, while completely print media is processed feebly, or in some cases not at all).

15 Lyons and Larson, "A Systematic Analysis." Twenty-seven studies containing aggressive sexual stimuli and 30 studies containing nonaggressive stimuli (70 percent in all) showed clear evidence of positive effects while an

additional 10 studies (12 percent) showed positive but somewhat mixed results, described as "an effect immediately after exposure that dissipated over time."

16 Check and Malamuth (1983); Malamuth & Check (1980).

17 Zillmann & Bryant (1982); Linz, Donnerstein & Penrod, (1984): Malamuth, Haker, & Feshbach (1980); Mayerson & Taylor (1987).

18 Donnerstein (1980); Donnerstein & Berkowitz (1981).

19 Malamuth & Check (1980).

20 Baxter, Barbaree & Marshall (1986); Wydra, Marshall, Earls & Barbaree, (1983).

21 Ibid.

22 Ibid.

23 D. Zillmann, "Effects of Prolonged Consumption of Pornography," D. Zillmann and J. Bryant (eds) *Pornography: Research Advances & Policy Considerations* (Hillsdale, New Jersey: Lawrence Erlbaum Associates, 1989):147-151.

24 Ibid, 149. Figure reprinted with permission.

25 Ibid, 150.

26 J. V. P. Check and Ted H. Guloien, "Reported Proclivity for Coercive Sex Following Repeated Exposure to Sexually Violent Pornography, Nonviolent Dehumanizing Pornography, and Erotica," Zillmann & Bryant (eds) Pornography, 178.

27 Ibid., 179.

28 Judith A. Reisman, "Impact of Peer-Approved Research on Sex Industry Self-Censorship" (A paper written for but not presented at the NFF Media Workshop (November 1990).

Chapter 6 *Children and Pornography: A Deadly Combination*

1. Attorney General's Commission on Pornography, Washington,D.C. Hearing, June 1985, Vol 1, 180 (Hereafter AGCOP).

2. AGCOP, Chicago Hearing, July 1985, Vol. II, 95.

3. AGCOP, Miami Hearing, November 1985, Vol II, 20-21.

4. James Dobson, *Children At Risk* (Dallas: Word Publishing, 1990),3.

5. P. C. Glick, "Fifty years of Family Demography, A Period of Social Change," 50 (4) *Journal of Marriage and the Family* (1988):861-873.

6. U. S. Bureau of the Census, 1950-1988.

7. Ibid.

8. *American Family Under Siege* (1989),7-8.

9. National Center of Child Abuse and Neglect, Children's Bureau, U.S. Department of Health and Human Service, *Study of National Incidence and Prevalence on Child Abuse and Neglect* (1988),(NIS-2).

10. D. Campagna and D. Puffenberger, *The Sexual Trafficking in Children*, 1988.

11. David Finkelhor, U.S. Dept. Network News (Fall edition, 1985).

12. Texas Citizen's Report, December 1991.

13. Canadian Study by John Check (1985) in *Pornography: Research Advances* eds. Zillmann and Bryant, 49.

14. Recent survey in Anderson, Indiana.

15. Judith Reisman, "The Impact of One Content Analysis Study on Self-Censorship of Child Pornography and Rape Imagery by *Playboy*, *Penthouse* and *Hustler* Post 1984" (Paper delivered at the NFF Media Workshop, November 1990).

16. Judith Reisman, *"Soft Porn" Plays Hardball* (Lafayette, LA: Huntington House, 1991).

17. Judith Reisman (Presentation before the Attorney General's Commission on Pornography, Miami; *Playboy,* March 1978, p. 231; *Penthouse,* May 1984, 137.

18. Reisman, *"Soft Porn" Plays Hardball,* 114.

19. AP Release *The Modesto Bee,* Modesto, CA, May 1989.

20. Reisman, "The Impact of One Content Analysis."

21. Ibid.

22. Baron & Straus, "Sexual Stratification, Pornography and Rape in American States" (1983).

23. *AGCOP Report* (July 1986):405.

24. See 18 USC Section 2256 (1990). For a complete analysis summary of every state's laws against child sexual exploitation and pornography, see R. Showers, Child Sexual Exploitation and Pornography Reference Manual, 1, Appendix, National Center for Missing and Exploited Children, 1992.

25. See Kenneth Lanning, *Child Molesters: A Behavioral Analysis* (second ed., 1987), 18-19.

26. New York v. Ferber, 458 US 747 (1982): 759, n. 10.

27. Lanning, *Child Molesters,* 18.

28. William Marshall, *Report on the Use of Pornography by Sexual Offenders,* Report to the Federal Department of Justice, Ottawa Canada, 1983. See also W. Marshall, "Use of Sexually Explicit Stimuli by Rapists, Child Molesters and Non-Offenders," 25 *Journal of Sex Research* (1988): 267-288.

29. Personal conversation with Judge Gene Malpas, now working at the National Obscenity Law Center, Washington, D.C.

30. Marshall, "Report on the Use of Pornography."

31. U.S. Senate, Permanent Subcommittee on Investigations of the Committee on Governmental Affairs, *Child Pornography and Pedophilia,* 99th Congress, 1st Sess. (1986): 46 (Available at the U.S. Government Printing Office, Washington, D.C).

32. Ibid, 17-18.

33. J. Reisman, "Images of Children, Crime and Violence In *Playboy, Penthouse* and *Hustler* Magazines," Executive Summary (1987),8 (Available at the Office of Juvenile Justice and Delinquency Prevention, United States Department of Justice).

34. S. O'Brien, *Child Pornography* (1983),89-90; See Also Commission on Pornography, 138.

35. *The Effects of Pornography on Children and Women,* Hearings before the Subcommittee of Juvenile Justice, Committee on the Judiciary U. S. Senate (testimony of John Rabun, for the National Center for Missing and Exploited Children, 12 September 1984).

36. Lanning, *Child Molesters, 1-8;* See also M. Hertica, *Interviewing Sex Offenders,* The Police Chief (February 1991),30-41.

37. R. Bennett, The Relationship Between Pornography and Extrafamilial Child Sexual Abuse, The Police Chief, Feb. 1991, pp. 14, 19.

38. H. Davidson and G. Loken, *Child Pornography and Prostitution* 2-3 (National Center for Missing and Exploited Children 1987) (hereafter *Child Pornography); Child Pornography and Pedophilia,* 100-101.

39. Lanning, *Child Molesters,* v-vi.

40. U.S. Senate, Permanent Subcommittee on Investigations of the Committee on Governmental Affairs, *Child Pornography and Pedophilia,* 99th Congress, 1st Sess., 1986): 52-53.

41. Carter, *Use of Pornography In the Criminal and Developmental Histo-*

ries of Sexual Offenders, Report to the National Institute of Justice and National Institute of Mental Health, 1985, hereafter, *Use of Pornography*; see also *Surgeon General's Report*, 13.

42. G. Abel, *Sexual Aggressive Behavior*, 1986.

43. *Ferber*, 458 U.S., 758 n. 9.

44. J. MacDonald, *Rape Offenders and Their Victims* (1971), 120-145: Halleck, "Emotional Effects of Victimization," ed., R. Slovenko *Sexual Behavior and the Law (1986);* 684 J. Landis, "Experience of 500 children with adult sexual deviation," 30 *Psychiatric Quarterly* (1956): 100-103.

45. Prager, "Sexual Psychopathy and Child Molesters: The Experiment Fails," (1982): 49,62, *Journal of Juvenile Law,* Cerkovnik, "The Sexual Abuse of Children: Myths, Research, and Policy Implications," *Dickinson Law Review* (1985): 691-719.

46. S. O'Brien, *Child Abuse: A Crying Shame*, (1980), 18.

47. See D. Finkelhor, *Child Sexual Abuse: New Theory and Research* (1984), 47.

48. American Psychiatric Association, *Diagnostic and Statistical Manual of Mental Disorders*, 3rd ed. (1980), 271.

49. *AGCOP Report* (July 1986), 505.

50. G. Loken, "Juvenile Prostitution in America Today," in *Child Pornography and Prostitution* (National Center for Missing and Exploited Children, 1987), 51.

51. Davidson and Loken, Child Pornography and Prostitution

52. G. Loken, "Juvenile Prostitution," 52.

53. T. Davis Bunn, address to Morality in Media, Naples, FL (3 January 1992).

54. D.K. Weisburg, *Children of the Night: A Study of Adolescent Prostitution* (1985), 44-45 (64 percent males from broken homes); S. Harlan et al, *Male and Female Adolescent Prostitution* (1981), 11-16 (70 percent males and females from broken homes); Enablers, Inc. *Juvenile Prostitution in Minnesota* (1981), p. 22 (67 percent females from broken homes).

55. Harlan, *Male and Female*, 12, 18, 19, 21; Enablers, *Juvenile Prostitution*, 22; Weisburg, *Children of the Night*, 46-50; See also Loken, "Juvenile Prostitution," 32.

56. Badgley Report, 1198.

57. J. Scanlon and Price, Youth Prostitution in Child Sex Rings, 139.

58. J. Bryant, "Frequency of exposure, age of initial exposure, and reactions to initial exposure to pornography" (Testimony and Report before the AGCOP, Houston, Texas, March 1986).

59. Jennings Bryant and Don Brown, "Uses of Pornography", *Pornography: Research Advances and Policy Considerations*, eds. Dolf Zillmann and Jennings Bryant (Hillsdale, N.J.: Lawrence Erlbaum Associates 1989):45-47.

60. Aaron Hass, *Teenage Sexuality* (New York: Macmillan, 1979).

61. *AGCOP Report* July 1986, 42-44.

62. R. Hazelwood, "The Men Who Murdered," *FBI Law Enforcement Bulletin* (August 1985).

63. Report to the Michigan Legislature "Sexual Offenses by Youth of Michigan." (Safer Society Resources of Michigan: Detroit, 1988), Executive Summary.

64. Summary of Broadcasting and Cable, *Broadcasting* (8 January 1990):26.

65. Tipper Gore, "Hate, Rape and Rap," *Washington Post*, Jan. 8, 1990.

66. "Teenagers and Sex Crimes," *Time*, 5 June 1989, 60.

67. "Sexual Abuse by Adolescents on an Upswing," Deseret News, Salt Lake City, 4 April 1989, p. B1.

68. John Whitehead, *Stealing of America* (1983), 68.

69. Marie Winn, "The VCR, A New and Important Baby Sitter?" *New York Times*, vol 6, 27 August 1989,29.

70. Report of Enforcement of Prohibitions Against Broadcast Indecency 5 FCC, 18 USC Sec 1464, 5305, para 64, 1990.

71. Personal communication from one of the mothers involved.

72. Dr. Douglas Reed, Discussion at the NFF Media Workshop, November 1990.

73. Victor Cline, "Pornography Effects: Empirical & Clinical Evidence" (Paper delivered at the NFF Media Workshop, Pittsburgh, November 1990).

74. Robert Kubey, Discussion NFF Media Workshop.

Chapter 7 Women and Pornography

1. Andrea Dworkin testimony, *Final Report of the Attorney General's Commission on Pornography* (Nashville, TN: Rutledge Hill Press, 1986), 198-199, hereafter "AGCOP."

2. Tamar Lewin, "Canada Court Says Pornography Harms Women and Can Be Barred," *New York Times*, (28 February 1992): Al, B9.

3. Ibid.

4. Ibid.

5. Judge Frank H. Easterbrook of the United States Court of Appeals for the Seventh Circuit in Lewin, *New York Times* (28 February 1992).

6. John Elson, "Passions over Pornography," *Time* (30 March 1992),52.

7. Ted Bundy's videotaped interview with Dr. James Dobson the evening before his death.

8. Washington Watch, Vol 1, No. 8 (Family Research Council, May 1990); Personal letter from Senator Connie Mack (23 April 1990).

9. Summary of the Pornography Victims Compensation Act of 1989 (22 June 1989).

10. Illinois Commission on the Status of Women Report and Recommendations (February 1985).

11. Howard, Reifler and Liptzin (1971); Ceniti and Malamuth, (1984) as cited in James Weaver, "Understanding the Perceptual and Behavioral Consequences of Exposure to Pornography" (Paper delivered at the National Family Foundation Media Workshop, Pittsburgh, PA, November 1990) hereafter cited as "Consequences." Most of the research summaries and conclusions in this chapter are taken from this paper unless otherwise noted.

12. Brown et al (1973); Brown (1979); Kelly and Musialowski, (1986) in Weaver, "Consequences."

13. *New York Times* (4 February 1985).

14. Weaver, Masland and Zillmann (1984) as cited in Weaver, "Consequences."

15. Testimony of a woman caught in the nightmare of pornography from interviews on the "Montel Williams Show" and the "Phil Donahue Show."

16. Personal conversation.

17. From testimonies of women whose men are obsessed with pornography.

18. Gail Stevenson, "Tolerance of Porn Traumatizes Women," *Los Angeles Times* (28 May 1985) Part II, 5.

19. Victor Cline, "Pornography Effects: Empirical and Clinical Evidence" (Paper delivered at the National Family Foundation Media Workshop, Pittsburgh, PA, November 1990).

20. Doth Zillmann and Jane Weaver, "Pornography and Men's Sexual Callousness toward Women" N.D. Zillmann and J. Bryant (eds.) *Pornography Research Advisors and Policy Consideration* (Hillsdale N.J.: Lawerence Erlbaum

Associates 1989), 107.

21. Ibid, 108.

22. Ibid, 112.

23. Ibid, 114.

24. Ibid, 119.

25. A. Garry, "Pornography and Respect for Women," Social Theory and Practice, 4, 408 as quoted in Zillmann, *Pornography Research.*

26. Zillmann, *Pornography Research,* 120-121.

27. John Elson, "Passions over Pornography," *Time* (30 March 1992) 52.

28. "AGCOP," 220.

29. Elson, "Passions over Pornography," 52.

30. Ibid.

31. Zillmann, *Pornography Research,* 99.

32. Burt (1980) as cited in Weaver, "Consequences."

33. Palys (1984, 1986) as cited in Weaver, "Consequences."

34. Weaver, "Consequences."

35. McKenzie-Mahr and Zanna (1990) as cited in Weaver, "Consequences."

36. Leonard and Taylor (1983) as cited in Weaver, "Consequences."

37. Donnerstein and Berkowitz (1981) as cited in Weaver, "Consequences".

38. Koss (1987) as cited in Douglas Reed, "Pornography's Relationship to Rape and Aggression Toward Women" (Cincinnati, Ohio: National Coalition Against Pornography, 1989) Hereafter "Relationship to Rape."

39. Russell (1975, 1984) as cited in Reed, "Relationship to Rape."

40. Michael Clay Smith, "Coping with Crime on Campus, "American Council on Education/Macmillan Series on Higher Education (1988) as cited in Reed, "Relationship to Rape."

41. Russell (1984); Koss (1987) as cited in Reed, "Relationship to Rape."

42. Kanin, 1969; Mosher, 1971; Koss and Oros, 1982 as cited in Reed, "Relationship to Rape."

43. Rapaport and Burkhart (1984) in Reed, "Relationship to Rape."

44. Mary Koss as quoted in *Northeast Mississippi Daily Journal* (19 April 1989).

45. Briere (1987); Costin (1985); Kanin (1969, 1985); Koss, Leonard, Beezley, and Oros (1985); Rapaport and Burkhart (1984) in Weaver, "Consequences."

46. Zillmann and Weaver (1989) as cited in Weaver, "Consequences."

47. John Court, "Pornography and Sex Crimes," *International Journal of Criminology and Penology,* 5 (1977):129-157 as quoted in Cline, "Pornography Effects."

48. Kutschinsky, "Toward an Explanation of the Decrease in Registered Sex Crimes in Copenhagen," *Technical Report of Commission on Obscenity and Pornography,* Vol. VII (Washington, D.C., U.S. Government Printing Office, 1971) as reported in Cline, "Pornography Effects."

49. Groth (1979) as quoted in Zillmann, *Pornography Research,* 98.

50. *Newsweek* (23 July 1990), 51-52.

51. John Court, "Sex and Violence: A Ripple Effect," N. M. Malamuth and E. Donnerstein (eds.) *Pornography and Sexual Aggression* (Orlando, Florida: Academic Press, 1984):143-172.

52. J. E. Scott and L. A. Schwalm, "Rape Rates and the Circulation of Adult Magazines," *Journal of Sex Research, 24* (1988): 241-250.

53. L. Baron and M. A. Straus, "Sexual Stratification, Pornography, and Rape in the United States," N. M. Malamuth and E. Donnerstein (eds.) *Pornography and Sexual Aggression* (Orlando, Florida: Academic Press, 1984), 185-209.

54. Katha Pollitt, "Georgie Porgie Is a Bully," *Time* (Fall 1990),24.

55. National Crime Statistics reported by the Florida Department of Law Enforcement in Bill Graf Column, *Daily Commercial* (Lake County, FL, 3 November 1991).

56. National Crime Survey, U.S. Department of Justice as cited in Reed, "Relationship to Rape."

57. AP Release, *Naples Daily News* (23 November 1991).

58. 1991 Uniform Crime Reports, Law Enforcement and Crime (August, 1991):824-825.

59. National Women's Study, *Rape in America* 1-2 (National Victim Center, 23 April 1992). Forcible rape was very conservatively denied as an event that occurred without the women's consent, involved the use of force or threat of force and involved sexual penetration of the victim's vagina, mouth, or rectum.

60. Ibid., 2-3.

61. Ibid., 12.

62. Ibid., 8.

63. FBI Uniform Crime Report (1984) in Reed, "Relationship to Rape,"

64. Rape in America, 2-3.

65. Rape in America, 7-8.

66. Ibid.

67. Beth Knake, Director of Project Help in Naples, FL as quoted in Lori Davis, "Self-esteem Is the First Thing To Go," *Naples Daily News* (7 November 1990).

68. Silbert and Pines (1984) as cited in Weaver, "Consequences."

69. *Newsweek* (18 March 1985).

70. Goldstein (1980) as cited in Reed, "Relationship to Rape."

71. Marshall, (1983) as cited in Reed, "Relationship to Rape."

72. Malamuth (1981); Kass (1986) as cited in Reed," Relationship to Rape."

73. Surgeon General C. Everett Koop, M.D. as quoted in Reed, "Relationship to Rape."

Chapter 8 Pornography and Family Values

1. Judith Reisman, *Soft-porn Plays Hardball* (Lafayette, Louisiana: Huntington House, 1991),75.

2. Judith Reisman, "The Impact of One Content Analysis Study on Self-Censorship of Child Pornography and Rape Imagery by Playboy, Penthouse and Hustler Post 1984" (Paper delivered at the National Family Foundation Media Workshop, Pittsburgh, PA, November 1990).

3. Dolf Zillmann, "Erotica and Family Values" (Paper delivered at the NFF Media Workshop, Pittsburgh, PA, November 1990). The ideas in this chapter, unless otherwise noted, are taken from this presentation.

4. Cherlin, (1981); Rodgers and Thornton, (1985), U.S. Bureau of Census, (1987) as cited in Zillmann, "Erotica and Family Values."

5. Weitzman (1985), as cited in Zillmann, "Erotica and Family Values."

6. Thornton, (1988); Thornton & Freedman (1982), as cited in Zillmann, "Erotica and Family Values."

7. Finkelhor, (1986); Gelles (1974); Gil (1973), as cited in Zillmann, "Erotica and Family Values."

8. White, (1987) as cited in Zillmann, "Erotica and Family Values."

9. Pagelow, (1984); Shupe, Stacey, and Hazlewood (1987), as cited in Zillmann, "Erotica and Family Values."

10. Dobash and Dobash (1979), Dutton (1987); Gelles (1979), as cited in Zillmann, "Erotica and Family Values."

11. James Weaver, "Understanding the Perceptual and Behavioral Consequences of Exposure to Pornography (Paper delivered at the NFF Media Workshop, November 1990).

12. Dolf Zillmann and Jennings Bryant, "Effects of prolonged consumption of pornography on family values," *Journal of Family Issues,* 9 (4) (1988):521.

13. Brosius, Staab, and Weaver (1990); Palys (1844), as cited in Zillmann, "Erotica and Family Values."

14. Zillmann, "Erotica and Family Values."

15. Thornton (1989):873 as quoted in Zillmann, "Erotica and Family Values".

16. Bergman (1982) as cited in Douglas Reed, "Pornography's Relationship to Abnormal Sexual Behavior/Sexual Offenders" (1989).

17. Zillmann and Bryant (1989).

18. Howard, Reifler, and Liptzin (1971) as cited in Zillmann, "Erotica and Family Values."

19. Zillmann and Bryant (1982), as cited in Zillmann, "Erotica and Family Values."

20. Dolf Zillmann "Perceptual and Dispositional Consequences of Pornography Consumption," p. 3.

21. Phyllis Schlafly column, 14 June, 1984.

22. Ibid.

23. Finkelhor and Yllo (1985) as reported in Douglas Reed, "Pornography's Relation to Rape and Aggression Toward Women," (1989).

24. Russell (1982) and Finkelhor and Yllo (1985) as reported in Douglas Reed, "Pornography's Relationship to Rape," (National Coalition Against Pornography, 1989).

25. Edward Donnerstein, *Journal of Communication* (Summer 1984).

26. "Erotic Encounters," *Penthouse,* May 1984.

27. James Dobson and Gary Bauer, *Children at Risk* (Word Publishing, 1990),6-7.

Chapter 9 Pornography Addiction: Key to the Pornography Explosion

1. Stephen Arterburn, Addicted to "Love" (Ann Arbor, Michigan: Stewart Publications, 1991), 107-108.

2. Ibid., 108.

3. Personal conversation with a former pornography addict.

4. Arterburn, *Addicted to "Love,"* 108-110. This section was taken from this book unless otherwise noted.

5. Douglas Reed, "Pornography and Addictive Compulsive Sexual Behaviors" (Paper delivered at NFF Media Workshop, Pittsburgh, PA, 1990).

6. P. J. Carnes, "Sexual Addiction: Progress, Criticism, Challenges," S. N. Barton & P. J. Carnes, eds, *American Journal of Preventative Psychiatry and Neurology,* Vol. 3, No.2 (Ridgewood Psychiatric Centers, PA 1990):5.

7. Reed, "The Role of Pornography."

8. D. M. Donovan and G. A. Marlatt, *Assessment of Addictive Behaviors* New York, Guilford Press, 1988):5.

9. "700 Club" Survey (1988).

10. Miami Herald (13 January 1988).

11. Coleman, "Sexual Compulsivity," 197.

12. J. L. Herman, "Sex Offenders: A Feminist Perspective," W.L. Marshall, et al., *Handbook of Sexual Assault: Issues, Theories and Treatment of Offenders*

(New York: Plenum, 1990):257-285.

13. Ibid.

14. Carnes, "Sexual Addiction."

15. Donovan and Marlatt, *Assessment of Addictive Behaviors* 5.

16. Reed, "The Role of Pornography."

17. D. Zillmann and J. Bryant, *Pornography: Recent Research, Interpretations and Policy Considerations* (Hillsdale, New Jersey, Lawrence Erlbaum Publishers, 1990).

18. *Final Report of the Attorney General's Commission on Pornography* (Nashville, Tennessee, Rutledge Hill Press, 1986).

19. P. J. Carnes, *Out of the Shadows: Understanding Sexual Addiction* (Minneapolis, Camp Care Publishers 1983),4.

20. H. Milkman and S. Sunderwirth, Craving for Ecstasy: The Consciousness and Chemistry of Escape (Lexington, Massachusetts, Lexington book 1987),6.

21. E. Coleman, Compulsive Sexual Behavior, 12.

22. In Torrance, CA. Reed, "The Role of Pornography."

23. Donovan and Marlatt, *Assessment of Addictive Behaviors*, 6.

24. See generally, W.L. Marshall et al, *Handbook on Sexual Assault* (New York: Plenum 1990), and S. Banton and Plaines, *American Journal of Preventive Psychiatry and Neurology*, Vol 2, No. 3 (Ridgewood Psychiatry Centers, PA, 1990).

25. V. Cline, *Where Do You Draw the Line*, out of print, (1974). The four steps are taken from this book.

26. Arterburn, *Addicted to "Love,"* 115-126. The four levels are taken from this book.

27. Arterburn, *Addicted to "Love,"* 126-129. The entire section is reprinted with only minimal changes from this book with the permission of the author.

28. Reed, "The Role of Pornography." The material in the next two sections has been taken primarily from this paper.

29. Ibid.

30. Marshall and Barbaree, in Marshall, ed. *Handbook of Sexual Assault,* 271.

31. Coleman, "Sexual Compulsivity," 197.

32. Douglas Reed, "Research on Pornography: The Evidence of Harm" (Cincinnati, Ohio: National Coalition Against Pornography, 1990).

33. Reed, "The Role of Pornography."

34. Discussion, NFF Media Workshop (1990).

35. Carnes, "Sexual Addiction."

36. R. Bennett, "The Relationship Between Pornography and Extrafamilial Child Sexual Abuse," *The Police Chief* (February 1991).

37. Ann Burgess, "A Study in Jefferson County, Kentucky," 1984 in Douglas Reed, "Pornography's Relationship to Child Sexual Exploitation and Abuse," (1990).

38. Murrin and Laws, 35.

39. Coleman, "Sexual Compulsivity," 197-199.

40. Carnes, Milkman and Sunderwirth, Lord, Baker, Wise, Collins-Dooley, and Robertson as cited in Reed, "The Role of Pornography."

41. Ibid.

42. R. J. McGuire, "Sexual Deviations as Conditioned Behavior: A Hypothesis," 2 *Behavior Research Therapy* (1965):185.

43. S. Rachman, "Experimentally induced sexual fetishism," 18 *Psychological Record* (1968):25.

44. J. N.. Marquis, "Orgasmic Reconditioning: Changing sexual object choice through controlling masturbation fantasies," 1 *Journal of Behavior*

Therapy and Experimental Psychiatry, (1970):263-271.

45. Evan, "Masturbating fantasy and sexual deviation," 6 *Behavior and Research Therapy* (1969):133. While conditioning by pornography and masturbation does cause sexual deviancy and increases the likelihood of acting out, counter conditioning to eliminate abnormal sexual behavior often fails. It is always extremely difficult because exposure to pornography has caused desensitization, escalation in taste for pornography, and loss of desire for sexual intimacy.

46. Ibid.

47. G. Abel, "Nature and Extent of Sexual Assault" in W.L. Marshall, in *Handbook of Sexual Assault and Treatment of the Offenders* (1990):9-21.

48. Ibid.

49. Reed, "The Role of Pornography." Such pornography should not be available to children under 18. This prohibition to minors could be accomplished by passage and enforcement of harmful matter per se laws. See Chapter 16.

50. Ibid.

Chapter 10 Media Violence—The Verdict Is In!

1. "A Session with Sessions," *Naples Daily News* (26 January 1992):5H.

2. Tani Hurley, "School Discipline," *Naples Daily News* (26 April 1992):1A.

3. Testimony of Chaplain of Los Angeles County jail, the largest jail in the country, and Prison Fellowship workers in Lorton Prison in Washington, D. C.

4. R. Kempley, "Making A Killing," *Washington Post*, 5 July 1992, G1,G4.

5. "Television and Behavior: Ten Years of Scientific Progress and Implications for the Eighties," Vol 1: Summary Report, National Institute of Mental Health (1982):37. The two Commissions were the 1969 President's Commission on the Causes and Prevention of Violence and the 1972 Surgeon General's Report on Media Violence.

6. Russell G. Geen, "Some Effects of Observing Violence Upon the Behavior of the Observer," *Progress in Experimental Personality Research*, Vol. 8. Academic Press, Inc. (1978):49; Russell G. Geen, "The Influence of the Mass Media"; *St. Louis Globe-Democrat* (20 September 1974).

7. Journal of the American Medical Association (1975), in Linnea Smith, M.D., "Distribution of Sadistic Videos to Minors" (Presentation to Juvenile Law Study Commission, 5 October 1990).

8. Berkowitz (1986), as quoted in Wendy Wood, Frank Y. Wong, and J. Gregory Chachere, "Effects of Media Violence on Viewers' Aggression in Unconstrained Social Interaction," *Psychological Bulletin*, Vol. 109. No. 3 (1991):371.

9. *New England Journal of Medicine*, 1976 in Smith, "Sadistic Videos."

10. Smith, "Sadistic Videos."

11. Gerbner et al as quoted in Susan Hearold, "A Synthesis of 1043 Effects of Television on Social Behavior," *Public Communication and Behavior*, Vol.1 (New York: Academic Press 1986):66.

12. "Television and Behavior":37.

13. Brandon Centerwall, "Exposure to Television As A Risk Factor For Violence," *American Journal of Epidemiology*, Vol. 129 (April 1989):644.

14. Jerome Singer and Dorothy Singer, "Television, Imagination and Aggression; A Study of Preschoolers" (Hillsdale, N. J.: Erlbaum, 1980) in "Television and Behavior": 38.

15. "Television and Behavior":6.

16. George Gerbner et al., "Violence Profile No. 9: Trends in network television drama and viewer conceptions of social reality" (1967-1977)

(Annenberg School of Communications, University of Pennsylvania, 1978) in "Television and Behavior":61.

17. "Television and Behavior":6.

18. G. T. Ellis and F. Sekyra, III, "The effect of aggressive cartoons on the behavior of first grade children," *Journal of Psychology* (1972) in "Television and Behavior":47.

19. Lynette Friedrich-Cofer and Aletha C. Huston, "Television Violence and Aggression: The Debate Continues," *Psychological Bulletin,* Vol. 100, No. 3 (1986):364-371.

20. "Television and Behavior":29.

21. From a mailing of the National Federation of Decency, now the American Family Association, in early 1984.

22. Friedrich-Cofer and Huston, "Television Violence and Aggression":365.

23. Russell G. Geen, "Some Recent Developments in the Study of the Effects of Violence in the Mass Media" (Paper delivered at the National Family Foundation Media Workshop, Pittsburgh, PA, November, 1990.)

24. Friedrich-Cofer and Huston, "Television Violence and Aggression":365.

25. Discussion, National Family Foundation Media Workshop, Friedrich-Cofer and Huston, Wood et al, Cook et al.

26. Huesmann, Eron, Lefkowitz and Walder (1984) in Geen, "Recent Developments."

27. "Television and Behavior":29.

28. Singer and Singer (1981) in Geen, "Recent Developments."

29. Huesmann and Eron (1986) in Geen, "Recent Developments."

30. Ibid.

31. Milavsky, Stipp, Kessler and Rubens (1982) in Geen, "Recent Developments."

32. Dorothy Singer, Discussion, National Family Foundation Media Workshop (November, 1990).

33. Thomas D. Cook, Deborah A. Kendzierski and Stephen V. Thomas, "The Implicit Assumptions of Television Research: An Analysis of the 1982 NIMH Report on Television and Behavior," *Public Opinion Quarterly,* Vol. 47 (1983):161-201.

34. Discussion, National Family Foundation Media Workshop (November, 1990).

35. AP Release, *Naples Daily News* (5 August 1991).

36. Anthony Lewis, "Execution Debate," *Naples Daily News* (24 April 1992):7A.

37. Mona Charen, "Unsupervised children: A threat and a tragedy," *Naples Daily News* (7 May 1990).

38. Linnea Smith, "Child Victimization and Sexually Explicit Mainstream Mass Media" (Presentation to Michigan Senate Juvenile Justice Advisory Committee, 1986).

39. *Wall Street Journal* (13 June 1991).

40. AP Release, *Naples Daily News,* 9 April 1990; Washington Press Release, 29 April 1991; AP Release, *Naples Daily News* 20 April 1992.

41. *Toronto Star,* 26 February 1992.

42. D.P. Phillips (1986), in Geen, "Recent Developments."

43. Centerwall, "Exposure to Television".

44. Ibid., 649.

45. Ibid., 651.

46. Associated Press, *Miami Herald,* (3 November, 1985).

47. Task Force on Families in Crisis Figures from "Confronting Domestic Violence: A Guide for Criminal Justice Agencies" (July, 1986).

48. Huesmann, Eron, Lekowitz and Walder, (1984) in Friedrich-Cafer and Huston, "Television Violence and Aggression":369.

49. Jill Smolowe, "Can't We Talk This Over," *Time* magazine, (7 January 1991).

50. U.S. Department of Education statement reported in Intercessors for America.

51. William Woo, "The Love and respect among generations," *Naples Daily News* (12 April 1992):3H.

52. Rod Nordland, "Deadly Lessons," *Newsweek* (9 March, 1992),22-30.

53. Ibid.

54. AP Release, *Naples Daily News*, (3 January 1992).

55. AP Release, *Naples Daily News*, (7 January 1992).

56. Senator Joseph Biden, Jr., Chairman, U.S. Senate Judiciary Committee.

57. Anthony Lewis, Execution Debate, Naples Daily News (24 April 1992):7A.

58. L. Smith, "Sadistic Videos."

59. Mona Charen Commentary, *Naples Daily News* (25 March 1992):7A.

60. Mona Charen Commentary, *Naples Daily News* (7 May 1990):7A.

61. Philip G. Ney, "The Repetitious Reenactment of Conflicts In Families Engendered by the Violent Words and Behavior Portrayed by the Media" (Paper delivered at the National Family Foundation Media Workshop, Pittsburgh, PA, November, 1990).

62. J. L. Freedman, "Effect of television violence on aggressiveness," *Psychological Bulletin*, 96 (1984):227-246.

63. Wood, Wong and Chachere, "Effects of Media Violence": 371-373.

64. Ibid., 378-380.

65. Bower (1981); Lang, (1979) as cited in Geen, "Recent Developments."

66. Geen, "Recent Developments." All the materials about learning scripts, priming, and individual differences have been taken from Dr. Geen's paper.

67. Ibid.

68. Ibid.

69. Aletha Huston and Dolf Zillmann, Discussion, National Family Foundation Media Workshop (November 1990).

70. Dolf Zillmann and James Weaver, "Effects of Prolonged Exposure to Gratuitous Media Violence."

71. H. J. Eysenck and S. B. G. Eysenck, "Psychoticism as a dimension of personality," London: University of London Press, 1976).

72. Richard Frost and John Stauffer, "The Effects of Social Class, Gender, and Personality on Physiological Responses to Filmed Violence."

73. Ibid.

74. Geen, "Recent Developments."

75. Ibid.

76. Ibid.

77. Kempley, "Making A Killing."

Chapter 11 *The Influence of Heavy Metal Music and MTV*

1. Bob DeMoss," Rising to the Challenge," a video produced by Parent's Music Resource Center and Teen Vision, Inc.

2. Ibid.

3. Barry L. Sherman and Laurence W. Etling, "Perceiving and Processing Music Television," *Responding to the Screen*, (eds.) Jennings Bryant and Dolf

Zillmann (Hillsdale, N.J.: Lawrence Earlbaum Associates),386.

4. Snow (1987), p. 326 as quoted in Sherman and Etling, "Perceiving and Processing," 373.

5. Nielsen Television Information, *Broadcasting* (February 1992).

6. DeMoss, "Rising to the Challenge."

7. "BA, BS" (1988), as cited in Sherman and Etling, "Perceiving and Processing," 376.

8. DeMoss, "Rising to the Challenge."

9. Joseph Stuessy, Record Labeling, Hearing Before the Senate Committee on Commerce, Science and Transportation, 99th Congress, 1st Session (19 September 1985):124 as cited in Thomas L Jipping, "Heavy Metal, Rap, and America's Youth: Issues and Alternatives" (Free Congress Foundation, 1992):8.

10 Thomas L. Jipping, "Heavy Metal, Rap and America's Youth." Cites music critic Al Menconi and quotes Cal Thomas, "Guns N' Roses: The Band From Hell," *Human Events* (12 October 1991):15.

11. Robert Kubey, "Media Use and Its Implications for the Quality of Family Life" (Paper delivered at the NFF Media Workshop, November 1990).

12. Bradley Hayton, "The Effects of Indecent Broadcast Programming Upon Children" (Paper delivered at the NFF Media Workshop, November 1990).

13. *New York Times* (13 March, 1987):B1.

14. Thomas Jipping, Personal conversation regarding his report on "Heavy Metal, Rap and America's Youth: Issues and Alternatives" (May 1991).

15. Hayton, "The Effects of Indecent Broadcast."

16. Kotarba & Wells (1987) p. 398 as cited in Sherman and Etling, "Perceiving and Processing," 374.

17. Frith (1981) p. 27 as cited in Sherman and Etling, "Perceiving and Processing," 374.

18. Ward, Stokes and Tucker (1986), p. 107 as cited in Sherman & Etling, "Perceiving and Processing," 374.

19. Larson & Kubey (1983), p. 14 as cited in Sherman & Etling, "Perceiving and Processing," 380.

20. The American Medical Association Group on Science and Technology Report, "Adolescents and Their Music," *Journal of the American Medical Association* (22 September, 1989).

21. DeMoss, "Rising to the Challenge."

22. Jipping, "Heavy Metal, Rap, and America's Youth," 13-15.

23. Leo, "Rock 'n' Roll's Hatemongering," U. S. News & World Report (19 March 1990).17 as quoted in Jipping, "Heavy Metal, Rap, and America's Youth," 16.

24. Jipping, "Heavy Metal, Rap, and America's Youth," 16.

25. DeMoss, "Rising to the Challenge," The 5 categories are those used in this video. These same subjects are found in almost all articles which describe heavy metal rock music. Most videos contain at least two or more of these in combination.

26. "The World of Dark Rock", *The New American* (17 February, 1986).

27. Paul King, M.D. "Heavy Metal Music and Drug Abuse in Adolescents, Vol 83/No.5/ *Postgraduate Medicine*, (McGraw-Hill, Inc., April, 1988):295.

28. *Circus* (30 June, 1981),28-29.

29. King, "Heavy Metal Music," 295.

30. Ibid., 298.

31. UPI Release (Los Angeles, 2 September 1985).

32. "The World of Dark Rock".

33. Hannelore Wass et al, "Adolescents and Destructive Themes in Rock

Music: A Follow-up" accepted for publication in *Omega*).

34. Phyllis Schlafly, "Rock Music and Teenage Suicide," The Union Leader (Manchester, N.H., 18 July 1985).

35. Ibid.

36. Hayton, "The Effects of Indecent Broadcast."

37. The *Washington Post* (9 July, 1984) A1, 14.

38. 20/20 investigation recorded in the Senate Congressional Record (26 September 1985, 99th Cong. 1st Sess. 131 Cong Rec S 12168).

39. Orange County Register (28 September, 1986):B1.

40. Miami Herald (13 January, 1985):5A.

41. DeMoss, "Rising to the Challenge."

42. Kandy Stroud, "Stop Pornographic Rock," *Newsweek* (6 May 1985),14.

43. Dolores Curran, "Video Images of Women Related to Rise in Sexual Violence," *St. Louis Review* (21 February 1992).

44 Sut Jhally, "Dreamworlds: Desire/Sex/Power in Rock Video"/ Foundation for Media Education/ P. O. Box 2008/ Amherst, MA 01004-2008; Bob DeMoss, "Rising to the Challenge"/ *Focus on the Family*/ P.O. Box 35500/ Colorado Springs, Co 80935; Eric Holmberg, "Hell's Bells"/ Reel to Reel Ministries/ P.O. Box 4145, Gainesville, FL 32613; The Peters Brothers, Truth About Rock/ P.O. Box 9272/ St. Paul, MN 55109.

45. John Leland, "Rap and Race," *Newsweek*, 29 June 1992, 46-52.

46. Ibid.

47. Chris McKenna, "Police Group: New Rap Album Urges Bush Slaying," *New York Post*, 2 July 1992.

48. Pittman (1985): 34 as cited in Sherman and Etling, "Perceiving and Processing," 378.

49. Kaplan (1984) p. 4 as cited in Sherman and Etling, "Perceiving and Processing," 378.

50. Kaplan (1987) p. 63 as quoted in Sherman and Etling, "Perceiving and Processing," 380.

51. Burns and Thompson (1987) p. 15 as quoted in Sherman and Etling, "Perceiving and Processing," 381.

52. Ibid.

53. Levy (1983) p. 33 as cited in Sherman and Etling, "Perceiving and Processing," 377.

54. Levy (1983) p. 76 as cited in Sherman and Etling, "Perceiving and Processing," 381.

55. Sherman and Dominisck (1986): 92 as quoted in Sherman and Etling, "Perceiving and Processing," 383.

56. Vincent, Davis, and Boruszkowski (1987) as cited in Sherman and Etling, "Perceiving and Processing," 383.

57. C.H. Hanson and R.D. Hanson, "Rock Music Videos and Antisocial Behavior," Basic and Applied Social Psychology, Vol. 10, No. 4 (December 1989).

58. Sherman and Etling, "Perceiving and Processing," 383.

59. UPI Releases (26 June 1991 and 2 July 1991); FCC Communications Daily (28 June 1991).

60. AP Release (4 December 1990).

61. Gerbner (1973); Gross and Morgan (1985) as cited in Sherman and Etling, "Perceiving and Processing." 384-385.

62. Leming (1987) p. 363 as quoted in Sherman and Etling, "Perceiving and Processing," 385.

63. Sherman and Etling, "Perceiving and Processing." 385.

64. Thomas (1988) p. 18 as quoted in Sherman and Etling. "Perceiving and

Processing," 386.

65. Charles Ashbach (Presentation to the National Family Foundation Board of Directors, October 1988).

66. Hannelore Wass et al, "Adolescents' Interest In and Views of Destructive Themes in Rock Music" (Baywood Publishing Co. Inc., 1988) Omega, Vol 19(3) (1988-89):179.

67. Hannelore Wass et al, "Adolescent and Destructive Themes in Rock Music: A Follow-up (Accepted for Publication in Omega).

68. C.H. Hansen and R.D. Hansen, "The Influence of Sex and Violence on the Appeal of Rock Music Videos," *Communications Research*, Vol 17, No. 2 (Sage Publications, Inc., April 1990): 212-234.

69. Zillmann and Murdorf (1987) as cited in Hansen and Hansen "The Influence of Sex," 228.

70. Hansen and Hansen, "The Influence of Sex," 229.

71. Berkowitz and Rogers (1986); Geen and Thomas (1986); Greeson and Williams (1986); Huesman (1986) Rosenthal (1986); Singer and Singer (1980) as cited in Hansen and Hansen, "The Influence of Sex," 232.

72. Hansen and Hansen, "The Influence of Sex," 232.

73. Ibid.

74. Donna Marie Beck as quoted in DeMoss, "Rising to the Challenge."

75. Dr. Mark Miller, John Hopkins University, The Public Mind with Bill Moyers, "Consuming Images" as quoted in Eric Holmberg, *All Rapped Up* (Gainesville, FL: Reel to Real Ministries), 25-26.

76. King, "Heavy Metal Music," 301.

Chapter 12 Understanding the Appeal of Horror Movies

1. Kim Newman, *Nightmare Movies, A Critical Guide to Contemporary Horror Films* (New York: Harmony Books, 1988), xii.

2. Ron Tamborini, "Responding to Horror" in *Responding to the Screen,* Eds J. Bryant and D. Zillmann (Hillsdale, New Jersey: Lawrence Erlbaum Associates, 1991),305-328.

3. Tamborini, "Responding to Horror," 317-321.

4. Morris Dickstein, "The Aesthetics of Fright," *American Film* (September, 1980),32-34.

5. Ibid., 59.

6. Ibid., 1987, Study by Dr. Tamborini.

7. King, 1981, p. 87 as quoted in Tamborini, "Responding to Horror."

8. Tamborini, "Responding to Horror," 307.

9. Personal interview, June,1991.

10 This information has been taken from a series of Press Releases and newscasts. The most complete description of his murders is found in a United Press International Release, 9 Sept. 1991. His background is detailed in *Newsweek,* Feb. 3, 1992.

11. Andre Derdeyn, M.D. and Jeffrey M. Turley, M.D., "Television, Films and the Emotional Life of Children" (Paper delivered at the National Family Foundation Media Workshop (November 1990) and published in the *Journal of the American Academy of Child and Adolescent Psychiatry*, Vol. 29, No. 6 (November, 1990) 942-945.

12. Newman, *Nightmare Movies*, 146.

13. Zillmann, Discussion, NFF Media Workshop (November 1990).

14. Dorothy Singer, Discussion, NFF Media Workshop (November, 1990).

15. Tamborini, "Responding to Horror," 308.

16. Ibid., 309-310.

17. James Weaver, personal interview, June 1991.

18. Zillmann, Discussion, National Family Foundation Media Workshop (November 1990).

19. Derdeyn and Turley, "Films and Emotional Life."

20. Charles Ashbach, "The Inner Image and the Outer World; Media Influences and Personality Development" (Paper delivered at the National Family Foundation Media Workshop, (November 1990).

21. Ibid.

22. Ashbach, "The Inner Image."

23. Derdeyn, Discussion, NFF Media Workshop (November 1990).

24. Ibid.

25. Donnerstein and Linz, 1984, in Tamborini, "Responding to Horror."

26. Logas, 1981, p. 21 as quoted in Tamborini, "Responding to Horror."

27. Zillmann, Discussion, NFF Media Workshop (November 1990).

28. Tamborini, "Responding to Horror," 310.

29. Zillmann's deductions from research on violent and pornographic media, Personal Conversation, October 1991.

30. Personal conversation with Graduate Film Student at School of Communications, Regent University.

31. Symposium on Media Violence and Pornography Proceedings and Resource Book, ed. David Scott (1984) 82.

32. Park Elliott Dietz, M.D. in David Armstrong, Intelligent Look at Pornography, *San Francisco Chronicle* (22 November 1991).

33. Douglas Reed, "The Role of Pornography in Compulsive or Addictive Sexual Behaviors" (Paper delivered at the National Family Foundation Media Workshop (November 1990).

34. "Porno-Violence Addict Charged With Assault," Morality in Media Newsletter Vol. 24, No. 2 (March 1985),4.

35. National Coalition on Television Violence Survey as cited in *American Family Association Journal* (September 1989):5.

36. Ibid.

37. *American Family Association Journal* (November-December 1989):13.

38. *American Family Association Journal* (July 1988): 16.

39. *American Family Association Journal* (January 1989): 9.

40. Graduate film student, School of Communications, Regent University, January, 1992; Bob DeMoss, Generation At Risk Seminar, Tampa, FL (4 November 1991).

41. Tamborini, "Responding to Horror," 314.

42. Ibid., 315.

43. James Weaver, "A content analysis of ten commercially successful 'teenage slasher' horror films" (Paper delivered at the Speech Communication Association annual meeting, New Orleans, LA, 1988).

44. James Weaver, "Understanding The Perceptual and Behavioral Consequences of Exposure to Pornography" (November 1990) footnote 4.

45. Tamborini, "Responding to Horror," 316.

46. Ibid., 317.

47. Roger Ebert, "Why Movie Audiences Aren't Safe Anymore," *American Film* (March 1981),54-56.

48. Ibid., 55.

49. Ashbach, "The Inner Image."

50. Tamborini, "Responding to Horror."

51. Derdeyn, Discussion at the NFF Media Workshop, (November 1990).

52. Derdeyn and Turley, "Films and Emotional Life."

Chapter 13 Prosocial Programming—A Vision for the Future

1. Author Robert Showers attended the meetings in which these questions were raised and discussed in January 1992.

2. Peter Marshall and David Manuel, *The Light and the Glory* (Old Tappan, N.J.: Fleming H. Revell Company, 1977),351-352.

3. Ted Baehr as quoted in Paul Thigpen, Cleaning up Hollywood, *Charisma* (December 1991),37.

4. Ernest E. Allen, "Strategies for the 90s: Using the Media for Good", (Paper delivered at the National Family Foundation Media Workshop (Pittsburgh, PA, November 1990), the ideas in the section on Making the Media a Partner are all taken from this paper.

5. *Public Opinion Magazine*, January 1982.

6. Norm Alster, "Crude Doesn't Sell," *Forbes Magazine* (21 January 1991).

7. Discussion at the NFF Media Workshop (1990).

8. Dorothy G. Singer, "Evaluation of School Showings and Discussions of a Television Series, Degrassi Junior High" (Paper delivered at the NFF Media Workshop (Pittsburgh, PA, November, 1990). The ideas and quotes in the section on Programming about Everyday People are taken from this paper unless otherwise noted.

9. Bruns & Geist, "Stressful life events and drug use among adolescents," *Journal of Human Stress, 10* (1984):135-139. 1984; T. A. Wills, "Stress, coping, and tobacco and alcohol use in early adolescence," Shiffman and Wills eds., *Coping and Substance Abuse* (New York: Academic Press (1985).

10. S.M. Dornbusch et al. "Single parents, extended households, and control of adolescents," Child Development, 56 (1985):326-341.

11. J. Philippe Rushton, "Effects of Prosocial Television and Film Material on the Behavior of Viewers." In L. Berkowitz (Ed.), *Advances in Experimental Social Psychology*, Vol. 12., (New York, NY: Academic Press, Inc., 1979):321-351. The ideas and quotes in this section are taken from Dr. Rushton's paper unless otherwise noted.

12. R.W. Winett, "Prosocial Television: Effective Elements, Barriers to Broadcasting." *In Information and Behavior: Systems of Influence* (Hillsdale, N.J.: Lawrence Erlbaum Associates, Inc., 1986):29.

13. R.J. Harris, "Prosocial Uses of Media." In *A Cognitive Psychology of Mass Communication* (Hillsdale, NJ: Lawrence Erlbaum Associates, 1989):221.

14. Jennings Bryant, Alison F. Alexander and Dan Brown, "Learning from Education Television Programs." In M. J. A. Howe, *Learning from Television* (London: Academic Press, 1983):14-15.

15. Ibid., 15-16.

16. Ibid., 17-19.

17. Johnston and Ettema (1982) as cited in Bryant, Alexander, and Brown, "Learning from Education Television," 19.

18. Winett, "Prosocial Television," 36-37.

19. Bryant, Alexander and Brown, "Learning from Education Television."

20. Winett, "Prosocial Television," 43.

21. Coates, Pusser, and Goodman (1976) as cited in Rushton, "Effects of Prosocial Television," 337-338.

22. Sprafkin and Rubenstein (1982) in Winett, "Prosocial Television," 37-40.

23. Harris, "Prosocial Uses of Media," 227.

24. Harris, 225.

25. Ibid., 226.

26. Ibid., 227.

27. Winett, "Prosocial Television," 31.

28. Jerome Johnston and James S. Ettema, "Using Television to Best Advantage: Research for Prosocial Television." In Jennings Bryant & Dolf Zillmann (Eds.) *Perspectives on Media Effects*, (Hillsdale, NJ.: Lawrence Erlbaum Associates, 1986):152.

29. Bryant, Alexander and Brown, "Learning from Education Television," 26-27.

30. Johnston and Ettema, "Using Television to Best Advantage," 143.

Chapter 14 The Family Market—A Constituency to Be Courted

1. *Newsweek* (April 1935) as cited in R. W. Winett, "Prosocial Television: Effective Elements, Barriers to Broadcasting," *Information and Behavior: Systems of Influence* (Hillsdale, N.J.: Lawrence Erlbaum Associates, Inc., 1986):55.

2. Paul Harvey, "Call it the 'gaper's block', *Johnson City Press* (Johnson City, TN, 22 November 1991).

3. John Underwood, "How Nasty Do We Wanna Be, Reflections on Censorship and a Civilized Society," *Miami Herald*, (22 July 1990).

4. Personal communication from John Underwood.

5. Louis Sullivan, "Emphasis on Saving Families," Washington Times (28 November 1990).

6. Richard Stevenson, "And Now a Message from an Advocacy," *New York Times* (27 May 1990):H29.

7. Stevenson, "And Now a Message," H21.

8. Caryn Mandabach, president of the Carsey Werner Company as quoted in Stevenson, "And Now a Message," H21.

9. TV Guide (March 1992) as cited in *Citizen Magazine* (Focus on the Family, 18 May 1992),8.

10. Paul Thigpen, "Cleaning Up Hollywood" *Charisma Magazine* (December 1991),37-38.

11. Bill Carten, "Cosby's Cliff Huxtable Has Said His Piece," *Naples Daily News* (26 April 1992):6E.

12. Much of the information about the Family Channel was taken from a series of press releases and a personal interview with Earl Weirich, V.P. of Public Relations.

13. Jane Wollman, "The Family Way," *Emmy* (December 1991), 30.

14. Daniel B. Wood, "Family Channel Focuses on the Inoffensive," *The Christian Science Monitor.*

15. Wollman, "The Family Way," 32.

16. Laura Landro, "Family Cable Channel Switches Signals from Religious to Entertainment Fare," *The Wall Street Journal* (24 July 1990).

17. Wollman, "The Family Way," 32.

18. Greg Ptacek, Indies Cater to Growing Market for Family Films, *Hollywood Reporter* (9 April 1991).

19. Report of the Family Vision Foundation (March 1992),2-3.

20. Greg Ptacek, "Growing Market for Family Films."

21. AP, *Union Leader* (Monesco, CA, 14 February 1992).

22. Joanna Lipman, "ABC Retreats On Bid to Relax Ad Guidelines," *Wall Street Journal* (13 March 1992):B1.B3.

23. Morton Kondracke as quoted in James J. Kilpatrick, "Media Leading Society Downhill," Universal Press Syndicated column.

24. Ellen Goodman, "AIDS and the New-Found Fear of Sex," *Naples Daily News* (5 April 1992):3H.

Chapter 15 Research, Public Policy, and Law: Combination for Change

1. *Report of the Commission on Obscenity and Pornography* (Washington, D.C., U.S. Government Printing Office 1970).

2. Ibid. D. Zillmann, "Research and Public Policy", *Pornography, Research Advances and Policy Considerations* (Hillsdale, New Jersey: Lawrence Erlbaum Associates, 1989): 388-389. (From the outset, it was clear that its verdict of "no ill effects" was based on few and tentative findings many of which were lately generated by the Commission itself to justify its biased conclusions).

3. Victor Cline, *Where Do You Draw the Line* (Salt Lake City, Utah, Brigham Young University Press, 1974); see also E. Donnerstein *Pornography and Violence Against Women* 347 Annals of N.Y. Academy of Sciences (1988):277-299; N.M. Malamuth "Rape Productivity Among Males," 37(4) *Journal of Social Issues* (1981):138-157; D. Zillmann and J. Bryant, "Pornography, Sexual Callousness and the Trivialization of Rape," 32(4) *Journal of Communication* (1982):10-21. E. Donnerstein "Erotica and Human Aggression," in R. Geen and E. Donnerstein (eds.) *Aggression: Theoretical and Empirical Reviews*, Vol. 2 (New York: Academic Press, 1983):127-154; N.M. Malamuth, "Aggression Against Women," *Pornography and Sexual Aggression* Orlando, Florida: Academic Press, 1984):19-52.

4. *Final Report of the Attorney General's Commission on Pornography* (Nashville, Tennessee: Rutledge Hill Press (1986):40, (hereafter 1986 Pornography Commission.)

5. See *Final Report of the Surgeon General's Workshop on Pornography and Public Health* (Washington, D.C., U.S. Government Printing Office, 1986) (hereafter Surgeon General's Report).

6. *1986 Pornography Commission* (1989):284; P. Dietz, "Pornography Imagery and Prevalence of Paraphilia," 139 *American Journal of Psychology* (1988):1493-95.

7. Ibid. See *Surgeon General's Report.*

8. *Surgeon General's Report,* 1499-1802.

9. *Presidential Commission Report on Pornography Technics.* Vol VI (1970); *Surgeon General's Report,* 2-10; *1986 Pornography Commission,* 343-344.

10. Ibid.

11. Attorney General's Organized Crime Report in California, 7 (1986).

12. U.S. Department of Justice, Bureau of Justice Statistics, *Lifetime Likelihood of Victimization* (1987).

13. American Family Association, *Pornography: A Report,* 4 (1989)

14. L. Baron and M. Strauss, "Pornography and Rape in American States" in *Pornography and Sexual Aggression,* 185-209; Scott and Schwalm, "Rape rates and the circulation rates of Adult Magazines, *Journal of Sex Research* (1989); see also J. H. Court, Pornography and Sex Crimes, *International Journal of Criminology and Penology* (1977):129-157.

15. J. Mason, Speech to Religious Alliance Against Pornography, Washington, D.C., (October 1987).

16. See P. Schlafly, *Victim Testimony Before the Pornography Commission,* (1987); *USA Today,* "Porn Victims Need This Bill," (21 April 1992):10A.

17. R. Hazelwood, *The Men Who Murdered,* FBI Law Enforcement Bulle-

tin (August 1985).

18. D. Pope, Testimony before the Select Committee on Children, Youth and Family, "Hearing on Women, Violence and the Law" (16 September 1987).

19. J. Rabin, Testimony before the Subcommittee on Juvenile Justice, Judiciary Committee, U.S. Senate (12 September 1984).

20. U.S. Department of Justice Press Release, "National Task Force on Child Exploitation and Pornography Created," (Feb 21, 1987). See also National Law Center for Children and Families Fact Sheet on Harms of Pornography (Alexandria, Virginia 1992)' R. Showers, *Myths and Misconceptions of Pornography*, Christian Legal Society Quarterly 9 (Fall 1988).

21. J. Lyons and D. Larsen, "A Systematic Analysis of the Social Science Research on the Effects of Violent and Non-Violent Pornography (Paper delivered at the National Family Foundation Media Workshop, November 1990) (in publication 1992).

22. Donnerstein, E., Linz, D., & Penrod. S., *The Question of Pornography: Research Findings and Policy Implications*. (New York: Free Press, 1987).

23. President Bush's Public Comments to Religious Alliance Against Pornography (October 1991).

24. *Ferber v. New York* 458 U.S. 747, 757 (1982).

25. *Osborne v. Ohio*, 495 U.S., 108 S. Ct. 1691 (1990).

26. Amici Brief of National Coalition Against Pornography, Concerned Women for America, *Focus on the Family*, et al. at 3 in *Osborne v. Ohio*, N. 88-5986 (October Term 1989).

27. *Maryland v. Craig*, 497 U.S., 111 L. Ed. 2nd 666 (1990).

28. *Fort Wayne Books*, 489 US 46 (1989), *United States v. Pryba*. (1990)

29. *Playtime Theaters v. Renton*, 475 US 41 (1986), *Arcara v. Cloud Books, Inc.,* 478 US 697 (1986).

30. R. Showers and G. Malpas, *Child Sexual Exploitation and Child Pornography* (in publication National Center for missing and Exploited children 1992).

31. See Report of FCC in Indecent Broadcasting (1991); See also *Action for Children's Television v. FCC*, (Act I) 852 F. 2d 1332 (D.C. Cir. 1988), Act II, 932 F. 2d 1504 (1991). See also *Action Children's Television v. FCC* (Act III) 117 L. Ed 2d 507, *cert denied* (March 2, 1992).

32. *Sable Communication of California v. FCC* 492 U.S. 115 (1989).

33. FCC Comments of Religious Alliance Against Pornography in the Regulation of Telephone Dial-a-Porn (1990).

34. Tennessee and Missouri. See note 41.

35. See Chapter 10, Media Violence: The Verdict Is In.

36. Porn Victim Compensation Act, S. 1521 (1992) sponsored by Senators McConnell (Kentucky) and Grassley (Iowa).

37. B. Taylor, "Obscenity, Per Se," *Michigan Law Journal* (1990).

38. Ibid.

Chapter 16 Consensus and Recommendations for the 1990s

1. "TV's Biggest-Ever Shakeup," Star, 24 March 1992, 7.

2. Robert Kubey, "Media Use and its Implications for the Quality of Family Life" (Paper delivered at the National Family Foundation Media Workshop, Pittsburgh, PA, November 1990).

3. Discussion, NFF Media Workshop.

4. Peggy Charren, "Kidvid: Doing Battle with G. I. Joe," *New York Times*, 26 January 1992.

5. Margaret Andreasen, "Patterns of Family Life and Television Consumption from 1945 to 1990," (Paper delivered at NFF Media Workshop).

6. Discussion, NFF Media Workshop.

7. *National Catholic Register*, Los Angeles, CA, 16 February 1992.

8. Paul Thigpen, "Cleaning Up Hollywood," *Charisma* (December 1992),36.

9. Bob Pierce, "Does Morality Scare Hollywood?" *Movieguide* (1992).

10. John Evan Frook, "Mahoney unveils pic, TV code to curb sex, crime," *Variety*, 3 February 1992.

11. Burns and Murphy, "Is TV Going Too Far?" 20.

12. Pierce, "Does Morality Scare Hollywood?"

13. Bill Britton, "Is TV Offensive?" *Programming* (3 August 1991), 123.

ORDER THESE HUNTINGTON HOUSE BOOKS !

_____	America Betrayed—Marlin Maddoux	$6.99 _____
_____	Angel Vision (A Novel)—Jim Carroll with Jay Gaines	5.99 _____
_____	*Battle Plan: Equipping the Church for the 90s—Chris Stanton	7.99 _____
_____	Blessings of Liberty—Charles C. Heath	8.99 _____
_____	Cover of Darkness (A Novel)—J. Carroll	7.99 _____
_____	Crystalline Connection (A Novel)—Bob Maddux	8.99 _____
_____	Deadly Deception: Freemasonry—Tom McKenney	7.99 _____
_____	The Delicate Balance—John Zajac	8.99 _____
_____	Dinosaurs and the Bible—Dave Unfred	12.99 _____
_____	*Don't Touch That Dial—Barbara Hattemer & Robert Showers	9.99/19.99 _____
_____	En Route to Global Occupation—Gary Kah	9.99 _____
_____	Exposing the AIDS Scandal—Dr. Paul Cameron	7.99 _____
_____	Face the Wind—Gloria Delaney	9.99 _____
_____	*False Security—Jerry Parks	9.99 _____
_____	From Rock to Rock—Eric Barger	8.99 _____
_____	Hidden Dangers of the Rainbow—Constance Cumbey	8.99 _____
_____	*Hitler and the New Age—Bob Rosio	9.99 _____
_____	The Image of the Ages—David Webber	7.99 _____
_____	Inside the New Age Nightmare—Randall Baer	8.99 _____
_____	*A Jewish Conservative Looks at Pagan America—Don Feder	9.99/19.99 _____
_____	*Journey Into Darkness—Stephen Arrington	9.99 _____
_____	Kinsey, Sex and Fraud—Dr. Judith A. Reisman & Edward Eichel (Hard cover)	8.99/19.99 _____
_____	Last Days Collection—Last Days Ministries	8.95 _____
_____	Legend of the Holy Lance (A Novel)—William T. Still	8.99/16.99 _____
_____	New World Order—William T. Still	8.99 _____
_____	*One Year to a College Degree—Lynette Long & Eileen Hershberger	9.99 _____
_____	*Political Correctness—David Thibodaux	9.99 _____
_____	Psychic Phenomena Unveiled—John Anderson	8.99 _____
_____	Seduction of the Innocent Revisited—John Fulce	8.99 _____
_____	"Soft Porn" Plays Hardball—Dr. Judith A. Reisman	8.99/16.99 _____
_____	*Subtle Serpent—Darylann Whitemarsh & Bill Reisman	9.99 _____
_____	Teens and Devil-Worship—Charles G.B. Evans	8.99 _____
_____	To Grow By Storybook Readers—Janet Friend	44.95 per set _____
_____	Touching the Face of God—Bob Russell (Paper/Hardcover)	8.99/18.99 _____
_____	Twisted Cross—Joseph Carr	9.99 _____
_____	*When the Wicked Seize a City—Chuck & Donna McIlhenny with Frank York	9.99 _____
_____	Who Will Rule the Future?—Paul McGuire	8.99 _____
_____	*You Hit Like a Girl—Elsa Houtz & William J. Ferkile	9.99 _____

New Title

Shipping and Handling _____
Total _____

AVAILABLE AT BOOKSTORES EVERYWHERE or order direct from:
Huntington House Publishers • P.O. Box 53788 • Lafayette, LA 70505
Send check/money order. For faster service use VISA/MASTERCARD
call toll-free 1-800-749-4009.

Add: Freight and handling, $3.50 for the first book ordered, and $.50 for each additional book up to 5 books.

Enclosed is $————— including postage.
VISA/MASTERCARD#_____ Exp. Date ———
Name _____
Address _____
City, State, Zip code_____

Media\Internet
302